AF264339

Ancient Asian History

Forgotten Stories of India, China, and Japan

Free Bonus from Captivating History (Available for a Limited time)

Hi History Lovers!

Now you have a chance to join our exclusive history list so you can get your first history ebook for free as well as discounts and a potential to get more history books for free!

Simply visit the link below to join.

Or, Scan the QR code!

captivatinghistory.com/ebook

Also, make sure to follow us on Facebook, X, and YouTube by searching for Captivating History.

Table of Contents

Part 1: Ancient India

Discovering Lost Stories from Indian History

Introduction

The Indian subcontinent was already alive around the same time the great pyramids were beginning to rise along the Nile. By the third millennium BCE, cities began to dot along the Indus and its tributaries, transforming the region completely. Some would consider these cities ahead of their time, as they were constructed with meticulous details.

More often than not, their streets were laid out on a grid, straight and evenly measured. Houses typically featured private wells and bathing areas. Most of the cities even had their own drainage system that ran beneath the streets, concealed with bricks and cleaned through inspection points. This was something the world would not see again in most places for thousands of years! It's safe to say that the Indus was one of the world's earliest urban civilizations, yet sadly, many people today know far less about it than they do about Egypt or Mesopotamia.

The reason behind this is rather simple. Unlike the history of the Greeks or the Egyptians, much of early Indian history was not written down in a steady line of records. Instead, the people of the Indus Valley preserved their past in different ways. Although foreign visitors kept records of what they saw across the subcontinent, these came from their own viewpoints. Greek writers described the lands they reached in the time of Alexander, while Chinese pilgrims wrote about their travels to Buddhist centers. The subcontinent was also mentioned in Persian records, though they were merely described as territories the Persians sought to influence. True, these accounts are useful, but they show India through outside eyes.

Within India itself, memory often lived in stories. This is where major epics like the *Rāmāyaṇa* and the *Mahābhārata* come in. These accounts are more than just long poems and mystical tales. In fact, they belong to a tradition called *Itihasa*—directly translated as "thus indeed it was." Importantly, *Itihasa* does not separate history from meaning in the same way modern books do. Instead, it carries memories of the past woven together with questions of duty, belief, and the nature of the world.

Of course, this does not mean that India lacked real events or real kingdoms. It simply means that storytelling was one of the ways people understood their past. Some characters may be based on historical figures. Some battles may mirror real conflicts. Over time, these memories blended with spiritual lessons and symbolic ideas. The result is a landscape where the line between what happened and what was believed is not rigid but fluid, understood differently depending on the tradition.

But it is this blending of history and story that makes ancient India so fascinating. Rather than relying only on dusty records or monuments, it invites us to explore a world where poetry, ritual, memory, and power all shaped the way people saw themselves. In the following pages, we'll explore what archaeology has uncovered, what foreign visitors have observed, what Indian traditions have preserved in their own voices, and of course, the interpretations of modern scholars.

Some tales are well known. Others are rarely retold, overshadowed by mainstream history. Together, they reveal a civilization that has continued to evolve for thousands of years, carrying its stories forward even when its cities fell silent.

Chapter 1 – Porus and Alexander the Great

The old ones called the river flowing through India and Pakistan the Parushni. To us, it's the Ravi River. And about three thousand years ago, along its banks, stood two great coalitions of men. On one side stood King Sudas of the Bharatas. He was young, but he commanded a clan that guarded the heart of the Punjab. Meanwhile, on the other side were ten kings who had joined arms, bound more by jealousy than by friendship. These kings were eager to see one thing: a blade buried deep into the heart of King Sudas and his men.

The Ravi River today.[1]

The ten came from every horizon. While Purus and Druhyus rode all the way from the west, Yadus and Turvaśas came from the south and Anus from the north. These, however, were the only names that survived the test of time, mentioned in the *Rigveda* (the oldest of the sacred books of Hinduism).

This rivalry with King Sudas and the Bharatas was not always there. Interestingly, the Bharatas (an early Vedic tribe prominent especially in the latter half of the second millennium BCE) had once been part of the alliance. But when Sudas's power grew tremendously, eventually threatening the old balance of power in the region, resentment began to brew. Then came priestly rivalry, which eventually sparked the conflict. It boiled to the maximum temperature when the Bharatas' king replaced his former chief priest, Vishwamitra, with his own favored priest, Vasishtha.

Swearing revenge, Vishwamitra orchestrated the battle. He began whispering into the ears of the leaders of neighboring clans, reminding them of the havoc that would engulf the region as long as Sudas sat on the throne. He urged them to unite against the Bharatas' king. And so, the ten gathered their forces and strength and crossed the river plains. They were confident that their numbers alone could easily drown Sudas's small but disciplined force. The story, however, had another ending for them.

One could only imagine the air before the battle broke out. The priests of Sudas turned to the divine, burning ghee upon the sacred fire and praying to Indra (the Hindu deity of weather) for divine intervention. The opposing kings chanted for the same god's favor, hoping Indra would be on their side as they obliterated their enemy.

When the battle opened at dawn, the sky shivered with thunder. Arrows hissed as the atmosphere was filled with the sounds of spears striking shields and chariots charging across the riverbanks. According to the *Rigveda,* divine intervention did occur. Rain soon came pouring down, swelling the Parushni and threatening the forces of the ten kings. It seemed as if the gods were siding with the Bharatas after all. The floods rose suddenly, cutting off their retreat. Chariots sank into the mud, horses neighed desperately for life, and men were swallowed whole by the torrent. Sudas's warriors pressed the attack, and when the waters receded, the ten kings lay broken.

The victory was absolute. Sudas emerged as the mightiest ruler of the Vedic world, and the Bharatas became the dominant tribe of the northern plains. The defeated tribes scattered to other lands. While some merged with distant peoples, others vanished altogether into the dust of history.

The hymns that spoke of the battle made it sound completely divine, as if gods had chosen a side. But historians would absolutely agree that its roots were purely human. It all revolved around power, pride, and the shifting sands of allegiance. It is safe to say that India, even in her earliest age, was never a land of stillness. Kingdoms rose and fell along the rivers; priests and kings competed for favor and survival. And in the memory of the people, this particular event is remembered as India's first great war ever recorded.

But of course, the Battle of the Ten Kings was not the only one that once shook India. Many centuries later, another wave of news began to drift across the desert winds, coming from far beyond the mountains. It spoke of a certain conqueror who had been mercilessly marching from the far west. He had crushed Persia, crowned himself pharaoh of the Egyptians lands, and burned cities in Bactria. Some called him "Master of the World," while those who knew him personally knew him by his name, Alexander of Macedon.

When Alexander's scouts first glimpsed the shining waters of the Hydaspes, they thought they were entering an unknown world. But the rivers of India had long witnessed wars before the Greeks were ever a people. The Parushni had swallowed ten kings. The Hydaspes would soon test another greater one.

The Threat from the West

When the people along the Indus learned more and more about the impending threat that loomed over them, they began to feel a surge of panic. Merchants closed their accounts early, and village headmen gathered at the temples, while the holy priests continued to read omens in the smoke. They were certain that the age of great invasions was returning, testing the courage of the people once more—though this time, the invader came not from a rival tribe or a neighboring kingdom, as during the Vedic wars. He came from the edge of the known world.

The chroniclers of Gandhara wrote that the first scouts appeared like ghosts at dawn. They were not Persians, though some wore Persian armor. Their shields were round, their spears long, and they marched in straight ranks that moved as one. No local chiefs had ever seen soldiers with such discipline and organization. The most feared of all was the Macedonian phalanx. This solid wall of men armed with long spears was known to advance against the enemy in a tight formation so closely packed that only a few could slip between their shields without being struck down. Then came the horsemen, typically placed behind the phalanx. The Macedonians also had engineers, scribes, and baggage trains that stretched for miles. The sight of this foreign force was as impressive as it was unnerving.

But the Indians were not easily deterred. It took more than numbers and a display of discipline to break warriors who had faced floods, rival clans, wandering raiders, and the wild strength of their own land since childhood.

However, not all were ready to repel any attacks laid by this mighty invader—especially those in the northwest region of the Indian subcontinent, who were growing weary each day. There, the rulers gathered their counselors to debate. Some envoys urged caution; others spoke of alliance. To resist such an army, they said, would bring ruin. To submit might bring reward.

The people of Taxila, for one, preferred to get on the invaders' good side rather than standing their ground. The city was one of the wealthiest in the region. It was a melting pot of scholars and traders, a place where Greek, Persian, and Indian merchants met in peace, exchanging goods and ideas. Its ruler, King Ambhi (known to the Greeks as Taxiles) was already aware of Alexander's many victories and had also heard rumors of the conqueror's generous treatment to those who willingly submitted. So, the decision was clear. Without wasting more time, Ambhi sent gifts of gold, fine linen, and other sorts of wealth to the foreigner. And when the Macedonian army finally reached his borders, he extended his arms, welcoming them as allies.

Meanwhile, east of the Hydaspes River was another man whose stance contrasted greatly with Ambhi's. Known as Porus, he was the lord of the tribe called Paurava. According to ancient sources, he was not only older than Ambhi but also prouder. He descended from a line of warriors who had ruled the land since the time when Sudas fought against his ten rivals on the banks of Parushni. His people were described to be tall and his elephants mighty. It was not surprising that his court was fierce in its independence. So, when his messengers returned with news of Ambhi's surrender, Porus chose to stand his ground. He was headstrong in ensuring that no foreign ruler would ever cross his river alive.

So, a battle was on the horizon. The Indian armies under Porus were as varied as the lands they defended. Unlike the rigid Macedonian phalanx, which moved like a single creature, the Indian forces were like a living mosaic. There were infantry archers, chariot riders from the plains, mercenaries from the hills, and cavalry trained to fight alongside towering elephants.

Ever since his major campaign against the Persian Empire, Alexander and his men had been campaigning almost continuously for roughly seven to eight years. He eventually crossed the Hindu Kush and entered the Indus region sometime in mid-326 BCE, right as the monsoon season was beginning. This was a time of violent storms, swollen rivers, and heavy rain that undoubtedly disrupted movement. Coupling this with the exhaustion that came from the long campaigns and the unfamiliar terrain in India, Alexander's men were growing unimaginably weary. Still, Alexander was not planning to turn back.

The Hydaspes, already swollen by the monsoon, flowed between the two forces. Porus stood on the eastern bank, where he could be seen walking among his war elephants. Around him, the camp moved quietly. Archers could be seen repairing and fixing their bowstrings by dim lamplight, while on the other corner, warriors sat cross-legged, drawing symbols of protection on the wet sand. Old priests muttered prayers while burning incense, its smoke curling upward and vanished into the mist a minute later.

The Macedonians were also busy with their work on the other side of the river. The men labored in silence under the dark sky, hauling logs and lashing them into rafts. Despite the heavy rain that came and went in bursts, flattening their campfires and wetting the canvas of their tents, the soldiers never complained. Some cleaned their weapons; others stared into the water, listening to the hiss of rain on the current.

By midnight, the rain eased. The clouds began to thin, and the moon appeared, pale and uncertain, over the horizon. Porus returned to his tent, but with the looming battle, he failed to sleep. For days, Alexander had made his life difficult. Alexander had been sending small detachments to feign crossing at different points along the Hydaspes. Each time, Porus's scouts sounded the alarm, and the cavalry thundered to the banks. Yet when the Macedonians withdrew again and again, Porus began to believe that these were nothing more than tricks to wear him down. Then, one night, the deception became real.

Alexander led a large force upstream, far from the main camp. Their movement could barely be heard since the rain muffled the sound of hooves and oars. Under the cover of night and guided by willing locals, the men made their way toward a wooded island that divided the river. When thunder rolled across the heavens at first light, the Macedonians wasted no time. They slipped into the water, shields above their heads and their horses swimming beside them. By the time the first Indian sentries noticed the glint of bronze through the fog, it was already too late.

The very moment the alarm was sounded, Porus made haste. He mounted his elephant and rode to the front. The ancient Greek historian Plutarch, for one, described how Porus stood like a tower on his massive elephant, directing his army from its back. His army was said to have assembled with remarkable speed. They did not panic despite the surprise attack, but rather, they moved like a trained machine. The elephants took their places in the center, forming a living wall. Behind them, archers lined up in dense ranks, bows strung and ready. The chariots rolled onto the plain, their wheels slicing through the wet soil. Cavalry gathered at both flanks, spears tipped with iron that gleamed even through the mist.

Although they had been through dozens of wars and battles throughout the many campaigns, the Macedonians had never seen an army like this. In their eyes, the Indian formation was equally strange and magnificent. The elephants swayed in place, their tusks sheathed in bronze. When their mahouts (traditional elephant riders) called, the elephants raised their trunks in unison as a response. It was indeed a sight to behold. When the massive creatures trumpeted, the sound was so deep and thunderous that some of the Macedonian horses responded by rearing and snorting.

When it was time for the battle, Alexander shouted orders to his phalanx. The long rows of spears then advanced, as steady as a tide. However, the ground soon proved to be a traitor to the Macedonians. The monsoon rains had turned the field into mud. So, their advance was not their proudest. Some slipped their shields; others found it hard to even walk as their sandals sank into the soft, wet ground.

Porus then unleashed his war elephants. They came at a lumbering charge, tusks lowered, trampling through mud and men alike. They crushed through the Macedonian front ranks, scattering the phalanx that had long been feared by many armies before. Even soldiers who had once faced the famed Persian Immortals now found themselves screaming at the sight of the towering elephants that were busy tossing men aside like rag dolls. Then came the volleys of arrows from the Indian lines, which almost immediately darkened the sky. Chariots sped forward, striking at the enemy flanks while cavalry wheeled around in sweeping arcs.

Porus charging into battle on his war elephant.[2]

The Macedonians tried to regroup, but Porus's men were everywhere. Although some were beginning to lose faith and hope, Alexander refused to retreat. He did not lose his composure. Ever observant, he managed to study every motion of the battlefield and every movement of his enemy. Despite the chaos, he noticed how the elephants, despite being fearsome, created gaps between their ranks as they advanced. Seeing this as an opportunity to turn the tides, he sent forward his light infantry composed of Agrianians and archers from Crete. These men were known for their speed and precision. Their task was simple: aim for the mahouts, who were perching high on the elephants' necks.

Now that the beasts began to falter, Alexander pressed on, accompanied by his Companion Cavalry. These horsemen circled wide, drawing the Indian riders into pursuit. Then he turned suddenly and struck at their flank. This, however, was not the end of the battle; in fact, it stretched for hours.

Porus, atop his elephant, fought at the center of the battlefield, visible to all. Arrows had struck his armor, and a spear had already grazed his shoulder, yet he paid no mind, refusing to descend and submit. When his mahout had been killed, Porus steered the creature himself, guiding it with his knees while he hurled spears into the flesh of his enemies with a strength that inspired his men.

Still, the Macedonians pressed harder, and eventually, the Indian lines began to weaken. The chariots soon became useless in the mud as their wheels stuck fast. Many elephants were wounded, and when panicked, they tended to turn on their own ranks. Porus watched as his formation began to break. Yet he would not yield.

The climax of the episode came when a spear finally pierced Porus's thigh. Blood ran down his armor. The great elephant beneath him began to show signs of collapse, as it had suffered multiple wounds. However, Porus remained mounted, striking down those who came near. His guards eventually fell one by one. Those few who remained quickly formed a ring around their king, swearing to protect him at all costs. But unfortunately, the Macedonians proved to be a mighty adversary after all. When the fighting ended, the field was a sea of broken weapons and fallen beasts. The riverbank was littered with bodies, their blood only washed away into the soil when rain returned later. The Macedonians had likewise suffered a great loss during the battle, but they had prevailed once more.

A painting depicting Alexander approaching Porus.[8]

Alexander himself rode through the wreckage on his trusty yet wounded steed, Bucephalus. He only came to a halt when he saw Porus on his elephant. True, he was visibly wounded and bleeding down his thigh, but Porus seemed unbroken. Ancient writers described how Alexander approached his opponent slowly. Soldiers from both sides stepped aside, uncertain whether they were witnessing the end of a battle or the meeting of equals. Porus, proud even in defeat, looked down at the invader who had crossed half the world to fight him.

"How do you wish to be treated?" Alexander may have asked the Indian king, perhaps through an interpreter.

Porus's reply was calm and steady. "Like a king."

"So shall it be," the conqueror said. Some said he even smiled, not in mockery but in respect.

Holding to his word, Alexander ordered that Porus's wounds be treated. Interestingly, the conqueror restored the lands to him. Alexander had long understood that ruling newly conquered territory required loyal local kings, not foreign administrators who knew nothing of the land. What's more, Porus had displayed great courage and discipline. It was clear that his people highly respected him. These qualities made him far more valuable as an ally than a defeated enemy. By granting him his kingdom, Alexander hoped to not only ensure stability on his eastern frontier but also place the region under a leader whose strength and authority would serve his ambitions without requiring his own constant presence.

Alexander planned to expand his influence deeper into the subcontinent. But fate seemed to disagree with his plans. First came the death of his horse shortly after the battle. Alexander then founded a city on the riverbank of Hydaspes and named it after Bucephalus. Next came the famous mutiny.

Although the Macedonians had won once more, their spirits had dulled. Many had seen death closer than ever before. They whispered that if one Porus could fight like a hundred men, what would await them deeper in India where mightier kingdoms still stood?

The Macedonians had heard stories of what lay beyond the rivers. The Nanda Empire, a realm so vast and rich, was said to possess armies that numbered in the thousands, with many more elephants. The soldiers grew silent when they heard the rumor. They were certain that Hydaspes was the beginning of their end.

Still, Alexander called on his generals and expressed his wish of new conquests. He spoke about marching east until they reached the edge of the ocean. To him, the horizon was never enough. His men had been loyal to him for years, but they, too, had their limits. After all those years of hardship, they longed to see home.

So, at the banks of the Hyphasis River, they halted, refusing to advance any further. It was a rebellion driven purely by exhaustion. For the first time, the conqueror faced an enemy he could not defeat, and it was his own weary army. Perhaps disappointed, the mighty conqueror withdrew to his tent. There he remained for three days, refusing food and speech. Outside, his soldiers waited, their resolve unshaken. When he finally emerged, his voice was calm, but his eyes had lost their fire.

"We will return," he said simply. "But we will return by another road."

The march back was more somber than triumphant. The army split into columns, with some sailing down the Indus and others cutting through the merciless desert. Disease and thirst claimed more lives than battle ever had. Villages that once watched in awe now turned away as the foreigners passed. Alexander himself was wounded again during a siege, struck by an arrow that pierced his lung. Though he recovered, the invincible image that had carried him across continents began to fade. Perhaps his men were right all along: Hydaspes was the beginning of the end.

When he finally reached Babylon, years later, he was nothing but a shadow of the man who had confidently crossed the Hydaspes. The great empire he had built stretched from Greece to India. True, it was vast, but it was also difficult to hold. Still, he spoke again of campaigns, this time into Arabia or even the western sea, but his body was already failing. Fever took him soon after, at only thirty-two years old.

Porus led a longer life than the Macedonian king, although his name was not immortalized as much as Alexander's. For a time, he ruled peacefully under Macedonian oversight, keeping order in the lands between the Hydaspes and the Acesines. What happened afterward, however, is rather blurry. A few Greek writers claim that Porus was later killed by another governor named Eudemus during the struggles that followed Alexander's death.

Even to this day, Porus remains one of the most debated figures in the history of ancient India. His name is known almost entirely through Greek records, and even those do not agree on who he truly was. The name "Porus" is generally seen as a Greek form of Paurava, a ruler from the Paurava kingdom that may have descended from the ancient Puru tribe mentioned in the *Rigveda*. This would connect him to the same Purus who fought King Sudas in the Battle of Ten Kings, the earliest recorded war in India.

The Puru people were an important tribe during the Vedic period. They controlled parts of what is now Punjab, a region rich in water and fertile land. By the fourth century BCE, these old tribal divisions had developed into small kingdoms. The Paurava realm, if it was indeed ruled by Porus, likely stood between the rivers Hydaspes and Acesines in the area now called Jhelum in modern Pakistan. It was known for its elephants, horses, and strong agricultural base. Its location made it an important link between Central Asia and the Indian plains.

Historians do not agree on the size or importance of Porus's kingdom. Some believe he ruled a wide territory that included nearby regions such as Taxila, while others think his power was more limited but still strategically significant. There is also a theory that the name Porus was not personal but a title used for several rulers in the area, which may explain the confusion in Greek writings. To them, all the local kings might have appeared as parts of a single resistance against Alexander.

What makes Porus mysterious is how little he is mentioned in Indian sources. The Vedic hymns, the later Puranas, and the early Buddhist texts all remain silent about him. This absence has led to questions. The most frequently asked is how could a king who faced one of history's most famous conquerors vanish from local memory so completely?

Several explanations exist. One is that his region soon came under new rulers after Alexander's departure, first under the Greek governors and later under Chandragupta Maurya. As the Mauryan Empire rose, Porus's legacy may have merged into a broader story of unification rather than remaining an individual legend. Another explanation is that Indian writers of that time preferred to record continuity and moral order instead of the personal heroism that Greek historians admired. Kings were remembered not for single acts of bravery but for maintaining stability and justice within their realms.

Still, Porus endures as a figure of quiet strength. Even through Greek descriptions, he appears as a tall and dignified ruler who met Alexander not as a defeated enemy but as an equal. Whether his true name was Paurava or something that time has erased, he came to represent the courage and endurance of India itself.

Chapter 2 – The Harappan Civilization

The rivers that once witnessed the might of both Alexander and Porus still exist. For many centuries, they moved across the plains, steady and almost unchanged. While the Hydaspes and the Acesines wound their way into the great Indus, the Ravi flowed through fields and villages scattered around the Punjab plains, passing from the hills of Himachal into the heart of what is now India and Pakistan. The battles of the past had long faded, but these rivers were destined to witness yet another figure who would leave a mark on history—though this time, he was neither native to the land nor arriving for battle. His name was James Lewis, a soldier of the British East India Company, though he did not keep that name for long.

We do not know much about his early life except for the fact that he enlisted young, at the age of twenty-one. This was common back then, especially for those who sought steady pay. Unsurprisingly, the Company was strict. One of the most serious crimes was dissertation. Lewis was well aware of this, yet in 1827, he deserted his post in Agra. Why he did so remains uncertain, but many suggest he had simply had enough of the experience. Whatever the cause, once he fled, he became a wanted man.

To survive, Lewis had to create a new identity. And so, he began to introduce himself as Charles Masson. With this new name, he embarked on multiple explorations. He wore simple clothing, carried little, and kept to himself. When questioned about his origins, he changed his story with ease.

Masson knew that he could not wander forever. At some point, he would have to face the Company he had deserted. But, if he had information or discoveries valuable enough, he could bargain for a pardon—or at least a lighter punishment. And thus began his mission across the Punjab into regions once crossed by Alexander's army.

He followed the Ravi River through the countryside, arriving at sites where ancient battles had once taken place. Masson was an avid reader of classical historians, so he was well-versed in the history of the lands. He had read Arrian and Quintus Curtius. He knew the stories of the Macedonian army crossing the rivers, fighting elephants, and meeting Porus in battle. These were the very stories that fired his imagination, and he hoped to find coins, weapons, or ruins that could be linked to that famous campaign.

Masson would walk along the banks with a small notebook in hand, jotting down every detail he saw. He noted the shape of old roads, the patterns of the abandoned brickwork, and any other sign of ancient settlements—no matter how small. He imagined Alexander's soldiers marching across these same fields, looking for a place to cross the river. He knew that many British scholars admired the Greeks, and bringing back evidence connected to Alexander would surely improve his chance of securing forgiveness. But it did not happen the way he expected.

One day, while passing a small settlement near the Ravi, Masson noticed several large mounds. They looked far from natural. They stood out clearly against the surrounding plain, rising in gentle slopes of baked earth and scattered debris. From afar, they resembled nothing more than low hills. However, the closer he got, it was clear that they were built not by mother nature but by human hands.

Masson returned to these strange mounds several times in the following months, convinced they were remnants of a forgotten past. Bricks lay everywhere, though most of them were either broken or covered in thick dust. However, each was the same shape and size. Weirdly enough, only Masson thought the site was special. Villagers nearby would walk over the mounds freely, often collecting what they needed for building walls, stables, and even roads. Even the British later did the same. No one thought the mounds were a part of an ancient site; they were simply convenient sources of material.

Still convinced he was a step closer to a great discovery, Masson continued to find proof. He examined the bricks with care and searched through the surface debris for hours. Patience is indeed a virtue: Masson eventually found small objects buried in the soil, including pottery shards with smooth finishes, bits of terracotta, and pieces of painted wares. The most intriguing of all were a few tiny seals carved with animals and symbols that were completely unfamiliar to a foreigner like himself. None of them matched the Greek or Persian traditions he knew from history books.

At the time, archaeology in India was almost nonexistent. There were no formal excavations, no trained teams, and no scientific surveys like those in Europe. Much of India's ancient past was understood through classical writers who mentioned Alexander or the Persians, or through Sanskrit texts that described early kingdoms and rituals.

Masson kept detailed notes of his findings—from the dimensions of the bricks to the patterns of the exposed walls, and even the distribution of pottery fragments. His days were often filled with sorting through the seals repeatedly. Some featured a unicorn-like creature, while others had an image of a bull or rows of peculiar symbols with no obvious meaning. These notes, along with his observations, would eventually form part of his published work called the *Narrative of Various Journeys in Balochistan, Afghanistan and the Panjab.*

Baked seals belonging to the Indus civilization.'

Masson compared these findings with what he knew of the region. Upon countless hours of study, he found that the style of the artifacts had no match in known Indian history. They weren't Mauryan, Kushan, or Gupta. They were certainly not from the period of Alexander, either. Their uniformity suggested a society that used standard construction methods, something far more organized than a temporary settlement. The more he saw, the more convinced he became that the ruins belonged to a civilization far older than any known kingdom in northern India.

Masson reported his discoveries to British officials in the region, yet he received a disappointing (but not surprising) response. As usual, the colonial officers were more interested in sites connected to Greece, Rome, or Persia—the mainstream colossal forces of the ancient world. In their point of view, a forgotten city with no connection to classical texts held little, if any, value. Without inscriptions they could understand, the ruins seemed unimportant. So, the mounds remained untouched.

Masson moved on with his other explorations. Later, in 1834, his identity was almost blown when he was visiting a town in the Persian Gulf. Luckily, he managed to deceive the British authorities by claiming he was an American traveler from Kentucky who had been exploring the world for a decade. Interestingly, the authorities not only believed his false identity but also befriended him. Intelligence was precious back then, so knowing that he had been traveling, the British asked Masson to write a report detailing everything about the countries he had visited. He complied, and eventually, the authorities pieced together his real identity. However, since he provided them with valuable information from his travels, Masson was pardoned. Later, he was given funds to launch excavations and expeditions across Afghanistan and the wider frontier regions the Company sought to understand.

A part of the excavation site at Harappa.[5]

It was only decades later that the site Masson discovered was formally excavated and gained a name. It all began during the construction of the railway line between Lahore and Multan when engineers and workers noticed the large mounds and the endless supply of sturdy bricks. They initially used them to build the railway beds and stations. Only afterward did scholars realize that they had destroyed parts of the ruins Masson had first recorded. The station built nearby was called Harappa, the name that would eventually be given to the entire ancient culture.

Major excavations at Harappa began in 1921, and shortly after, archaeologists also uncovered another city known as Mohenjo Daro. These two cities were roughly five hundred kilometers apart, but both belonged to the same civilization. (Harappa is in modern-day Punjab, while Mohenjo Daro is in Sindh.) They followed the same grid pattern; their streets were typically laid out in straight lines that intersected at right angles, forming blocks much like those found in modern towns. Their main avenues were broad enough to accommodate carts and foot traffic. The smaller lanes that branched from them are believed to have led into residential areas.

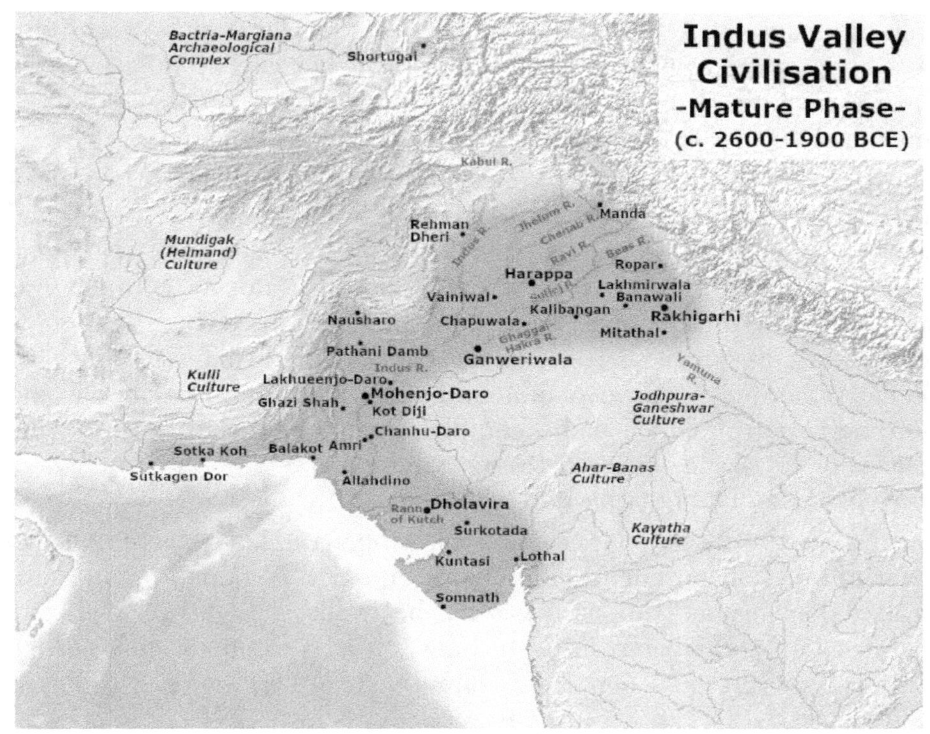

A map of the Indus Valley.[6]

Since they'd been built during the height of the Indus Valley world (c. 3000 BCE), it is not surprising that the houses were constructed with remarkable consistency. Every one of the bricks that formed the structures followed a standard size that appeared across the entire civilization—from Gujarat in the south to Punjab in the north.

However, one of the most impressive features of these cities was not the buildings themselves but the drainage system. Every house, even the smallest, was connected to a covered drain that ran beneath the streets. These drains were built with tightly fitted bricks and inspection points at regular intervals. This allowed wastewater to flow from homes into the main channels and out of the city. It is safe to say that only a few ancient civilizations gave such attention to public sanitation. Even in many modern towns, such careful planning would be considered advanced.

The excavations of public buildings in these cities also proved that the people paid attention to organized life. Harappa once had large granaries that were raised on platforms. They also featured ventilation channels to keep stored grain dry and safe. The scale suggested a system of food collection and distribution run by officials or councils. Nearby workshops possibly produced pottery, beads, and tools. Their layout indicated craft districts where artisans worked in regulated spaces rather than scattered individual huts.

Mohenjo Daro was home to one of the most remarkable structures of the ancient world, the Great Bath. This large rectangular pool was lined with finely fitted bricks, coated with a sealant to make them watertight. Stairs descended into the water from both ends, and the complex was surrounded by small rooms. While the purpose of the Great Bath is not fully known, its design suggests some form of ritual washing or controlled public gathering. About two thousand years later, Roman cities would become famous for their baths, complete with heated rooms, pools, and spaces for social life. Those baths were often places of leisure, trade, and conversation, built in marble and decorated with statues.

In comparison, the Great Bath of Mohenjo Daro was simpler in appearance. It featured no columns or mosaics. Where Roman baths projected luxury and imperial power, the Indus bath projected careful construction and shared use. It hints at a community that valued cleanliness, order, and perhaps a common ritual life, long before Rome existed.

Some scholars agree that this Indus civilization stood out for its distinctive approach—especially when compared with other ancient cultures. While the ancient Egyptians built upward, with their pyramids and obelisks that pierced the sky, Harappa preferred to build outward. This civilization created cities that stretched across the plains with careful planning and repeated patterns.

The Mesopotamia civilization was known for recording the deeds of kings and laws on clay tablets. The Indus people, however, had a different method: they carved their symbols on small seals, leaving behind scripts that mostly remain undeciphered to this day.

The Greeks loved to celebrate their heroes and legends in their art and literature, while the people of the Indus Valley left no statues of kings and heroes. Their achievements seem to speak of collective effort rather than personal glory.

Even though the civilization did not seem to glorify luxury or sophistication as much as the other popular ancient cultures, the Indus cities were not isolated. Trade connected them to the wider world.

Records from Mesopotamia mentioned a place called Meluhha. Historians and scholars alike believe they were referring to the lands of the Indus. The reason is simple. Meluhha lay beyond Magan and Dilmun, across the sea to the east, exactly where the Indus cities stood. The Mesopotamian texts also mentioned goods they obtained from Meluhha, like carnelian beads, ivory, and timber, which were all typically found in Harappan workshops. Indus-style seals and weights have also been unearthed in Mesopotamian cities, further cementing the theory that the two civilizations were in contact through long distance trade.

When systematic excavations began in the Indus Valley in the early twentieth century, one of the first major findings came from the work of Sir John Marshall. The director of the Archaeological Survey of India, Marshall had an extensive portfolio; he had already worked in Greece and the Near East. So, when he first approached the mounds of Harappa and Mohenjo Daro, he expected to find things he was familiar with. But, alongside another archaeologist, Ernest John Henry Mackay, what he uncovered was different from anything he had seen before.

Harappan weights, now stored in the National Museum of New Delhi.[7]

What stunned these men the most was how different the Indus cities were from other ancient sites already known to archaeology. Egypt had massive temples and elaborate tombs built specifically for pharaohs and his families. Mesopotamia was popular for its towering ziggurats and palaces. At those sites, authority was carved in stone and raised high above the common streets.

Marshall and Mackay expected these when they first excavated the Indus cities. But instead, as we've mentioned, Harappa and Mohenjo Daro left behind no sprawling palaces, no obvious temples, and no monuments that celebrated kings or priests. The buildings were practical, with a focus on houses, storage areas, workshops, and civic structures.

Some scholars now suggest that the absence of grand palaces or temples does not mean the absence of strong leadership. Instead, it may indicate a different kind of political structure. It's plausible that the Indus cities were governed by councils made up of merchants, landholders, and elders rather than by single rulers who displayed their authority through monuments. Power may have been expressed through consistency, planning, and control of resources rather than through statues and royal buildings.

Archaeologists even found it difficult to unearth weapons. Instead of war equipment and weapons, they only uncovered small copper knives, a few arrowheads, and tools that seemed more suited to craft work, daily tasks, and hunting. No large stores of spears or swords were ever discovered. Excavators also saw no traces of major battle, no layers of ash that mark the burning of a city, and no mass graves that serve as proof of a violent end. Although some citadel mounds existed, they lacked the heavy defensive walls and towers that characterized the fortified cities of Mesopotamia or Egypt.

If conflicts occurred, they were not turned into public monuments or detailed written records that have survived. There are no known scenes of battle, no praise poems for generals, and no reliefs showing armies in formation. It appears that this culture did not glorify war in the same way. Disputes or struggles, if they took place, may have been smaller in scale or handled within the framework of local communities and councils rather than large imperial campaigns. Here the contrast with Greece, Rome, and Mesopotamia becomes clearer. Greek and Roman cultures recorded their conflicts in detail. Writers such as Herodotus, Thucydides, Polybius, and Livy never shy away from vividly recording battles, campaigns, coups, and shifting alliances. These stories of conquests and victories were recorded not only in scrolls but also their cities' arches, columns, and temples. War was undeniably central to their identity and public memory. In Mesopotamia, kings carved their victories on stone stelae, boasted of defeated enemies, and built enormous structures that projected strength. Conflict and rulership were displayed openly and deliberately.

And so, in 1931, Marshall and Mackay concluded in their report that the people of Mohenjo Daro and other Indus cities were neither warlike nor fearful of invasion. Their view shaped the early image of the Indus Valley Civilization as a peaceful and cooperative society.

Later research, however, made this picture more complex. Modern scholars emphasize that the limited number of weapons in the Indus Valley's archaeological record does not necessarily rule out violence. Many Indus tools and objects were made from copper, wood, and other materials that decay over time. Weapons made of perishable materials would not survive thousands of years in the soil. In addition, later excavations at some sites have uncovered skeletons with injuries, including skull fractures and other trauma, which point to episodes of interpersonal violence or unrest. These remains do not suggest great wars but do show that life was not entirely free from conflict.

Environmental and social pressures were a likely source of conflict. Studies of ancient river systems show that the courses of the Indus and related rivers shifted over time. Flooding, drought, and the drying of certain channels would have threatened crops and trade. A society that depended on careful management of water and agriculture would have felt these changes sharply. Competition for land and resources could have led to disputes.

There is also evidence that some Indus cities contained elements of controlled access and protection. Citadel mounds created raised areas that were easier to defend. Gateways regulated entry into certain sectors. The grid layout of streets, while practical, also allowed movement to be watched and directed. These features suggest that the people of Harappa and Mohenjo Daro understood risk and took measures to manage it, even if they did not surround their cities with massive stone walls.

Taken together, the evidence suggests that the Indus Valley Civilization was stable and highly organized but not entirely free from tension or danger. It differed from Greece, Rome, and Mesopotamia not because it lacked conflict but because it did not celebrate or monumentalize it. Authority seems to have been quieter, spread through systems and planning rather than embodied in a single visible ruler.

Labeling the Indus Valley as a purely peaceful civilization oversimplifies reality. The people of the Indus Valley may not have sought glory through war, yet they understood power, order, and survival.

The Vanishing of the Ancient Cities

It is believed that around 1900 BCE, Harappa and Mohenjo Daro, cities once bustling with craftsmen, merchants, and traders, went through early signs of decline. Streets that had been regularly maintained began to fill with debris. Workshops fell silent. Public buildings were no longer repaired. But the change was gradual rather than sudden, and no evidence suggests that invading armies were responsible.

What remains of Mohenjo Daro.[8]

The reasons behind this decline are complex, but the largest culprit could be mother nature and time. As mentioned, studies of ancient river systems show that the Indus and its tributaries shifted their courses over time. Some rivers dried; others moved far from the cities they once supported. This unfortunate change undoubtedly threatened agriculture, which depended on the predictable cycles of flooding and irrigation. Eventually, fields that had once been fertile turned dry, making it difficult to cultivate. In some regions, signs of over-farming and soil exhaustion appear in the archaeological record.

There was a clear domino effect. With less water and failing harvests, trade networks weakened. The long-distance exchange that had once connected the Indus Valley to Mesopotamia and Central Asia began to shrink. Merchants lost the stability that had once allowed them to move goods across wide regions.

As resources thinned, people gradually left the cities in search of more reliable land. Small groups and families began moving east toward the Gangetic Plain, which offered more dependable rainfall and open areas for settlement. Of course, the movement was not an organized migration but more of a slow dispersal over many years. As people spread out, the large cities were abandoned. Brick by brick, time and weather reduced them to the mounds that Charles Masson later explored.

It is safe to assume that no single culture replaced the Indus world immediately. Instead, new patterns of life emerged in the north and east, forming the early stages of what would later become known as the Vedic age. The people who lived in the Ganges region built different kinds of settlements, used new forms of pottery, and developed new social structures. Still, it is likely that elements of the Indus tradition survived among the communities that carried the memory of the old cities with them.

The influence of the Indus Valley can be seen in the persistence of standardized weights and measures in later periods, in certain craft techniques, and possibly in symbols that appear in later religious traditions. The careful planning of Harappa and Mohenjo Daro, with their regulated streets and civic management, may have shaped later Indian ideas of order, balance, and communal responsibility. So, even without written records, the Indus world left traces in the way its towns were organized and in the value placed on collective life.

By the time the first Vedic settlements grew into chiefdoms, the Indus cities were already memories buried deep beneath earth and sand. But their foundations, both physical and cultural, helped shape the next chapters of India's story. The disappearance of this early civilization made room for the rise of new kingdoms, new beliefs, and new leaders.

Chapter 3 – Chanakya, the Key to Chandragupta's Rise

The Nanda Empire was founded by Mahapadma Nanda sometime between 345 to 340 BCE—a time when India was experiencing remarkable growth. Based in Magadha, with its capital at Pataliputra, the empire controlled some of the richest lands in the subcontinent.

The Gangetic Plain produced grain in such abundance that it could feed multiple cities and armies at once. The empire also had its hands on many mines that were full of gold and other precious stones. Trade routes connected Magadha to distant regions, allowing various goods and tributes to travel directly into its treasury. From these resources, the Nandas built what Greek writers later described as one of the largest military forces of the ancient world. They wrote of thousands of infantry and cavalry, long lines of chariots, and elephants that marched like moving towers.

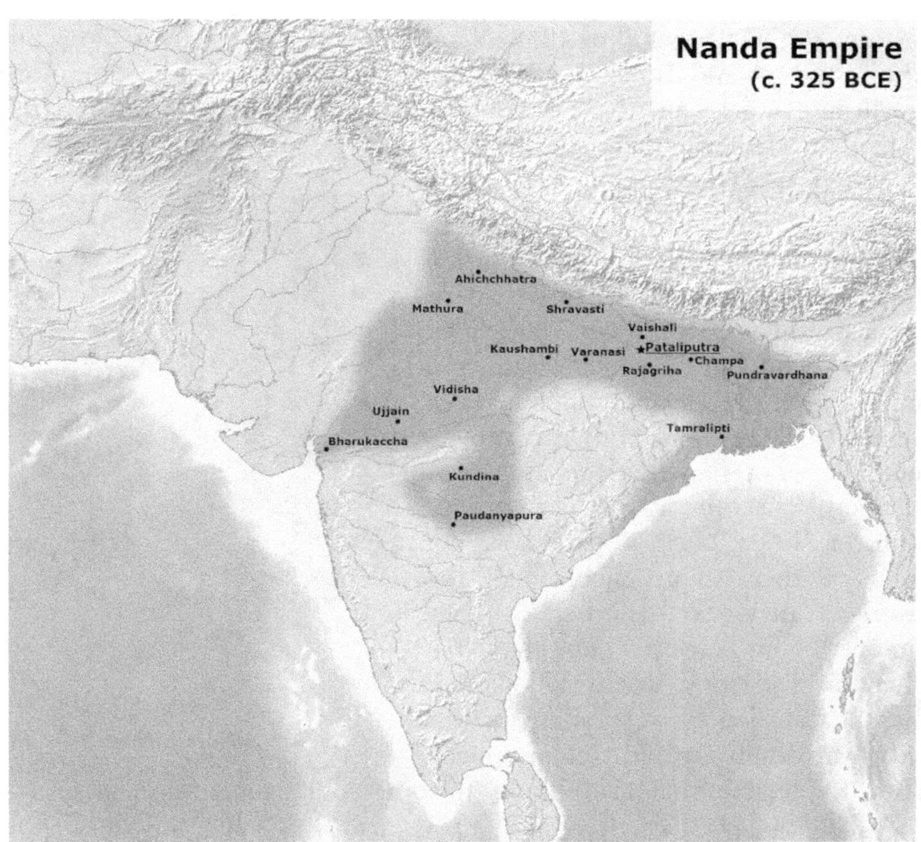

The extent of the Nanda Empire circa 325 BCE.[9]

Of course, every empire had its own set of challenges. Despite its power and wealth, there was distance between the empire's ruler and its subjects. Maintaining a colossal army had always been costly, so taxes were heavy. Farmers had to pay substantial portions of their harvests. Merchants, though still active and influential, eventually found themselves navigating through layers of officials whose duties were tied closely to taxation. And so, especially in the countryside, many local rulers and clan chiefs began to resent Magadha's authority.

As if these problems were not enough, Magadha also featured a social order that further added to the tension. Indian society had several classes, each with traditional roles in religion, warfare, trade, and labor. One of these classes was known as the Brahmins, who were long seen as the caretakers of learning and rituals. They held influence in the Nanda Empire, but that influence was not constant; it varied from court to court. Some valued their counsel, using them as guides to craft policy and custom. Others, including the Nanda court, preferred to look to administrators and military commanders, whose priorities were more practical. As a result, these scholars were not always treated with the respect they believed their learning deserved.

A Brahmin named Chanakya experienced this mistreatment firsthand. He was often described in Brahminical stories as a brilliant scholar from Taxila. He was well-versed in not only ritual and religion but also statecraft and philosophy. Another legend spoke of Chanakya being born with a complete set of teeth—a sign that the child was destined to become a king. His parents, however, knew such a path was not easy. Rather than accepting the prophecy, they were disturbed. So, they removed his teeth, hoping that Chanakya's destiny would be altered. But the astrologers were adamant that the royal destiny would not disappear.

A depiction of Chanakya.[10]

They were certain that it would pass to someone he guided instead.

And it was true: Chanakya would soon become a king maker. This particular story began when he traveled to Magadha sometime near the end of the fourth century BCE. He was expecting the reception that a scholar of his rank usually received. But things went south when the Nanda king—possibly Dhana Nanda, the son of Mahapadma Nanda—mocked him. Legend has it that it was because of the Brahmin's lack of teeth or simply his less appealing appearance. Other sources disagree with this narrative, claiming that the king never mocked him but simply dismissed him outright without listening. Whatever the exact details, this moment was a turning point that set Chanakya on a new path. Soon after, he left the court with controlled anger and a promise. From then on, he had one mission: to topple down the Nanda Empire.

Chanakya made his way toward the city of Taxila, where many roads intersected, carrying merchants, envoys, teachers, and students from all over the distant lands. Interestingly, the city had no single ruler. It thrived mostly on trade, ideas, and the movement of people. Here Chanakya remained, teaching curious minds for some time. Meanwhile, he kept his eyes open and his ears sharp, listening intently to even the smallest news about the empire.

One day, he encountered a certain boy whom he believed had potential. His name was Chandragupta Maurya. Details of his background are murky; we do not have a single confirmed origin. The Jain tradition, for one, claimed Chandragupta belonged to the Maurya tribe, which was possibly part of the ancient Kshatriya (traditional warrior class of ancient India). Others wrote that he was raised among hunters or a group of herdsmen. Whatever his origins, he does not appear in the legends as a polished figure. The stories describe a boy who was bold, curious, and quick-thinking but also rough around the edges, untrained in the formalities of royal courts.

However, Chanakya did not approach the young Chandragupta immediately. He kept a close watch on him before finally interacting with him. Their early interactions were not sentimental. Chanakya did not take him as a son or as a prodigy to admire. He saw in him something useful—potential that could be shaped into a force capable of challenging a powerful dynasty. So, their relationship, as remembered in the narratives, was built on purpose rather than affection.

From Chanakya, Chandragupta learned the basics of statecraft, warfare, and the structure of kingdoms. He was told to observe the ways rulers gain and lose support. Chanakya also bestowed on him the art of alliances. He was taught how allies were important, especially in a land divided by many clans. Chanakya tested Chandragupta's memory with stories of ancient kings, often asking the young boy to repeat the lessons in his own words. Chanakya also instilled discipline in Chandragupta, emphasizing its importance in a strong leader. Whenever the young Chandragupta acted recklessly, Chanakya would correct him. In other words, the scholar was always by his side, working to refine his natural energy into direction and strategy.

Of course, the training in Taxila was not confined to lessons and conversations. As Chandragupta absorbed his teachings, Chanakya began laying the foundation of what would become a quiet but far-reaching campaign against the Nandas. He knew that confronting Magadha head on would mean certain death. He must ensure that the empire was weakened from within before making any direct challenge. And, as if the heavens were on his side, the opportunity was laid right in front of him.

Taxila was the perfect place to gather intelligence and build alliances due to the constant movement of merchants, monks, and foreign travelers. He shared meals with travelers who had passed through border towns and listened to their stories about discontent among local chiefs. Ancient sources also describe how Chanakya would dispatch men and women across the land, disguised as wandering ascetics, storytellers, healers, and traders. Unsuspected, these spies could observe the roads and settlements. They counted the number of soldiers, took note of their rotating shifts, and eavesdropped on rumors and reports about shortages of grain. Through these wandering men and women, Chanakya learned which officials were corrupt, which governors were resented by their subjects, and which towns were holding their anger as they were abandoned by the Nanda court.

Chanakya also made use of the merchants. Long distance trade was the lifeblood of the northwest, so those who moved goods across great distances often knew more about the state of the land than any court official. He spoke with merchants who carried goods to Pataliputra and never shied away from lending his ears when they complained about taxes that ate into their profits and were reportedly high enough to discourage long journeys. So, it was relatively easy for Chanakya to convince these merchants to aid him. They were willing to cooperate if they believed there was a chance for change. Through them, Chanakya gained contacts in market towns and ports, forming an informal network of traders who could carry news faster than most messengers.

Bribery and misinformation played their part as well. Once Chanakya knew which officials in the Nanda administration could be swayed and which commanders lacked loyalty, he began scheming with the help of his coin purse. Money sent through the right channels opened doors that would otherwise have remained shut. Rumors were also spread in places where they would cause friction, and doubts were planted among those who already felt neglected by the royal court. The aim was not chaos but erosion, a slow weakening of the structure that held the empire together.

Of course, spies and the cooperation of merchants were not enough to bring down an empire. It was crucial for Chanakya to gather more concrete supporters. So, he sought allegiance with the clans that lived beyond the direct clutch of Magadha—especially those who had lost autonomy under earlier Magadhan rulers and were forced to suppress their grievances with the Nandas. Knowing that these clans were only lying low until an opportunity came, Chanakya approached them with practical agreements. He offered future influence, trade advantages, and reduced taxes if the clans agreed to support him when the time came. One of his strongest allies was Parvataka, the king of the mountain kingdom known as Himavatkuta. In exchange for his alliance, Chanakya offered him half of Nanda's empire—but would soon resort to trickery to reverse the offer.

By the time Chanakya and his protege Chandragupta left Taxila, the empire's outer regions were slowly eroding. The heart of the empire still appeared strong, but beneath the surface, cracks had begun to form. And, interestingly, these cracks were not opened by fierce soldiers and large-scale battles but by a network of ordinary people who followed the whispers of a patient scholar.

Meanwhile, the future ruler, Chandragupta, had grown into a fine, more disciplined man. Many years following his first interaction with Chanakya, he began moving with small groups of followers. True, these were not large armies that could challenge the Nandas openly. But their numbers were strong enough to strike the empire's outposts and intercept supply lines. Over time, Chandragupta's name had become known by those who longed to see the empire crumble. His growing number of supporters, combined with the stories of his feats, allowed him to encourage local rulers to turn against Magadha.

As Chanakya's efforts continued to spread unease, the Nandas found themselves increasingly isolated. Dhana Nanda, remembered in later stories as a king who cared for nothing but his own wealth and pride, began to sense the nearing danger. But, with the size of his army and the riches of his treasury, the king was confident. He was certain Chandragupta was only a small thorn in the thicket. Little did he know, armies loyal to their source of pay often lose their spirit when stability falters, and riches offer little protection when the channels that carry them are disrupted.

With the help of Parvataka, Chanakya and Chandragupta made their major move. They marched their army and laid siege to the many cities scattered close to Pataliputra. One city, whose name has been lost to time, is said to have put up strong resistance. The old story describes how Chanakya successfully tricked the city into lowering their guards. Disguised as a Shaivite mendicant (holy person), he entered the city and offered a word of advice. He suggested that the heavens had spoken that the siege would only end if the idols of the seven mothers were removed from the town's temple. The defenders, ever superstitious and perhaps driven by desperation, quickly followed his suggestion. After the idols were removed, Chanakya quietly ordered his army to end the siege. The defenders, glad to have followed the humble mendicant's words, rejoiced and began celebrating their victory. This was the time: Chanakya's army launched a surprise attack and captured the city soon after.

It was only after subduing all the regions outside the capital that Chanakya and Chandragupta moved toward Pataliputra. They captured the capital city but spared the Nanda emperor. He was allowed to escape death by going into exile, taking nothing more than a cart of goods. Some Sanskrit texts say that when the emperor and his family were leaving the city, his daughter caught a glimpse of Chandragupta and immediately fell in love. She then chose him as her husband, following a traditional practice known as *svayamvara* in which a woman chooses her spouse herself. But as she stepped down from the cart to approach the new ruler, nine spokes of the cart's wheel mysteriously broke. Chanakya saw this incident as an omen, claiming that the Maurya dynasty, beginning with Chandragupta, would last for nine generations. Whether Chandragupta married the princess remains uncertain since no historical evidence was found to support the legend.

Meanwhile, Parvataka was also said to have fallen in love with one of Nanda's *visha kanyas* (legendary female assassins in ancient India who specialized in poisoning their targets). Ancient Sanskrit writings claim that Chanakya approved of the marriage. Unfortunately, Parvataka succumbed to poison when he touched the woman during their wedding. This was the moment Chanakya saw a chance to reverse his words to Parvataka years earlier. He urged Chandragupta to not call a physician and let Parvataka die.

With Parvataka now off the chess board, Chandragupta became the sole ruler of Nanda's territories. This was the birth of the Mauryan Empire, which lasted from 321 BCE to 186 BCE.

With the regions now under a new sovereign, reconstruction soon began. Although Chandragupta sat at the top of the hierarchy, Chanakya's influence could be felt in the early years of the Mauryan Empire. Vast experiences had taught him that a kingdom built on shifting alliances needed firm roots, so meticulous changes had to be made. Perhaps to keep Chankya's word, taxes were reorganized, ensuring fairness and consistency. Next, the fresh empire appointed new administrators who were screened for their skill and reliability rather than their connection to the court. Land was measured, surveyed, and recorded so that the state could further understand its own resources.

Even Pataliputra experienced change. The city that had served many earlier dynasties soon grew into a more structured administrative center. Its channels were cleared and its roads greatly repaired. New quarters were built to accommodate the increasing number of officials, scribes, and workers. Discipline had always been the most important quality in both Chanakya and Chandragupta's eyes. So, they expected to see this quality in the empire's system of governance. Reports from distant regions must be submitted on time, and revenue collection must follow measured rules instead of fluctuating demands. To eradicate corruption—or lessen it, at least—officials who served the crown worked under closer supervision.

Trade, which had shown signs of weakening under the Nandas, began to strengthen once more. The new administration system no longer treated the merchants as convenient sources of quick revenue. Farmers, too, could breathe easier as they were freed from excessive taxes and vague regulations.

Inscriptions and later accounts speak of an empire that grew more stable with each passing year. While Chandragupta provided the authority, Chanakya supplied the framework that allowed the new emperor to manage a large and diverse land. But as this order settled across the Gangetic Plain, events unfolding far to the west began to draw closer to India's borders.

Alexander's death brought chaos. His vast empire was fractured among his four generals, who were eager to carve out a domain from the territories he had conquered. One of the four generals was known as Seleucus. This seasoned commander claimed the former Persian lands that stretched from Babylon to the foothills of the Hindu Kush. And so, when news of the new Mauryan Empire reached his ears, Seleucus started strategizing.

Seleucus marched east sometime in 305 BCE, confident that he could assert control over a valley he believed to be a part of the Macedonian inheritance. However, when he reached the borders, what he witnessed surprised him. The Mauryan Empire was undeniably strong. It was unified and organized, complete with a massive army. This was far from the fragile, scattered territory he had expected. Historians wrote that war took place, but only for a short while. Details are unclear, but

Chandragupta eventually proved that the Mauryan Empire was not to be trifled with. Continuing the war would be unwise, so Seleucus chose to make a treaty with Chandragupta.

Through this treaty, they established diplomatic relations. Seleucus agreed to leave several eastern provinces (including the areas of modern Afghanistan and Pakistan) firmly in the hands of Chandragupta. In return, the Mauryan Empire gifted Seleucus with five hundred war elephants, which later became a major asset in Hellenistic warfare. These very elephants accompanied Seleucus in the Battle of Ipsus (301 BCE), in which he emerged victorious.

With peace achieved and another major conflict evaded, Seleucus sent Megasthenes to Pataliputra as an ambassador. His observations of the foreign lands, later compiled in *Indica*, introduced the Greek world to Indian cities, customs, and political organization. Through him, information traveled in both directions, creating one of the earliest formal links between the Mauryan state and the Mediterranean world.

As the empire strengthened its ties abroad, life within the court moved steadily into a new generation. Chandragupta's reign, shaped so deeply by Chanakya's guidance, was approaching its middle years when stories surrounding the birth of his son began to take form. These stories come from much later sources, yet they became some of the most widely repeated tales in Indian tradition.

Chanakya was determined to protect the king from poison, a common danger in ancient courts. It was believed that Chanakya would quietly add small amounts of poison to the king's meals to build immunity. But this resulted in a tragedy one day when the Mauryan emperor shared his meal with his pregnant queen. While Chandragupta could withstand the poison, a single bite was all it took for the queen to collapse to the floor. Chanakya, realizing what had happened, rushed to the queen's side. It was too late for the queen—but not her unborn child. Legend has it that Chanakya cut open the queen's womb and rescued the baby before the poison could spread further. However, a single drop managed to touch the child's forehead, leaving behind a dark mark. Apart from this permanent mark, the boy was unharmed. This drop of poison led to his name, Bindusara, which means "the strength of the drop."

As for Chandragupta, he did not remain on the throne until his death. Later traditions suggest that he withdrew from public life and surrounded himself with the teachings of Jain monks. In 298 BCE, he abdicated the throne and made a journey south to Karnataka. There, he lived the remainder of his life as an ascetic. Jain traditions also say that the former emperor later undertook a ritual fast to death.

Meanwhile, in Pataliputra, the matters of governance were left to his son, Bindusara, whose rise marked the second generation of Mauryan rule (out of nine). Mirroring his father before him, Bindusara was a capable ruler. He maintained the vast territories once secured by Chandragupta and built on the disciplined system that had been established. His reign is remembered as a time of stability. Relations with Hellenistic kingdoms continued, and the Mauryan court retained its reputation as a center of order and intelligence. Envoys traveled between India and the western realms, carrying messages, gifts, and news. And through all of this, Chanakya continued to work behind the scenes, advising the young king and ensuring that the structures of governance remained intact.

The ruins of Pataliputra.[11]

However, Chanakya's time was almost up. Many historians agree that he died in 275 BCE, but they are uncertain about the manner of his death. Some records say that political tension began to take place within the court. Bindusara is said to have shunned the old Chanakya after listening to an accusation made by a courtier named Subandhu. The courtier, jealous of the advisor and wishing to remove him from power, told the emperor about his mother's death, whispering that Chanakya purposely poisoned the queen.

Driven by anger, Bindusara dismissed Chanakya, who went on to live quietly in a forest. But Subandhu still could not rest easy; he was afraid that Chanakya would soon plan his return. So, he arranged for the humble hut where Chanakya was staying to be burned to ashes. His plan worked, and the ninety-two-year-old Chanakya died. Bindusara eventually regretted his decision. He arranged for a reconciliation, but all was too late.

Chapter 4 – Ashoka's Unique Transformation

Being good is not easy. And trying to uphold benevolence while at the top of the hierarchy is even harder. Wearing a crown unsurprisingly comes with a myriad of responsibilities: managing lands and taxes, commanding armies, judging disputes, punishing treason, settling succession, holding fragile coalitions together, and determining the fate of thousands with a single decision. Absolute power also amplifies impulses. Fear could easily turn into extreme paranoia, caution into blind suspicion, and discipline into cruelty. Even a well-intentioned king could slip into brutality when put under pressure.

History has endless pages that illustrate this pattern. In China, the first emperor, Qin Shi Huang, was credited with unifying the warring states. But alongside this contribution to civilization, he also went down in history for harsh legalism, mass executions, and (allegedly) the burning of books. It is safe to say that his achievements and his violence are inseparable in historical memory.

Mesopotamia had rulers such as Naram-Sin of Akkad who embraced divine kingship, invoking their heavenly mandate while suppressing revolts with overwhelming force. Their absolute authority justified absolute retaliation. The famous Persian king Cambyses II was also a favorite subject of discussion among Greek writers. They often described him as a cruel and unstable ruler who never hesitated to destroy anything that lay in his path to victory—though these accounts were likely exaggerated by his enemies. And Rome, too, was put under the leadership of notorious emperors many times across history. Nero, Caligula, and Caracalla were said to have been extremely paranoid, constantly thinking about their own assassinations.

Ancient traditions tended to remember rulers in extremes. Everyone was either a heroic conqueror or a monstrous tyrant—nothing in between. Only a few kings remained in the gray area. The combination of immense power, constant threats, and the need to validate authority pushed many leaders toward decisions that later generations judged harshly. And it was rare for kings to grow gentler as they aged. Often, they tightened control, punished dissent more heavily, and relied increasingly on fear to stabilize their rule.

The same, however, cannot be said of the third emperor of the Mauryan Empire, Ashoka. Admittedly, his early reputation fits perfectly alongside the names of other harsh figures of antiquity. Later Buddhist texts even referred to him as "Chandashoka," which simply means "Ashoka the Cruel." But interestingly, his story does not follow the usual arc. Instead of being remembered for increasing ruthlessness in the later years of his reign, Ashoka eventually became known as the emperor who transformed for the better.

The Violent Path to the Throne

The Mauryan Empire had grown tremendously under Chandragupta and Bindusara, but it was also politically complex. Succession within such a huge state was rarely smooth, and Ashoka's ascent became one of the most brutal episodes preserved in India's historical memory.

Ashoka was not the next in line. The designated heir was his older brother, Crown Prince Susima. Although both held significant influence in court—Susima was backed by important nobles, and Ashoka's military capabilities were acknowledged—Ashoka's unstable temper made him inferior to his brother. He was respected but at the same time feared.

Still, Ashoka would not accept defeat. Buddhist sources such as *Ashokavadana* and *Divyāvadāna* claim that a violent struggle ensued after Bindusara's passing. According to these writings, Ashoka did not hold back. He is said to have killed ninety-nine of his brothers, which was almost every rival who stood in his path.

Of course, modern historians view these numbers with skepticism. The number ninety-nine is typically used to emphasize dramatic moral transformation rather than literal events. Buddhist authors purposely wrote their narratives this way to portray Ashoka as a man who sank deeply into violence before rising into virtue. But still, their exaggeration was not baseless. The Mauryan succession was contested, and bloodshed was not uncommon in ancient royal households. Eliminating rivals—be it brothers, cousins, or influential ministers who had served the court for decades—was always a real possibility in the struggle for power. Whether Ashoka killed dozens or only a few, the underlying truth is that his ascent was marked by force and violence.

A depiction of Ashoka riding his chariot, carved on the Sanchi Stupa.[12]

Once the throne was his, the new Mauryan emperor moved quickly to consolidate his power. This was the period when his ruthless side took over almost completely. He imposed strict governance, demanding absolute obedience from both officials and commoners. Multiple traditions portray him as an autocratic ruler whose early decisions were often shaped by a combination of suspicion and a desire to assert complete control. Although few administrative details from this period survive in inscriptions, later accounts suggest he was harsh with dissenters and swift in meting out punishment to those who defied imperial authority.

One of the most infamous stories that details his brutality was recorded in the *Ashokavadana*. The story says Ashoka once ordered the massacre of 18,000 wandering ascetics in Bengal. These people were Ajivikas, a sect considered heretics by the orthodox Vedic traditions of ancient India.

Of course, as with many dramatic ancient stories, this episode must be approached with caution. Interestingly, the massacre does not appear in any contemporary inscription. Even the number—18,000—is suspiciously rounded, a typical feature of ancient storytelling. Scholars see this story as an example of polemical literature. It was designed to portray Ashoka as a zealous king who punished rival faiths and to explain the decline of the Ajivika sect.

Ashoka's Legends of Cruelty

This massacre was not the only legend preserved by Buddhist authors to frame Ashoka's life as a dramatic journey from brutality to moral awakening. While the legends' historicity is doubtful, their place in the tradition is significant, revealing how later storytellers understood and reshaped the image of the emperor.

The most memorable and daunting of all is the story of "Ashoka's Hell." This account speaks of Ashoka, said to be a sadistic ruler, building an elaborate torture chamber. Before launching the construction project, Ashoka dispatched his men across the empire with the task of finding a suitable man to become the empire's official executioner. Ashoka's men eventually found the perfect candidate, who went by the name of Girika. He was so vicious that when his parents tried to stop him from taking the position, Girika mercilessly murdered them. This was perhaps viewed as loyalty by the emperor, who swiftly appointed him as the empire's official executioner.

The executioner advised the emperor to build the torture chamber based on the suffering endured by people reborn in Buddhist hell. Ancient texts described the structure in full detail. It had a rather deceptive exterior. To those unaware of the purpose of the building, it appeared pleasing in the eyes. Its entrance was indistinguishable from that of a well-kept palace building. This beauty, however, ended at the gate.

Inside, there were horrors modeled on the five torments of Buddhist hell. The interior was said to contain boiling pits for immersing prisoners, heated metal floors meant to scorch anyone who stepped inside, hidden blades, and other violent contraptions meant to prolong suffering. Some versions add that Ashoka decreed that anyone who entered the building, whether prisoner or visitor, would never leave alive—including himself.

Weirdly enough, none of these details about the chamber appear in Ashoka's inscriptions. Scholars have also unearthed no archaeological evidence that could prove the existence of this torture complex. So, many scholars have deduced that the torture chamber was nothing more than a moral allegory—a literary device designed to represent the cruelty that Buddhist storytellers believed characterized Ashoka's early rule.

Another legend written in the *Divyāvadāna* emphasizes that Ashoka's cruelty revolved around his officials. This episode began with Ashoka assembling his ministers and ordering them to do something rather peculiar. He told them to cut down every flowering and fruit-bearing tree in the royal gardens, leaving only the trees full of thorns.

Baffled, the ministers responded with utter silence at first. Flowering trees provided shade, color, and fruit. Thorny trees, on the other hand, had no benefits and were considered nuisances. Unsure of the rationale behind their emperor's orders, the ministers approached him to seek clarification. According to ancient sources, they asked Ashoka not once but three times, hoping for an explanation or perhaps permission to disregard the command. Ashoka, however, interpreted their repeated questioning as insubordination. In a fit of rage, the emperor unsheathed his sword and beheaded five hundred of his ministers.

As with the story of the torture chamber, the details here are also far from historical. Scholars also point at the rounded number—five hundred—which was a symbolic figure commonly used in ancient storytelling. The lack of Mauryan-era sources also cements the conclusion that this episode was created by later Buddhist authors to shape readers' imagination about how Ashoka reigned in his early years. The flower trees could have represented prosperity, beauty, and generosity, while the thorny trees could have symbolized severity and harm. The emperor's preference for thorns over blossoms could be a metaphor for his moral state, and his violent reaction to questioning reflects a ruler whose authority rested on fear rather than respect.

The Transformation

All these stories, taken literally, describe a tyrant of almost theatrical cruelty. By portraying Ashoka at his worst, the storytellers create the foundation for one of antiquity's most extraordinary reversals. The greater the cruelty attributed to Chandashoka, the more astonishing the emergence of Dhammashoka appears in the narrative arc that follows.

The incident that led to his reversal varies depending on the source. One lesser-known narrative speaks of the involvement of a monk named Samudra. According to the story, Samudra was seized by Girika and imprisoned in the infamous torture chamber. There, the monk was subjected to many kinds of unthinkable punishments. Girika himself inflicted various torments on him, yet the monk remained mysteriously unscathed.

When Ashoka heard of this event, he made haste to see the monk in person. The story goes that, during their meeting, the monk directly rebuked Ashoka, speaking without fear, and confronted him with the suffering his rule had unleashed. The rebuke struck Ashoka hard enough to break through whatever indifference or cruelty had previously guided him. Samudra's admonition included the instruction to build stupas (sacred Buddhist monuments) across the empire and to ensure the protection of all living beings. The tale concludes with Ashoka burning the torture chamber to the ground. He then burned the merciless Girika to death and vowed to rule with righteousness instead of violence from then on.

In this narrative, Ashoka's transformation is instantaneous, triggered by the authority of a holy man. Whether or not such an event occurred, the story reflects a long-standing attempt to explain how someone remembered for cruelty could alter his life so dramatically.

The second version of the story, however, is more historically grounded. According to this version, Ashoka's transformation for the better was triggered by neither the acts of a holy man nor a magical incident. The emperor began to change his rule at the end of the Kalinga War.

Kalinga was once a prosperous coastal state with a strong tradition of independence. For a long time, it resisted Mauryan expansion, refusing to bid its independence goodbye. But when Ashoka launched an invasion around 260 BCE, Kalinga was forced to go through a period of terrible chaos. The campaign eventually ended in a decisive Mauryan victory. But what distinguishes this war from countless others in ancient history is the emperor's own testimony about its aftermath.

According to Ashoka's later reflections, the fighting resulted in an unimaginable loss of life. He records that approximately 100,000 people died. Another 150,000 were taken captive or deported. Many more perished from famine, displacement, and disease in the chaos that followed.

Ashoka reportedly visited the affected regions after the campaign ended. The burned settlements, scattered corpses, and sight of countless families grieving the death of their loved ones stirred his stony heart. His later reflections describe a moment when the enormity of the destruction overcame him, and remorse seized his mind with a force he had not expected.

From this experience, an internal shift began to take place. Ashoka didn't merely regret the cost of the war in administrative terms, nor did he frame it as a political miscalculation. Interestingly, the language, preserved in various forms, expresses a more personal sense of sorrow. He realized that the conquest had brought grief rather than glory and that the human cost far exceeded any strategic benefit. It is this emotional and moral turning point—not a miraculous intervention or a political necessity—that many historians view as the genuine beginning of his transformation.

Whatever mixture of personal guilt, ethical awakening, or pragmatic realization shaped Ashoka at this moment, it marked a clear departure from his earlier reputation. The emperor once remembered for eliminating his rivals without thinking twice, enforcing harsh punishments, and allowing (or at least accepting) the violence of conquest now felt the consequences of his own actions. The transformation did not require external miracles or symbolic stories; it emerged from the confrontation between his authority and the suffering that authority had produced.

The Benevolent Emperor's Policies

Ashoka's transformation did not remain an internal turning point. Over the years that followed, it reshaped the principles by which he governed. This gave rise to what later tradition called Dhammashoka, "Ashoka of Dhamma." The word "dhamma" in this context did not refer to a strictly Buddhist doctrine, nor was it a religious code meant for monks. Ashoka used it to describe a practical moral policy for the empire. This was a code of conduct that emphasized compassion, restraint, fairness in justice, and mutual respect among different social and religious groups. It was a guiding principle intended for everyone— ordinary people, officials, and even the royal household.

In the emperor's new point of view, justice required three simple things: moderation, patience, and avoiding unnecessary harshness. To ensure these ideals were put into practice, Ashoka reshuffled his administrative machinery. He appointed groups of officers he referred to as *dhamma-mahamattas*. Their duty was straightforward: they must promote moral welfare across the empire. These officials were expected to travel from province to province, keeping their eyes open for disputes and other conflicts that could result in violence if left unchecked. They advised on proper conduct and ensured that vulnerable groups, particularly the poor, the elderly, and those without family support, were not neglected. Some would say the creation of this position was one of the biggest signs of the empire's departure from conventional ancient statecraft. Instead of dedicating administrative resources to collecting taxes or suppressing never-ending rebellion, Ashoka used them to advocate for ethical behavior.

Ashoka's reforms also extended to areas that earlier rulers rarely addressed. He ordered a reduction in animal slaughter, particularly in royal kitchens, and encouraged alternatives to killing for food or ritual. He supported planting trees along roadsides, digging wells for travelers and villagers, and establishing rest houses for people journeying across the vast Mauryan territories. True, these measures might seem minor, but they reflected a broader principle: governance should strive not only to maintain order but also to ease hardship and improve the daily lives of the people who depended on it.

One of the most distinctive features of Ashoka's dhamma policy was his religious tolerance. Although he personally favored Buddhism after his transformation, the emperor refrained from imposing his beliefs on his subjects. Several of his inscriptions repeatedly emphasize that respect should be shown to all religious sects. He warned against boasting of one's own faith while disparaging another's, insisting that such behavior caused harm and hindered mutual understanding. This deliberate promotion of cross-sect dialogue was unusual in a world where religious competition often shaped political allegiance. For Ashoka, harmony among diverse traditions was a political necessity and a moral imperative.

The Dhauli Major Rock Inscription of Ashoka, with its front shaped like an elephant head.[18]

Despite this emphasis on tolerance, Ashoka's patronage played a significant role in the spread of Buddhism. He supported monastic institutions, encouraged the settlement of monks in different parts of the empire, and is traditionally associated with the convening of the Third Buddhist Council. According to later sources, the council sought to purify the monastic community by removing doctrinal disagreements and reinforcing discipline. Whether or not Ashoka directly sponsored such a council, his reign undeniably strengthened the position of Buddhism in the subcontinent.

The most far-reaching effect of his patronage was the dispatch of Buddhist envoys to regions beyond the Mauryan realm. Traditional accounts describe missions being sent to Sri Lanka, the Himalayan regions, Central Asia, and even to faraway lands under Hellenistic influence. These missions helped establish Buddhist communities abroad, laying foundations for the religion's long-term expansion. In India itself, Ashoka supported the construction of stupas and monasteries, many of which became important centers of learning and pilgrimage long after his death.

For several decades, Ashoka's efforts reshaped both the moral and religious landscape of the Mauryan Empire. Of course, it's impossible to know whether every ideal was fully implemented. But his inscriptions and administrative changes reflect a ruler who consciously attempted to reshape imperial authority through principles rarely associated with ancient monarchs.

Ashoka died sometime in 232 BCE. Despite leaving behind an empire that was still intact, his successors did not share the same moral vision. The empire bid farewell to the stability that Ashoka had maintained. Succession disputes emerged almost immediately, as different factions supported different heirs. In a vast empire that depended on strong central leadership, uncertainty at the top encouraged provincial governors to assert increasing autonomy. Some territories, especially in the south and borderlands, drifted toward practical independence, maintaining only nominal allegiance to the center. External threats soon manifested and grew too big to curb following the reign of Dasharatha (the grandson of Ashoka and the fourth Mauryan emperor).

This political decline had significant consequences for Buddhism. Regional rulers who emerged in former Mauryan territories did not inherit Ashoka's personal commitment to Buddhism. Many belonged to communities aligned with older Brahmanical traditions. As they established or revived their courts, they naturally promoted the religious practices and institutions familiar to their own lineages.

Without state sponsorship, Buddhism's position in the subcontinent changed, though it did not vanish immediately. Its influence gradually receded from the heartlands where Ashoka had once elevated it. Monasteries eventually lost royal funding, missionary activity slowed, and the religion's intellectual centers faced increasing competition from resurgent Brahmanical schools.

Over time, Buddhism became more prominent in the northwest and in regions connected to trade routes, even as it diminished in the Gangetic Plain. Meanwhile, the missions associated with Ashoka's patronage had taken root abroad, helping Buddhist thought spread to regions where it would endure long after it faded from much of India.

The enduring impact of Ashoka's transformation lies not only in his personal shift but in the scale at which he attempted to implement it. The memory of Ashoka's transformation was immortalized, shaping how later generations understood the possibilities and limits of power guided by conscience.

Chapter 5 – What Goes Around Comes Around

At a glance, life in the royal courts of the ancient world might seem like a dream without worries. Luxury and power were both included in the package, but so was danger. These royal courts were where power shifted, often without clear warning. In some halls, the change came with a shout, while in others, it emerged in complete silence—at times carried out by the very hands that once swore loyalty.

Rome, for one, knew this game too well. Several of its emperors met their fate at the hands of the Praetorian Guard, the ones ironically responsible for keeping them safe at all costs. Persia also watched its kings fall, not to foreign invasions but to generals who called themselves Persian. Even the old kingdoms of the Nile once witnessed episodes in which the pharaohs succumbed to the plots of their own attendants or viziers.

Of course, scenes like these were not confined to the western world. In the far east, across the plains of northern India, the courts of Magadha carried their own history of sudden turns. The walls of Pataliputra, no matter how high, could not completely defend its rulers against the dangers within.

One such story from this subcontinent took place in the late sixth century BCE, long before the rise of the Mauryan Empire. It was a time when the kingdom of Magadha was run by its first major ruling house, the Haryanka dynasty.

The King Killed by His Own Flesh and Blood

The throne belonged to King Bimbisara, whose reputation was pristine; he was considered one of the most respected rulers of his age. His court was known for its steady administration, and the king himself was often praised for his ability to manage alliances without constant warfare. To this day, Bimbisara is remembered for many contributions, especially annexing the kingdom of Anga to the east, which set the foundation for the rise of the Mauryan Empire. He was also believed to have been a stout protector of Buddhism. (Bimbisara was the king who built Rajagriha, a city often mentioned in Buddhist writings.)

But despite ruling the kingdom for over five decades, the king was never free from silent threats from his own court. The crown prince, Ajatashatru, had grown restless as he watched his father's long and stable reign. Some nobles and advisors in the court spread the rumor that Bimbisara favored his younger son, while others whispered to the crown prince that it was high time he claimed the crown. They pledged their loyalty to Ajatashatru not because they believed in his potential but because they hoped to increase their own power through the prince. And so, bit by bit, bigger ambition took root. Ajatashatru began to see his father as an obstacle.

Bimbisara was so focused on the kingdom that he did not fully sense the change in his son. Tension in the palace grew quietly. When the prince finally reached the point of no return—knowing he had steady support from certain court factions—he seized control of the palace guards and confronted his father. The crown prince held the king under arrest at first. He is believed to have been confined in a chamber away from the court. Only then did Ajatashatru murder him. His cause of death, however, remains a subject of debate. While some say he was starved, others say he died of shock after being tortured.

The ruins of a prison in Rajgir, believed to be the one that held King Bimbisara.[14]

Ajatashatru took the throne soon after, sometime around 492 BCE. The act that placed him there remained unspoken in public, but it shaped the atmosphere of the court. Regardless of what had happened, the new king was determined to expand Magadha's power. While Bimbisara had favored alliance and negotiation, Ajatashatru preferred to rely on military strength. He became one of the most forceful rulers of his time, launching campaigns that changed the political map of northern India. He went to war with the kingdom of Kosala, fought the powerful Licchavi confederacy, and built impressive fortifications to protect Magadha's borders. His ambition pushed the kingdom outward in every direction.

Ajatashatru reigned for about thirty-two years. However, when it was clear that the calm unity of Bimbisara's time had never fully returned, the court advisors' view of the king began to shift. Other powerful nobles soon followed suit, aligning themselves with factions rather than the throne. Ajatashatru ruled with determination, but the bond between the royal family and the court had been weakened by the act that gave him the crown.

Around 460 BCE, the king's son, Udayin, turned against him. With the support of factions within the palace, Udayin struck down his father and seized the throne. The pattern that had begun with Bimbisara repeated almost exactly, as if the palace itself had grown accustomed to resolving succession through the bloody removal of the king.

Unfortunately, after Ajatashatru's death, Magadha went through a period of decline. There were rapid changes in leadership. Udayin was later killed by a minister, and the kings who followed him ruled only briefly. Some reigned for a few years, others for only months, and many met their end through the same quiet violence that had claimed their predecessors.

Pushyamitra's Rise after Bloodshed

As you may remember, a short while after Chandragupta Maurya rose to the throne around 322 BCE, Chanakya predicted that the dynasty would last for nine generations. This was neither a curse nor a blessing—merely a statement made by a man who understood deeply how quickly loyalty could shift in the royal palace. And as the years passed, his words seemed to come truth.

After Ashoka's long reign, the throne was passed to Dasharatha. He inherited a vast realm, and keeping such an empire under complete control was never easy. His rule covered regions that still carried the Mauryan name, but it was clear that each province moved at its own pace. Southern territories became more distant, western satraps hesitated over tribute, and even the military had slowly lost the discipline that had defined the days of Chandragupta.

After Dasharatha, the empire was ruled by Samprati, who attempted his best to restore order. Some ancient sources describe how he traveled across regions, hoping he could mend strained alliances and unite the people. However, a king could only do so much; the realm he governed was no longer the mighty empire of earlier times. Skirmishes and conflicts among frontier clans became more common, and the governors entrusted to keep order often acted more on their own judgment than on instructions from Pataliputra. Although trade still resumed, enriching the empire, there were clear changes. The roads, once patrolled by loyal officials, began to see more local toll collectors and self-appointed guardians. Eventually, the empire had trouble maintaining its far-flung provinces.

During this period of decline, Brihadratha came to the throne. His authority extended over Magadha and nearby regions, but beyond that, obedience depended on negotiation rather than command. But, as the ninth emperor of the Mauryan Empire, Brihadratha was not planning to sit still as his realm collapsed around him. He spent long hours surrounded by advisors as he studied reports that came from distant towns and held audiences to reassure both nobles and common citizens that the empire was standing firm.

It's unfair to label Brihadratha a weak ruler, as it is clear he was in a difficult position. His court was divided into groups that cooperated only when necessary. Senior ministers who once served under his predecessors still carried influence, but they were more cautious than loyal. They could easily shift their loyalty, siding especially with those who seemed capable of protecting their interests. Messages sent to distant provinces returned slowly or not at all, and Brihadratha often found himself making decisions without knowing whether his orders would be respected.

Brihadratha tried all means to mend these fractures. He offered gestures of reconciliation to rival court factions and attempted to strengthen ties with regional leaders through marriage alliances and diplomatic exchanges. But each effort met with only partial success. Some nobles accepted his authority, but their concern that the empire would soon crumble never left their thoughts. Others respected him but doubted whether the Mauryan name still carried enough weight to keep the realm steady.

Even the army, once the strongest pillar of the empire, reflected the same uncertainty. The soldiers acknowledged Brihadratha's rule but preferred to look to their commanders for direction. After all, their pay was no longer as regular as before, and supplies often arrived late. Officers disagreed about priorities: whether to defend the weakening western frontier, assist local disputes in the east, or hold position and wait for clearer instructions. The soldiers felt the shift and naturally responded only to leaders who were decisive.

Brihadratha was well aware of this; he knew that it was the army that gave order to the empire. This was the reason he placed great trust in a general named Pushyamitra.

Born into a Brahmin family known for learning and strict practice, Pushyamitra chose to become a soldier early in his life. After years of disciplined service, he rose through the ranks and became a commander who valued clarity and structure—the two qualities he carried into every unit he led. When he took charge of a unit, he began with simple measures that everyone in the camp noticed. Reports were to be written and delivered at fixed times rather than whenever an officer remembered. Orders were given in plain language, repeated until even the last line in the formation understood them. When confusion broke out at a frontier post over who was responsible for supplies, he redrew the chain of command and named a single officer in charge, making it clear who answered for what. These were not dramatic reforms, but they turned scattered groups of soldiers into a force that could move as one when needed.

So, it is not surprising that the soldiers respected him. They had served under kings who once commanded absolute obedience, but they could sense that Brihadratha lacked confidence. In contrast, Pushyamitra stood before them with certainty.

However, Brihadratha saw this as a blessing. With the court no longer united and the trust of regional leaders gradually faltering, the emperor valued Pushyamitra's steady presence. Pushyamitra became his sole hope, often summoned for counsel and suggestions. Even when Brihadratha had to attend official ceremonies, he wanted Pushyamitra at his side. The Mauryan emperor knew that the public held the general in high regard but failed to notice that the soldiers' respect and loyalty ended with the general.

As the years passed, the empire moved closer to imminent ruin. There were growing dangers at the borders. The northwestern frontier, in particular, never stopped facing pressure from ambitious local powers. For many years, the Indo-Greek kingdoms had also been causing trouble there. Kings like Demetrius and Menander had been taking advantage of the weakening state of the Mauryan Empire. Some ancient writers blamed Brihadratha, who showed no signs of resistance. Because of this, the enemy managed to push through Punjab and Mathura, eventually laying attacks on Saket and Pataliputra.

Pushyamitra became convinced there was nothing the emperor could do to save his world. The only solution was to eradicate the ruler he deemed incapable and place himself on the throne. After all, he knew he had the ultimate support of his men. Brihadratha, however, remained oblivious; he strongly believed that Pushyamitra stood behind him.

One day, Brihadratha decided to hold a grand parade of the army. Historians generally agree that he held this occasion simply as a display of confidence, to show the public that the Mauryan throne still held authority and that the soldiers still marched under the royal banner. Officials welcomed the idea, and court officers accepted the invitation politely. While the army obeyed the announcement, their quiet glances clearly revealed where their respect had settled.

This was the last day the people of Magadha ever saw their emperor well and alive. At first, the parade seemed like just another grand royal celebration. The parade ground stretched wide, packed with long lines of infantry, archers, and cavalry. Elephants stood at the edges, with their keepers guiding them into position. The loud rhythm of drums could be heard across the field as the units arranged themselves in perfect rows. The banners of the Mauryan Empire proudly fluttered above them. However, even before the ceremony began, many soldiers looked not toward the royal pavilion but toward Pushyamitra, who inspected the formation with his sharp gaze.

The emperor entered last, riding in a chariot. Some say he wore no excessive decoration, choosing to appear steady and humble rather than grand. As he stepped down, attendants parted the way, and the murmur of his arrival moved through the ranks. He walked along the front lines, greeting commanders with confidence and offering brief acknowledgments to the troops. To untrained eyes, his posture carried dignity, but those who paid attention could see the strain behind it.

Pushyamitra followed a short distance behind, neither too close nor too far. He wore formal armor polished to a dull shine, his sword at his side. Those who knew him recognized the calm focus in his movements as he approached the king, ready to continue the ceremonial inspection that followed every such occasion.

When Brihadratha signaled for him to come forward, Pushyamitra stepped ahead, confident and obedient. To the spectators, it seemed like nothing more than the usual exchange between the king and his most trusted commander-in-chief. The soldiers watched in silence, accustomed to seeing the two men stand side by side during official events. The court officials who were gathering at the edge of the field also observed the interaction, unaware of what would unfold just a few moments later.

The general bowed in the expected manner, and Brihadratha leaned slightly forward, prepared to hear whatever report or respectful greeting Pushyamitra was about to deliver. In that moment of closeness, before any words were spoken, Pushyamitra unsheathed his sword. Brihadratha saw his movement, but it all happened so quickly that he failed to react in time. Without hesitance, Pushyamitra plunged his weapon straight into the ruler whose trust in him was as deep as the vast ocean. Brihadratha staggered. Perhaps shock overtook him before pain did. His attendants shouted, but none reached him in time.

Brihadratha's lifeless body collapsed to the ground, but Pushyamitra did not move a muscle. He did not attempt to flee or defend himself for the bloody act he had committed. Instead, he stood upright, still clutching his sword in one of his hands, as if he had simply accomplished a kill on the battlefield. The parade ground fell into a long, terrible stillness. Thousands of soldiers watched their emperor fall at the hands of his own commander, yet not a single rank broke formation. Not an arrow was drawn. Not a spear shifted. Some looked uneasy; others stunned, but none stepped forward to challenge the man who had led them through years of decline. The grim silence was the clearest sign of how far the empire had slipped from its old foundations. It seemed as if they accepted the death of the last Mauryan emperor with an open heart.

Brihadratha's body was carried away, and Pushyamitra immediately shouted commands to secure the palace and prevent confusion in the city. The troops obeyed at once. No riot or resistance broke throughout the empire. By the end of the day, the gates of Pataliputra opened for the general who had become the new ruler of Magadha. Just as Chanakya had predicted, the Mauryan dynasty ended with the death of Brihadratha in 185 BCE, the ninth generation.

Pushyamitra moved quickly once he entered the palace. He knew all too well that assassinating the incapable king was only the beginning. A new ruler needed soldiers who would obey his instructions, nobles who would cooperate without question, and administrators who would carry out orders without hesitation. Therefore, his first few moves were to consolidate his standings in Pataliputra.

To officially assert his authority in the eyes of both nobles and rival kings, the new emperor undertook the Ashvamedha, one of the most important Vedic royal rituals of ancient India. The rite involved a sacred horse, which was handpicked by Pushyamitra. He then released the horse to wander freely for a full year. Any king who stopped it had to fight the royal army. In Pushyamitra's case, the horse was left completely unharmed and returned to him safe and sound—showing that his authority was unchallenged. To end the ritual, he sacrificed the horse during a major ceremony that included feasting.

Then, Pushyamitra focused on restoring discipline within the army. Pushyamitra placed trusted officers in charge of key units, refreshed the chain of command, and ensured that supplies finally reached distant posts on time. The soldiers responded immediately. They had followed him while he served as general and continued to do so now that he stood at the center of authority.

One of his biggest challenges was the threat imposed by the Indo-Greek rulers. Now that Pushyamitra was at the forefront of the empire, it was time to retaliate. Headstrong as ever, the new ruler of Magadha refused to let the borders crumble any further. So, without hesitation, he sent detachments to reinforce the western regions and counter-attacked the threats laid by the Indo-Greeks. He even personally coordinated the movement of larger forces from the center of the kingdom. The conflicts that followed were violent, but they did not expand into extended campaigns. Pushyamitra pushed back the Indo-Greek advances and reminded neighboring states that Magadha still possessed strength.

Apart from issues on the border, Pushyamitra also focused his attention inward toward older practices he believed would help his efforts to stabilize the kingdom. He revived Vedic rituals that had been less prominent during the later Mauryan years. These ceremonies involved Brahmin priests, generous gifts, and the recitation of ancient verses. However, not everyone viewed this revival positively. Several Buddhist texts, particularly those written generations after Pushyamitra's rule, describe him in a more negative light. They speak of his harsh decisions: Pushyamitra allegedly destroyed monasteries and ordered the executions of many monks. Some accounts describe his raids on Buddhist centers and how he often offered rewards for killing Buddhist monks.

These accounts, however, are not completely reliable. Later historians, especially, have debated these claims. While some believe these stories mirror the real conflicts between religious communities at that time, others argue that they were shaped by later political tensions rather than the events of Pushyamitra's reign. What's more, archaeologists have found evidence of continued Buddhist building activity during Pushyamitra's reign, suggesting that the situation may have been more complex than the accounts describe. Still, the presence of such stories reveals that Pushyamitra's rule left strong impressions.

One fact is certain. Pushyamitra succeeded in bringing Magadha back to its feet. He strengthened tax collection in the core territories, reorganized local councils, and appointed officials who would not challenge his authority. Roads were also repaired, reviving trade activities, and borders were fortified.

Pushyamitra wore the crown for approximately thirty-six years, eventually establishing a dynasty known as the Shunga. He was then succeeded by Agnimitra in 149 BCE. As the son of Pushyamitra, Agnimitra was a capable ruler. He had served the empire earlier as governor, so he was well versed in the matters of the court by the time of his coronation. Agnimitra reigned for only eight years, but his contributions were impressive. Besides patronizing arts and literature, he is remembered for waging a successful war against the neighboring independent kingdom of Vidarbha. It's safe to assume that Agnimitra continued some of his father's policies while giving more attention to palace affairs and regional negotiations.

Unfortunately, after Agnimitra, the line of Shunga rulers grew weaker. Regional clans again grew bold to push for autonomy. There were signs of division among the court officials, and Pataliputra's nobles also began to prioritize their own positions over the stability of the empire. By the time Devabhuti inherited the throne in 83 BCE, the empire had once again lost much of the strength that Pushyamitra had built.

Devabhuti wasn't just the last king of his line. Many traditions describe him as inattentive to affairs of state. Some accounts record how he was easily distracted by court entertainment and found joy in the comforts of the palace. In other words, he was a ruler who preferred private pleasures to public responsibilities. Whether these descriptions were exaggerated by later writers or reflected his true nature remains uncertain, but the effect on the court is clear. When a king withdrew from his duties, others stepped forward to fill the space he left behind.

One person who took advantage of this was Vasudeva Kanva. As a senior minister, he held high influence in the court. He had already built connections among powerful nobles and aligned himself with those who believed the emperor had no desire to lead the empire. Vasudeva Kanva also oversaw messages that came in and out of the palace, managed the royal coffers, and had eyes on the movement of officials at all times. Unlike Devabhuti, Vasudeva paid close attention to the state's governance. Over time, many courtiers began to consult him rather than the ruler they were supposed to serve.

Ironically, the Shunga line ended in treachery—just like the Mauryan dynasty. According to Bāṇabhaṭṭa, a Sanskrit poet who lived many centuries later, Devabhuti was assassinated by Vasudeva Kanva, with the help of the daughter of a slave woman serving the emperor.

With the death of Devabhuti, Vasudeva Kanva made himself the new emperor of Magadha, establishing the Kanva dynasty. The Kanva rulers sat on the throne of Magadha from 73 BCE to 28 BCE. The Kanva's fall into the hands of the Satavahana dynasty marked the end of Magadha as a single, centralized power.

Chapter 6 – Women in Ancient India

One of the most popular epics of ancient India, the *Mahābhārata*, contains the story of a certain woman known by the name Draupadī. She is, in fact, one of the central characters of the ancient Sanskrit epic. Considered one of the most prominent figures in both Hindu and Indian culture, Draupadī is often noted for her beauty, courage, devotion, intelligence, resilience, and rhetorical skills. Even to this day, her story has been an inspiration for artists and performers alike.

According to the epic, Draupadī was a princess of the Panchala kingdom and the wife of the five royal Pāṇḍavas brothers named Yudhishthira,

An illustration of Draupadī and the Pāṇḍavas brothers.[15]

Bhima, Arjuna, Nakula, and Sahadeva. Their story, however, is not a romantic one, as it centers on a political disaster. The brothers were in a constant rivalry with their cousins, the Kauravas, who were described as deceitful.

One of the most famous episodes in the epic occurs when Yudhishthira, the eldest of the Pāṇḍava brothers, accepts a dice game proposed by the power-hungry Kauravas. Unaware that the game is rigged, he eventually gambles away everything he ever possessed. At first it's his wealth, then his kingdom, and finally, himself. Then, Draupadī enters the episode. She is dragged into the Sabha, the royal assembly hall, as part of the final wager. However, instead of responding with fear or submission, Draupadī remains composed. She asks nothing but a simple question:

"If my husband lost himself first, what legal rights does he have left to stake me?"

The Sabha is filled with powerful figures like Bhīṣma, the kingdom's senior statesman and authority on morality, Droṇa, the military commander, and Dhṛtarāṣṭra, the blind king presiding over the dispute. But none can answer her.

Her question breaks the court's moral paralysis. After a moment of prolonged silence, the blind king, Dhṛtarāṣṭra, responds. He grants her request for first Yudhishthira's freedom, then the freedom of the other Pāṇḍavas.

Of course, this story is literary, not historical. But it has shaped Indian cultural memory for centuries because it presents a woman who understands the mechanics of power better than the men around her.

Another major Indian epic, the *Rāmāyaṇa*, speaks of another female figure: Sītā, the wife of Rāma, a prince celebrated for his moral integrity and destined to be king. The story begins when Sītā is abducted by the ruler of Lanka, Rāvaṇa. With the support of his allies, Rāma eventually rescues her, but another conflict rises upon her return. Many doubt her purity. (This is a reflection of patriarchal expectations deeply embedded in the social values of the period. Often, a woman's honor was judged through standards imposed by the community rather than by her actions or intentions.)

An illustration of Sītā and her husband, Rāma.[16]

However, Sītā does not waste her time defending herself verbally. She knows that the only way to silence those who judge her is to show evidence. So, she chooses a response that defines her character for thousands of years: Sītā chooses to go through a test known as the *agniparikṣā*. In this trial by fire, Sītā steps into a burning pyre. There are many versions of the outcome, but the most popular one says that the fire deity, Agni, protects her. She emerges from the fire unharmed, proving her innocence. She is accepted back by Rāma and the court. The episode marks one of the most debated moments in the epic, reflecting the heavy moral expectations that women were often forced to shoulder.

Still, these two episodes illustrate something important about ancient Indian storytelling. Women are not merely background decorations. They serve as catalysts, challengers, and anchors for the moral and political dilemmas that drive both epics forward. Their actions are decisive, and the narrative revolves around their choices.

Needless to say, the historical reality of women in ancient India was complex. Their position was neither uniform nor static. Their status changed considerably across time, region, and social class, creating a landscape where empowerment and restriction often coexisted.

In the Early Vedic period (c. 1500–1000 BCE), textual evidence points to a society in which women were held in high regard. Not only were women of this period viewed as respected members of the household, but they were allowed to enjoy a degree of freedom that later eras refused to preserve. Young girls were given formal education, sometimes studying the same sacred texts as boys. Women were also given opportunities to participate in public rituals and philosophical discussions. In some cases, they composed hymns that made their way into the Vedic corpus.

Notable figures such as Gargī Vācaknavī, who debated metaphysics in the *Bṛhadāraṇyaka Upaniṣad*, and Maitreyī, who questioned the nature of immortality, appear in early texts as respected intellectuals.

Marriage also operated differently during this time. Women could choose their partners in certain contexts, and texts record forms of marriage where mutual consent was essential.

Religious life further reinforced this early pattern of respect. The worship of goddesses such as Sarasvatī (learning), Lakṣmī (prosperity), and Durgā (strength and protection) was already well established. These were far from being minor deities. In fact, these goddesses were considered central figures in ritual life, reflecting a worldview in which feminine power—*Śakti*—was seen as fundamental to cosmic order.

But as time passed, this landscape gradually changed. In the later Vedic and post-Vedic periods, women became subject to more rigid patriarchal norms. Legal and didactic texts from these eras began to define women primarily through their roles as daughters, wives, and mothers. The flexibility of earlier centuries gave way to greater emphasis on male authority and female obedience. Sadly, the freedoms and rights women once enjoyed became increasingly limited to specific communities or elite groups.

This change can also be seen in social practices that gained prominence in later periods. Child marriage became more common, narrowing the span of a woman's autonomy. The dowry system, though not uniform across the subcontinent, placed additional economic burdens on families with daughters. This also led to the perception of women as financial liabilities. In theory, property rights existed, particularly the concept of *strīdhan*, property gifted to a woman at marriage. But widows often lost inheritance claims, and remarriage was never a good option since it could strip them of earlier rights.

Despite these tightening restrictions, women did not disappear from political or administrative life. In certain dynasties and regional polities, women still exercised genuine authority. The kingdom of Magadha, for instance, felt the influence of powerful female figures such as Queen Nandini. She was often associated with diplomacy, intrigue, and political maneuvering during the era of the Nanda dynasty. Elsewhere, inscriptions and narratives mention queens managing estates, issuing land grants, or ruling as regents when political circumstances demanded it. These examples do not negate the broader decline in women's freedoms, but they show that female leadership was not entirely removed from the historical record.

The Controversial Story of Tishyarakshita

This story takes place during the reign of Ashoka. The emperor was said to have multiple queens who gave birth to several sons. Of course, each of these sons were backed by different circles of influence with their own interests. Ministers, attendants, and relatives all held different opinions on who should wear the crown next. It was during this period of tension that Tishyarakshita appears in the literary record.

An illustration of Tishyarakshita.[17]

Tishyarakshita's name did not come from administrative archives or inscriptions. Instead, her image comes almost entirely from Buddhist narrative texts such as the *Ashokavadana* and *Divyāvadāna,* both of which were written centuries after Ashoka's life. These sources are valuable, but they were also shaped by moral lessons, sectarian interests, and narrative convention. This means they must be approached with caution.

In these accounts, Tishyarakshita is introduced as a younger wife of Ashoka. She is described as intelligent, perceptive, and very involved in courtly matters. However, the Buddhist authors place her firmly in the role of an antagonistic queen, following a pattern seen in many South Asian literary traditions in which powerful royal women are depicted as jealous or dangerous to highlight a moral point. Her story centers on one of Ashoka's sons, Kunala. According to the Buddhist legends, he was exceptionally handsome, virtuous, and devoted to the principles of dhamma.

According to most Buddhist authors, this episode took place when Kunala visited a distant province to serve as the governor on behalf of Ashoka. Before he set out for this journey, he was stopped by Tishyarakshita. Some speak of their meeting in the palace, others during a ceremonial gathering. Whichever the venue, Tishyarakshita was believed to have developed an infatuation the moment she laid eyes on the prince. Kunala, however, rejected her advances, reminding her that she was his own stepmother.

Tishyarakshita was enraged by the rejection, though she did not exact revenge immediately. One day, while Ashoka was deeply asleep, she quietly took a letter the emperor had prepared to be sent to the ministers in Taxila, where Kunala was stationed. She altered the message, changing a word in the Prakrit script from *adheetaam* ("he must study") to *andheetaam* ("he must be blinded"). Tishyarakshita then sealed the letter carefully, making it appear as if it was untouched.

When the letter arrived in Taxila, the ministers were horrified. They showed signs of hesitation until Kunala strongly advised them to do as the emperor wished. According to another version, Kunala himself read the order and blinded himself with a hot iron as an act of obedience. Regardless, Tishyarakshita succeeded in her plan.

Kunala and his wife, Kanchanmala were left with no choice but to wander the land as beggars, surviving only by playing music. Ashoka eventually discovered what happened to his son. Overwhelmed by grief and enraged at his wife's treachery, the Mauryan emperor punished Tishyarakshita severely: she was executed.

But, as we said, this event is not corroborated by historical evidence. The complete silence on this in Ashoka's inscriptions suggests that the dramatic story preserved in Buddhist literature belongs to a later interpretive tradition. The Buddhist writers use this moment to reinforce the king's commitment to justice and the karmic consequences of unethical behavior.

There are also political explanations that fit the situation more plausibly. Ashoka had several sons, and Kunala was not the clear successor. His mother, according to some traditions, was not a principal queen, which may have weakened his position. A queen advocating for her own son's claim was not unusual. Neither was political maneuvering to diminish the influence of rival branches of the royal family. In this light, the story of Tishyarakshita's romantic jealousy could be a later embellishment imposed on what was originally a succession struggle. The Buddhist chroniclers, viewing the court from a moral lens, might have reframed political conflict as a tale of personal misconduct.

Still, the persistence of her story, however hostile the sources, implies that she was not a marginal figure. Even if the details are distorted, her presence in these legends indicates that she was remembered, however imperfectly, as someone whose actions influenced debates over succession and legitimacy. That alone places her among the women whose imprint on ancient Indian political life survived the centuries, even if only through the lens of those who disapproved of her.

Ambapālī, One of the Most Influential Women of Ancient Vaiśālī

Before the Mauryan Empire came to dominate northern India, the city of Vaiśālī was best known for its unique politics. Unlike most of the cities on the subcontinent, Vaiśālī was not ruled by a single monarch. Instead, it operated as a republic governed by an assembly of clan leaders known as the Licchavis. Under this system, certain public roles carried both prestige and responsibility. Among them was the position of *nagarvadhu*, a term that translates to either "bride of the city" or "the city courtesan."

Far from being marginalized, the *nagarvadhu* was an officially recognized figure representing refinement, culture, and artistic accomplishment. The title was reserved only for highly talented and beautiful courtesans in ancient India. They often performed at public events, acted as a patron of the arts, and of course, were expected to interact with the social and political elite.

Our main character, Ambapālī, belonged to this class. Her reputation was preserved in Buddhist texts and local traditions, which often described her as graceful, talented, and highly sought after by both nobles and visiting dignitaries. Her origins, however, vary depending on the source. According to one popular legend, she was discovered as an infant under a mango tree. This gave her the name Ambapālī, which simply meant "the mango-grove girl." This origin story is typical of literary traditions that seek to elevate a figure by giving them an unusual beginning.

An ivory carving depicting Ambapālī (right) greeting Buddha.[18]

A more grounded explanation suggests she was trained and appointed as the city courtesan because of her unparalleled skills. In a republic like Vaiśālī, where cultural events played a diplomatic role, the *nagarvadhu* needed to be not only educated but also musically accomplished and socially adept—and Ambapālī excelled in all these qualities.

One of the clearest signs of Ambapālī's standing was her ownership of her own estate, which included a well-known mango grove. This was unusual, especially when not all women were given the same property rights. Often, their rights depended on context and caste. According to traditional narratives, her estate was valuable enough that the Licchavi nobles sought to acquire it for themselves. Records preserved in Buddhist texts describe how they attempted to pressure her into relinquishing it by using their political authority to challenge her ownership.

But Ambapālī was always firm; she would not easily yield. She resisted the nobles' pressure by continuously asserting her legal rights and leveraging her public position. In the end, she retained her property. The dispute reveals how firmly she stood within Vaiśālī's political and social framework. Clearly, she was not merely an entertainer completely dependent on patrons. She was a figure with her own autonomy, wealth, and legal standing in one of the most powerful republics of the time.

Her interactions with nobility were not limited to local politics. Later, merchants and even kings sought her company not solely for pleasure but because an association with the *nagarvadhu* of Vaiśālī was a mark of prestige. This gave her a form of unwritten influence. People in high positions treated her with the same seriousness they reserved for political allies.

Ambapālī's later life is most clearly preserved through the *Therīgāthā*, an ancient anthology of poems composed by early Buddhist nuns. A set of verses attributed to her offers a rare first-person reflection on aging and the passage of time. These verses describe the fading of her youthful beauty without sentimentality. She lists specific parts of her body (hair, skin, limbs) and notes how they have changed. However, she frames her transformation as an inevitable process rather than a source of sorrow. The tone is introspective, matter of fact, and grounded in the Buddhist emphasis on impermanence.

These verses are also remarkable because they represent one of the earliest forms of women's autobiographical writing in India. Through them, Ambapālī speaks with her own voice, not filtered through the perspectives of male authors. They offer an unembellished glimpse into her self-understanding as a woman who once occupied a position of public admiration and later embraced a life of renunciation.

Bhadda Kundalakesa, the Woman Who Debated Anyone

Bhadda Kundalakesa was born into a wealthy merchant family. The beginning of her story, however, is intertwined with a certain boy. Unlike Bhadda, the boy's birth was accompanied with ominous signs—though the records never mention exact details. His parents, worried that he might bring misfortune, initially considered putting him to death. But they eventually had a change of heart and raised him.

Those signs later proved accurate. As he grew older, the boy developed a compulsive habit of stealing. He would take whatever he could reach without regard for consequences. His parents did everything to set him right. They scolded and punished him, but he continued stealing. When he reached adulthood and showed no ability beyond this compulsion, his father gave him the means to become a professional thief and left him to his own fate.

What followed was predictable. The young man broke into so many houses that news of his crimes reached the royal court. Enraged, the king gave his officers a single day to find the culprit or face execution themselves. Under such pressure, the thief was caught quickly and sentenced to death.

This is the moment Bhadda enters the story. As the thief was led through the city on the way to his punishment, Bhadda saw him. For reasons unknown, love manifested. Bhadda felt an intense attachment to him and immediately begged her father to interfere and secure his release. After being persuaded, the king granted a pardon, and the thief was made Bhadda's husband.

Unfortunately, even after coming close to death itself, the thief remained unchanged. He continued to steal, and soon, his target was none other than the person who had saved his life. He noticed that Bhadda always wore expensive ornaments, so he devised a plan to kill her and escape with her jewelry. He lured her to a remote spot at the edge of a cliff. His plan was to push her off the cliff and remove her ornaments. But Bhadda was quick to discover his schemes. And so, she acted first and killed him.

Returning to her family after killing her husband, despite it being self-defense, was not an option. Concerned with social fallout and the uncertainty of her position, Bhadda made a drastic decision. She renounced the world and joined a Jain ascetic order. (The stories note that Jain nuns had their own hermitages and traveled widely, suggesting that female renunciants were a recognized and visible presence in ancient India.) Bhadda entered their ranks, setting her on the path that would define her reputation for the rest of her life.

Once she embraced the ascetic life, Bhadda's sharp intelligence quickly became her defining trait. Wandering ascetics across different traditions frequently engaged in public debates, which were typically held in marketplaces, courtyards, or public parks. These debates drew large audiences and often shaped a sect's reputation.

Bhadda excelled in this environment, and her reputation grew tremendously. Early sources depict her as articulate and quick-thinking. She was adept at exposing weaknesses in opposing arguments. Bhadda would travel from town to town, challenging philosophers, priests, and other renunciants. Legends claim that she rarely lost.

Although embellished by tradition, these stories suggest an important historical core: Bhadda built a reputation not through noble birth or political marriage but through impressive intellectual prowess. She operated comfortably in a domain normally dominated by men, and she earned respect—as well as notoriety—on her own terms.

Her most prominent stage of life was when she crossed paths with Sāriputta. As expected, Bhadda invited him to a debate. She was confident that her reasoning could withstand any opponent, even one of the Buddha's foremost disciples. She threw question after question to Sāriputta, but he answered each one smoothly. When she finally lost the debate, Bhadda did not have a fit. Instead, she learned the limitations of her training. According to Buddhist texts, she realized that she had mastered argumentation, but argument alone could not provide the insight she sought. Impressed by Sāriputta's responses in the debate, she requested ordination in the Buddhist order.

Bhadda Kundalakesa's story, like many preserved in Buddhist literature, blends historical memory with a pinch or two of legend. The basic elements, including her marriage, the cliffside incident, her time with the Jainas, her debating career, and her eventual conversion, likely reflect real traditions about a well-known female ascetic. The dramatic framing of her defeat by Sāriputta, however, bears the imprint of didactic storytelling.

Even so, her presence across multiple sources and her own surviving verses show that she was remembered as a striking figure. To this day, she is viewed as an example of a woman of intellect, self-determination, and formidable presence in the debates that animated ancient India's religious landscape.

Chapter 7 – The Arrival of the Horsemen: A Reimagination

The Byzantines knew them as the Hephthalites. Others referred to them as White Huns. Indian sources, however, call them the Hunas. These people came all the way from a realm that stretched across the lands north of the Hindu Kush, touching regions known today as Kazakhstan, Uzbekistan, and the western edges of Xinjiang. They were also different from the Huns who troubled the Roman Empire.

These regions were challenging, shaped by harsh winters and open steppe. It was nearly impossible for the Hunas to stay in one place permanently. When supplies dwindled and mother nature turned into a challenge, they must search and move to another location, building everything from scratch once more. These people soon moved into India, wreaking havoc across the flourishing Gupta Empire.

It's safe to say that the Hunas were one of the fiercest groups of horsemen to ever exist in Central Asia. Their children were expected to learn to stay balanced on a galloping horse before they could even speak clearly. Apart from being skillful at maneuvering a lightning-fast steed, the Hunas were also described to be exceptional in mounted archery. These were some of the skills that allowed them to push into Bactria, contest with the other steppe groups, and even test the strength of the Persian kings. Victory was not always theirs, but they could always learn a lesson from each encounter.

Of course, raiding was not one of their hobbies. Nomadic tribes typically embarked on migrations or invasions when the plains they called home were growing crowded, exhausted, or threatened by new rising clans.

And so, when the Hunas heard word of a wealthy and fertile land that lay to the south beyond the jagged barrier of the Hindu Kush, they were quick to strategize their surprise arrival. The Gupta Empire appeared mighty to the untrained eye, but it was beginning to rot from within—and the Hunas knew this. An empire might be strong, but none were impregnable forever.

The riders mounted their horses and began their long descent to the south in the mid-fifth century CE. At this time, their name was still unknown in the lands they approached. But it wouldn't take long for that to change.

The State of the Gupta Empire

The Gupta Empire is considered India's classical golden age. It rose to prominence sometime in 320 CE under Chandragupta I and reached its zenith under his successors, Samudragupta and Chandragupta II. With its location lying across the Gangetic Plain, the dynasty was bestowed with luxurious gifts: fertile fields, busy trade routes, and old urban centers—all of which contributed to its massive wealth and authority.

The Gupta Empire was known for stability and refined administration. Under the reign of the Gupta rulers, cities like Pataliputra, Ujjain, and Mathura bloomed like never before. They transformed into important centers of learning, commerce, and religious activity.

Gupta rulers prioritized art, literature, and knowledge. They frequently supported poets, scholars, and artisans whose works shaped the memory of early Indian civilization. This period marked the flourishing of Sanskrit literature and the expansion of knowledge in astronomy and mathematics.

Sculptors and metalworkers also produced some of their best creations during this time. The seated Buddha from Sarnath (near Varanasi), for instance, is a prime example of the Gupta period's artistic style, which fascinates art historians to this day. Later images of the Buddha in India and Southeast Asia were heavily influenced by this very style.

Trade with lands to the west and across the Indian Ocean also kept markets active and ports bustling with color. To many within the core of the empire, it seemed like a period of confidence and cultural richness, a time when the world felt orderly and the boundaries of the kingdom secure. It was easy to fall into the illusion of security. Many believed that the empire's trouble ended at the borders and could never trespass into its great halls.

But the more influence and fame an empire secured, the bigger the threat it would soon face.

Rumor on the Frontier

It was just after sunrise that the man guarding the watchtower at the edge of Gandhara noticed approaching visitors. This frontier post was located far from the comforts of the big cities, so a single glance across the horizon could easily alert the guards.

However, this time, the guests were not enemies. It was a caravan that seemed more anxious than usual. The traders had dust on their clothing, and their animals looked tired, as if they had been pushing harder than usual. Suddenly, one of the merchants stepped forward, greeting the guards in a slow voice. He did not bring the usual chatter about markets, roads, or precious goods they had just traded. Instead, he brought a rumor-something that had shaken his men enough that they spoke of it only once they were inside the safety of the outpost walls.

The merchant claimed that, beyond the passes, a village had been burned to the ground. The attack must have been swift, he said, too fast for villagers to mount a defense. The raiders moved in and vanished before anyone could identify who they were. He also informed the guards about their strange discovery in the ashes: small metal pieces marked with unfamiliar patterns. They certainly did not belong to the Guptas or the Kushan. They were also not older coins from the northwest.

Then, another merchant added more detail to the news. He had heard rumors that these riders were not like the settled clans of the region. Instead, they rode smaller, tougher horses and were armed with bows that could bend farther than Indian archers believed possible.

The officer in charge of the outpost listened without interrupting. The news was not exactly surprising to him since he had heard vague hints of such riders in recent seasons. But this was the first time anyone had traveled directly from a burned settlement. Quickly, he ordered the guards to record the information shared by the weary traders and sent a messenger east with a report.

The Beginning of an End

There was no sign of unease in the east. Life in the capital at Pataliputra resumed as usual. The morning opened with the sound of conch shells, temple bells, and the low voices of scholars politely greeting one another in the shaded courtyards. The sky was clear, as if it was just another beautiful, uninterrupted day. The sunlight shone against the gilded ornaments atop palace roofs, making the city appear majestic, especially to newcomers.

Market stalls were already open along the main streets. They each displayed their best goods, ranging from spices to carved ivory, fine textiles, and metalwork that never failed to draw merchants from across the region. When caravans arrived from the ports of the west, they brought goods from Persia and lands farther still. Meanwhile, from the eastern roads came traders from Bengal, their boats often laden with cloth and grains.

The atmosphere inside the palace complex was even more vibrant. Courtiers could be seen making their way toward the audience chamber, while scribes were busy carrying bundles of palm leaf manuscripts to a meeting. There were artists who brought their pigments and boards, ready for another day's work in service of the court. Meanwhile, in a shaded alcove, a group of Brahmins were debating a philosophical question. A pair of Buddhist monks stood at another corner, discussing a line from a recent sermon.

Elsewhere in the palace, a poet recited a few new verses to a small audience of nobles. Among them was a man whose reputation was beginning to rise beyond the court. Known as Kalidasa, he would go down in history as the greatest Sanskrit poet and dramatist of all time. He listened to the young poet with a half smile, occasionally offering a suggestion to refine a line or strengthen an image.

In a hall where land grants were being issued, several officials could be seen gathering for a meeting. Brahmins and administrators had their days full of reviewing documents and recording the rights given to temples, scholars, and loyal officers.

At the edge of this hall, a lone messenger stood, freshly arrived from the frontier. In his hands was a report sealed with the mark of an outpost in Gandhara. He gently placed the scroll among the other documents, but unsurprisingly, none of the officials reached for it right away. After all, Pataliputra favored good news far more than warning. The officials were so absorbed in their discussions about lands and festivals for the coming season that they were certain that whatever news had come from the northwest could wait until the morning's work was done.

But the messenger waited, shifting his weight slowly from one foot to another. He watched as scribes moved past him without a glance. For a moment, he wondered if the court had grown too accustomed to peace, too certain of its own strength. But he said nothing. He had delivered his report, and its fate was no longer in his hands.

Fortunately, the warning did not fall entirely on deaf ears. Word of the disturbances soon reached a man who deeply understood the weight of such news better than most. A prince named Skandagupta, he was renowned for his discipline and resolve. He had grown up hearing stories of his forefathers' campaigns—tales of Samudragupta's sweeping victories and Chandragupta's steady rule. So, as the son of the Gupta emperor Kumaragupta I, he knew that it was his responsibility to protect the legacy he had inherited.

However, he received the report of the disturbances not from reading the scroll dropped by the messenger in Pataliputra but while overseeing military inspections in the western provinces. He knew that trouble was brewing. More reports came in later. The outpost at Gandhara had fallen mysteriously silent, a minor chief had shown signs of shifting his loyalty, and a merchant relay station had been destroyed. These confirmed his suspicions that something new had arrived at the fringes of the empire.

Without delay, Skandagupta summoned his council of generals. They gathered inside a fort that overlooked a dry valley. The meeting, however, opened with confusion rather than clarity. Some officers insisted that the enemy must be remnants of old regional clans they had previously defeated that were growing bolder once more. Others pointed to rebellious groups from beyond the Indus. But the descriptions brought by traders did not match any known enemy.

"If these rumors have truth to them, then it is best we make a move," one of the generals may have said.

Skandagupta agreed and immediately issued orders. He sent scouts and armies to the west. There was undoubtedly no room for caution. Skandagupta himself refused to remain behind the walls as his men set out. He marched at the head of a mixed force: infantry seasoned by earlier campaigns, cavalry units drawn from loyal chiefs, and a few elephant corps positioned to anchor the line.

Their first confrontation took place at dusk. It began with the return of Skandagupta's scouts, who warned the rest that the hostile riders were approaching. It is said that the prince barely had time to reposition his lines when the enemy swept down the slope, their steeds kicking up clouds of dust. They rode with astonishing speed. Their movements were fluid and scattered at the same time. Instead of forming a solid front, they broke into smaller groups, circling the Gupta ranks. Then, they released a rain of arrows from bows that bent far more than those used by Indian archers.

The attack took Skandagupta's forces by surprise. It scattered the units at first, but the prince quickly steadied them. He led the infantry forward and called the cavalry to flank the enemy. Then, the elephant corps made their move, leaving the riders no choice but to retreat from close engagement. After a tense and chaotic struggle, the raiders finally withdrew. Swiftly, they disappeared into the horizon. Skandagupta's men erupted in celebration as they watched their enemies retreat, but the prince remained quiet.

Bodies lay across the field, Gupta soldiers among them. Their armor was pierced by arrows that were lighter, sharper, and built for speed. Skandagupta took his time surveying the ground. He was now certain that these riders were not a familiar enemy simply testing the border. The battlefield belonged to him that day, but this skirmish was just the beginning of their problem—or perhaps, their collapse.

Not long after that first clash, the signs of strain reached the city of Mathura. The merchants in its sprawling bazaar had always been early risers, pulling open wooden shutters at dawn and calling for their apprentices to arrange their goods. But now their voices carried less confidence. News traveled along the trade roads fast, sometimes faster than caravans. By the time the first travelers from the northwest limped into Mathura, their stories were already being spread around.

A cloth merchant who had once greeted customers with a loud, cheerful call would now pause his activities whenever he heard hoofbeats echoing through the streets. He had heard from a passing caravan that a small market town to the north had been raided—not conquered or held, only struck, plundered, and left in the smoke. Nobody knew which settlement would be next. From that point on, the merchant found himself scanning the roads more often than the faces of buyers who browsed his stall.

Along the riverbanks, monks who had lived peacefully in small monasteries outside the city gates began arriving in groups. They carried little more than the robes on their backs and a few scrolls they refused to abandon. Their monasteries, they said, were too exposed. Too far from the safety of walls. They sought refuge in Mathura's larger temples, where they hoped the sound of chanting and the presence of travelers might offer some protection. Artisans followed the same path. Metalworkers and potters grew wary of the safety of their families, so they packed up their workshops and moved toward the crowded quarters near the main market.

Prices changed quickly. Grains cost more with each passing week. Caravans from the northwest arrived late or did not arrive at all. Spices that had once come regularly from mountain towns became rare. When they appeared, they were often sold for double the usual rate. Some merchants also spoke of coins marked with strange symbols carried by traders fleeing the frontier. Nobody recognized them at first, but eventually someone named the riders who minted them: the Huna.

The pressure was felt by everyone, even the city's chiefs. Their most important duty had long been to protect Mathura and keep its gates secure. However, now their decisions were tangled in doubt. Some urged loyalty to the Gupta throne in Pataliputra, insisting that reinforcements would soon arrive. Others believed that waiting for distant help was foolish. If the Huna reached Mathura, they argued, it would be safer for the city to negotiate its own survival. Quietly, a few chiefs began making their own preparations regardless of what the emperor decreed.

As Mathura braced itself for impending threats, another change was taking shape far to the east. Sometime in 450 CE, Emperor Kumaragupta I had died. He had worn the crown for slightly over a decade, and his early reign was often remembered as a period of stability and prosperity. His influence could be felt across the vast land, from Gujarat in the west to Bengal in the east. The emperor was also credited with founding the famous Nalanda University in Bihar. But as he stepped closer to the end of his life, uncertainty grew. Apart from the riders, the empire itself was also battling internal issues: governors in distant regions had become more independent.

So, the transition that followed Kumaragupta's passing was not as smooth as earlier successions. Court factions argued day and night, each shouting support to different claimants. For a moment, it was unclear who would take the throne and lead the empire back to its feet.

Inscriptions from Skandagupta's later years speak of how he eventually worked his way to the throne, becoming a worthy successor. After removing the other claimants, he secured the loyalty of the army, which remembered the discipline and resolve he had shown during the first clash with the riders. It did not take long for the officials, especially those who valued stability, to line up behind him. They were convinced that only a firm hand at the center could keep the empire from slipping further into disorder.

Skandagupta was accepted as the next Gupta emperor, yet his work did not end with his coronation. Reports from the northwest continued to arrive, each more troubling than the last. The riders who had tested the border while he was still a prince were returning with greater strength. This time, they had successfully taken Gandhara and established a firmer foothold.

And so, the emperor prepared for another campaign. Some would say that this disturbance accelerated his age. The weight of command had carved lines on his face, and sleepless nights had become familiar companions. He knew that his first clash with the Hunas years earlier was just a warning. This time, the riders had come prepared and were determined to push deeper into Gupta territory.

However, Skandagupta was never known to back down easily. He gathered what remained of his strongest units and advanced again to the northwest. The journey itself tested the men. Supplies were thinner, horses needed rest more often, and the treasury that once supported large armies had been depleted due to the succession struggle following the death of Kumaragupta I. It was a struggle to fund even a single campaign. Still, they moved on, driven by the knowledge that the frontier would not hold without them.

The next battle erupted somewhere near the Punjab region, where open fields coincided with rocky ground. The Huna riders struck at them with the same precision Skandagupta and his men remembered. Volleys of arrows filled the sky, and the riders circled the Guptas in sweeping arcs. Then, they vanished, leaving only clouds of dust, before reappearing again in sudden bursts. The Gupta infantry stood their ground. They raised their shields and waited for the perfect moment to counterattack.

It was a brutal struggle. Skandagupta fought in the center, rallying his men as lines bent under the force of the heavy charges. Hours passed before the tide finally turned. In the end, the Hunas retreated and made their way north, leaving behind their fallen.

Skandagupta had emerged victorious again, but it tasted strangely hollow. The battlefield was covered with bodies. Many were his own soldiers, men who would not return to their villages or families. Worse still was the cost that awaited him in the capital. The empire's treasury was nearly empty. To rebuild the army for the next threat, taxes would have to increase. Farmers would be the ones to suffer, as they had to pay more. Merchants, too, would not be excluded. Everyone would feel the burden of keeping the invaders away.

The brave emperor understood a truth that few dared to speak aloud. This latest victory was only temporary. He was merely holding back collapse, not restoring the empire that his ancestors had tirelessly built. Each campaign drained more strength than it returned. Even as the court celebrated his latest success, he knew that the future was slipping beyond his grasp. There was little he could do to permanently keep the Guptas from harm.

There are no exact details of his death, but historians agree that Skandagupta likely ruled until 468 CE. His death plunged the empire into a time of turmoil. Some say he left behind no heir to claim the throne, so it was passed to his half-brother, Purugupta. The Gupta dynasty remained in control for many more years, but none of the rulers that came after Skandagupta could reverse the damage the empire was suffering.

Internal issues continued to swell. Across the provinces, governors began acting as if they were kings in their own right. They collected taxes for themselves, not always for the court. They negotiated with border tribes without waiting for permission from Pataliputra. Some even raised personal armies. The unity that once defined the Mauryas and the early Guptas had clearly disappeared. Trade routes that had once carried merchants from city to city now felt unsafe. Caravans traveled in smaller groups, avoiding certain roads entirely. Farmers who once relied on stability to plant their crops found themselves subjected to new taxes imposed by whatever official claimed the land that year.

Half a century after Skandagupta's victory against the invaders, the Hunas returned to the borders once more. This time, they were led by a formidable warrior named Toramana. Under his command, the riders pushed deep into northern India, this time achieving major success. Towns fell, leaving behind only smoke and ashes. Local chiefs who valued their lives more than loyalty to Pataliputra either surrendered to the invaders or offered a hand to help them push deeper into the empire.

For a time, Toramana held sway over regions of central India, carving his authority into the land with surprising speed.

Then, around 515 CE, the torch of leadership was passed to his son, Mihirakula. This name was remembered especially by Buddhist chroniclers, who cited him as a harsh ruler. They described how he never thought twice about destroying monasteries as long as his invasion missions could make progress. Monks began to flee south the moment they heard rumors that the riders were closing in. Of course, these accounts tend to be exaggerated.

Other sources painted a more mixed picture. Some regions acknowledged Mihirakula as a legitimate king. Even his court soon displayed elements of Indian courtly culture. His coins carried symbols familiar to the people he ruled, and his use of elephants in battle suggested a growing acceptance of local military traditions.

By this time, the Guptas were already severely weakened and divided. With their economic strain and internal power struggles, it was impossible for them to push the Hunas back permanently. Historians suggest that environmental stress and potential climatic disasters further contributed to the empire's decline. Gradually, the Guptas authority shrank to small regions, then to single cities. In the end, the empire that had once produced the best poets, mathematicians, sculptors, and astronomers of all time dissolved into a constellation of smaller kingdoms.

Yet the Huna riders were never destined to rule the land forever. Resistance grew as regional rulers gathered strength. In the sixth century CE, coalitions of Indian kings made a move, slowly pushing back the invaders. In central India, leaders such as Yashodharman of Malwa successfully launched attacks that corroded Huna authority. Bit by bit, their strongholds were breached and broken. As a result, some Huna groups retreated toward the northwest, while others settled more quietly, blending into local communities.

With the Gupta empire now a thing of the past, India entered a new and more fragmented age. Smaller kingdoms rose in the regions once controlled by the Guptas. In the north, particularly in places like Magadha and Kanauj, new dynasties were born, each competing for complete influence. Meanwhile, in the west, rulers at Valabhi prioritized trade activities. They were the ones who guarded the trade routes and coastal ports. Farther east, different courts began to shape their own versions of kingship and culture. Although no single power replaced the

Guptas at once, many of these later states inherited their systems of administration, their styles of art, and even their memory of what a strong and orderly kingdom should look like.

Chapter 8 – What Life Was Really Like in the Gupta Empire

An Astronomer in Ujjain

Dawn had just made its first appearance of the day, shining its cool early light on the rooftops of Ujjain, the beating heart of arts and literature in the Gupta Empire. The Shipra River, a sacred river comparable to the Ganga River, still held the night's last chill. A few early risers walked down the *ghāṭ* (a flight of steps typically found by the riverbank) to perform their ablutions.

The Shipra River today.[19]

Meanwhile, on the city's northern hill stood a cluster of buildings belonging to a small school of astronomers. This was the place where calculations were made long before the day's bustle reached the markets, where scholars measured the heavens with the same seriousness kings devoted to politics. This was where our astronomer, Rishyashva, spent most of his time. He had been awake before the first light breached through the skies. Like many others in his discipline, he preferred the quiet hours when the mind felt unburdened.

Sitting cross-legged on a reed mat, Rishyashva was surrounded by palm-leaf manuscripts. He had a lot to go through today. So, he tied his cotton shawl more tightly around his shoulders and began reading through a manuscript containing a set of eclipse tables copied from an earlier *siddhānta* (textbook). It was another ordinary morning, but for an intellectual like him, no morning ever passed without a small thrill of responsibility.

A few hours later, a young apprentice arrived. He greeted Rishyashva with a small bow before inviting the middle-aged scholar outside. When Rishyashva stepped out into the courtyard, the eastern horizon had begun to shift from grey to pale gold. A few of his younger students were still rubbing their eyes as they prepared the instruments on the rooftop. One of the instruments was called a *śaṅku*. Planted upright on the polished stone floor, the *śaṅku* was a crucial tool to determine latitude, solstice drift, and midday shadows.

Rishyashva bent to examine the first shadow cast by the *śaṅku* while his apprentice marked its tip carefully with a charcoal dot. In time, they would compare the curve of these markings to yesterday's and the previous day's. Precision mattered. A single miscalculated angle could easily ruin a table of rising times, and a ruined table meant a flawed calendar, which in turn could disrupt temple festivals and ceremonial timing across the surrounding towns.

If the day was cloudy and no sunlight shone from the heavens, scholars would use another method to measure time. Known as the *ghaṭikā-yantra* (a water clock used to track time through controlled dripping), it was a simple device but remarkably reliable when handled with care. Used both in ancient times and the medieval era, this instrument featured a small thin metal bowl with a pin-sized hole at its base. The bowl was placed gently upon the surface of water inside a larger vessel.

Once set afloat, the bowl would begin to fill as water seeped in through the tiny hole. The rhythm of that seepage allowed scholars to mark the passage of fixed units of time. When the bowl finally sank, its descent signaled that one *ghaṭikā* had passed.

By mid-morning, Ujjain became even more lively. Women could be seen gathering at the *ghāṭ*, washing utensils and cloth. A few brought their children along to splash in the shallow waters. Merchants began to fill the marketplace, each hurriedly raising the shutters of his stalls, eager to start another day of business. On the other side of the city, priests walked briskly toward the temple with brass pots of water balanced on their hips.

Time seemed to never stop for Rishyashva as task after task arrived to fill his day. A messenger approached him, having traveled from a nearby shrine. He carried a clay tablet on which a question was etched in a rather hurried stroke. Rishyashva read it twice to fully absorb the inquiry. The priests wished to know the correct rising time of Jupiter for an upcoming consecration ceremony. Such requests were common, as many rituals depended on planetary positions.

Rishyashva walked over to a table where his manuscripts were neatly stacked. After scanning the latest position tables and comparing them with that morning's shadow measurements, he gave a faint smile. Jupiter was indeed cooperative this season. He dictated the calculations confidently to his apprentice, who wrote them on a fresh strip of palm leaf before dusting it with fine ash to dry the ink. The messenger took the document and thanked the scholars before hurrying off to deliver it to the priests.

Next, Rishyashva's routine brought him to another courtyard where students had already gathered. They were all seated under the neem tree with wooden writing boards ready in their laps. Although these young men were devoted learners of science and mathematics, they were no different from students anywhere else: the first row was attentive, the middle row hopeful, and the back row half-asleep.

Today's lesson revolved around *nakṣatras* (lunar mansions or constellations used to track the moon's monthly path). Rishyashva began the class by drawing a rough diagram and explaining how the moon's movement through the twenty-seven *nakṣatras* determined timing for certain rituals. He cited an older authority, then compared that authority with newer observations. Some students murmured agreement, while others frowned, struggling to reconcile theory with measurement. Rishyashva knew their struggle well. The heavens were consistent in their patterns, but human tools—be it rods, cords, or even human eyes—were far from perfect. Mistakes were bound to happen, but perhaps with knowledge, patience, repeated observation, and experience, they would not happen as often.

His lecture ended just before midday. This was the only time Rishyashva would sit and relax. He returned to the shaded veranda where a pot of buttermilk sat, cooling in a basin of water. The scholar drank slowly, appreciating what little free time he had that day. However, right after he took the first bite of his meal, a colleague arrived with a stack of palm leaves under his arm.

"A correction from Mathura," his colleague said, handing him the bundle. "Unfortunately, their calculation for the last eclipse does not match ours."

Rishyashva sighed. Harmonizing calculations across regions was perhaps the most tedious aspect of his work. Different academies used slightly different standards for the year's length, the moon's motion, and positional corrections. To say he was tired was an understatement, but he must see to the calculation. He made a mental note to review the discrepancy after lunch.

Ujjain's heat softened toward evening, and Rishyashva returned to the courtyard where the *śaṅku* stood once more for final observations. His apprentice, hardworking as ever, was already waiting for him, ready to jot down his observations. When the stars began to dot the dark sky, the two scholars would gather once more. This time, their station was on a platform built on the rooftop. Rishyashva would observe the position of the star while his apprentice recorded his reading meticulously.

Only after they finished the last of their measurements and readings did they descend the stairs, preparing themselves to end the day. By this time of day, Ujjain had grown quiet except for the sound of distant drums from a small shrine, marking the start of the evening ritual. There was nothing but oil lamps glowing in the doorways and other scholars calmly leaving the courtyard to return to their families. As for Rishyashva, he folded his palm-leaf manuscripts carefully before heading home, knowing that tomorrow he would return to the same chambers and courtyards once again, observing and calculating the universe.

The Guild Merchant from Uttarāpatha

Devendra jolted upright, startled by the sound of oxen shifting their yokes outside. He had spent the night in a rest house maintained by his guild—a low mud-brick structure located just off the main road east of Ujjain. Of course, comfort was minimal. The walls were bare and the floor hard. But at least there was a roof that kept Devendra from the dew and a doorway that faced a pleasing view of the Uttarāpatha—a major trade route bridging the city of Takshashila (modern Taxila) in the northwest to Tamralipti (modern Tamluk) on the Bay of Bengal in the east.

Immediately, Devendra reached for his ledger. This time, the bundle of goods was not large. But still, it was varied enough to matter. Some of these goods belonged to Devendra, while others were entrusted to him by fellow members of his *śrenī* (merchant guild that organized trade and protected its members). There were rolls of fine cotton sitting in the corner, beautifully dyed with indigo and madder. Next to the cotton rolls were three chests. One was full of strings of glass beads, another had packets of black pepper, and the last carried several small copper vessels, each polished to a soft shine.

After checking each item, ensuring that none were stolen or broken, Devendra stepped out into the courtyards. He was not alone; a few other merchants were already preparing their carts for the long journey ahead.

"Have you recorded everything?" the keeper of the rest house, a man with gray hair, asked Devendra. The merchant replied with a simple nod.

"And delivery in three days?" the keeper asked.

"Three days if weather permits," Devendra answered. "Four if the rains have softened the road."

The keeper grunted approval and made a small mark on his wooden board. The guild had always kept close track of journeys. Merchants traveled under its name as much as their own. If one of them failed or cheated, it reflected on all.

In less than an hour, Devendra finished preparing his cart. It was pulled by two oxen, their horns wrapped in strips of cloth to avoid chafing. He then climbed up to the driver's plank and flicked the reins lightly. The cart creaked forward, bringing Devendra onto the road outside Ujjain.

The route was alive in a quiet way. Not far into his journey, Devendra passed a group of farmers. Driving a herd of cattle with sticks, they were heading toward the city. Then, Devendra came upon a small group of monks. They wore nothing but simple robes. Their feet were bare, and each of them carried an alms bowl. The monks did not stop Devendra; they rarely asked merchants for anything directly. But often, merchants with a heart would slow their carts and offer a little something to these monks. Devendra took a small packet of grain from his supplies and passed it to the last monk in line. The monk accepted it with a bow and a small smile, then continued without a word. Devendra always reminded himself that giving a little away on the road never harmed a trader's fortunes. If anything, it kept the journey lighter in ways that did not show up in ledgers.

A few hours later, Devendra's journey brought him to a landscape of fields of millet and barley, accompanied by groves of neem and banyan. The road turned so narrow there that only one cart could pass at a time. Farther up, Devendra came across another convoy approaching from the opposite direction. There were three carts in total, each ladened with pottery and baskets of grain.

Their leader raised a hand in greeting. "How is the road east?" he asked when they drew close.

"Dry enough," Devendra replied. "But I heard from the keeper that a small bridge near the second ford has weakened. Cross with care."

"I see. Well, in the west, bandits have been seen near the old mango grove," the other merchant warned. "It is wise to travel with a company."

They exchanged no more than that. Information on the road was as valuable as any coin and traded just as carefully. The carts passed, each man carrying the other's warnings with him.

The temperature shot up by late morning, draining Devendra's energy. Knowing that exhaustion would soon come if he continued the journey, the merchant pulled the cart off the main road and headed toward a roadside shelter built by a local landholder. The resting spot was humble—nothing more than a raised platform with a thatched roof and a stone trough nearby. But it was enough to catch a break.

Devendra unyoked the oxen and led them to drink from the trough. He then sat on the platform to eat. His midday meal was simple: two pieces of wheat flatbread, a handful of lentils cooked the night before, and water carried in a leather bottle. As he chewed, he watched the road and weighed the remaining distance. If the oxen held steady, he would reach the next toll station by late afternoon.

When the worst of the midday heat had passed, he loaded the cart again and returned to the road. As he expected, by late afternoon, a small structure came into view. This was a toll point where local officials collected fees for the use of the road and the nearby river crossing.

"Where are you headed?" one of the officials asked, eyeing the cart.

"Toward the eastern market town," Devendra said, handing over a small tablet that listed his goods.

The man glanced at it, then at the bundles on the cart. "Cotton, pepper, copperware. Guild-registered?"

"Ujjain cloth merchants' śreṇī," Devendra confirmed.

The official nodded, then named the toll. Devendra counted out the coins from a cloth pouch, watching carefully as the man checked each piece. Toll keepers had been known to complain of short payment if a merchant did not pay attention. But today, the exchange was smooth. The barrier was lifted, and Devendra moved on.

After crossing a shallow river ford, the landscape changed once more. Small market villages appeared at intervals, each marked by a cluster of stalls and a shrine beneath a spreading tree. Textile dyers worked near the water, stirring vats of color that stained their hands deep blue and red. Potters' wheels spun lazily as the workers shaped wet clay into jars. Smiths could be seen hunching over small furnaces, expertly coaxing iron into tools and nails.

Devendra did not stop long in these villages. He had arrangements to keep farther along the route. Still, he noted prices overheard at stalls, glimpsed the quality of cloth on local looms, and stored away the faces of possible future buyers.

Only when sky began to turn purple did Devendra reach a familiar and modest market outpost. Merchants like himself often slept here precisely because it lay at the right distance for a three-day delivery. By the time Devendra arrived, the veranda was already full of guild merchants spreading out their beddings close to their carts and goods.

Devendra ended up spending several minutes searching for a spot for the night. He found a narrow corner beside a shop where iron tools hung from a wooden beam. After tending to his oxen, he opened his ledger by the light of an oil lamp set on a stone niche. He tallied the tolls paid, checked his coin pouch, and reviewed the route left for tomorrow. A fellow merchant leaned over, asking the price he planned to charge for his copper vessels. Devendra answered briefly, keeping his calculations precise. When he finally ate a bowl of warm rice and lentils from a local cook, he did so quickly, mindful of the distance still ahead. As the market outpost settled into quiet murmurs and flickering lamps, Devendra lay down on his mat. The Uttarāpatha stretched forward in the darkness, and he intended to follow it at first light. The delivery deadline was close, but it seemed like weather was indeed on his side. Devendra would certainly complete his delivery on time.

A Widow in a Gupta Household

Kamala was already awake before the rest of the house came alive. However, it was more out of habit than necessity. Years ago, when her husband was still alive, she had risen early to prepare for his day. But after his passing, she lived in her eldest son's home. Although her duties had become lighter, it seemed difficult for her to change her routine; it was as if she could not sit still.

And so, she wrapped her plain cotton *sārī* more tightly around her shoulders and made her way into the courtyard, toward the small household shrine set into a niche in the wall. A tiny stone image of Lakṣmī sat there between two oil lamps. The first thing she did was clean the niche. She removed the wilted flowers, relit the lamps, and placed a few grains of rice before the divine image. Then, she whispered her prayer; Kamala wished nothing more than a steady household where neither quarrels nor misfortunes would ever visit.

Then, she went to the kitchen area, where a faint crackle of kindling soothed her aged ears. Her daughter-in-law, Vatsalā, had just started the morning fire. Kamala walked over, not to take over but to watch and assist where needed. A few steps away from them was a younger maid who was busy grinding grain on the stone mill. Kamala warmly greeted her and checked the texture of the grain with her fingertips.

"Add a little more water, and it should bind better," Kamala said gently.

The young maid nodded and adjusted the mixture without complaint. She had always valued Kamala's advice and adored the old woman, for she never raised her voice.

The family began to wake one by one. Her son, Devadatta, stepped into the courtyard, adjusting his upper cloth and rubbing his eyes. He greeted his mother with a respectful morning wish, then moved toward the well for his own washing. A moment later, grandchildren burst from their room, eager to start the day. But Kamala was quick enough to intercept them, smoothing their hair and straightening their garments before they ran too far.

"You need to wash your face first," she said. "Only then may you argue over who sits where."

They smiled sheepishly and obeyed. Small directives like these were hers to give. Indeed, they were not commands of great consequence, but they kept the day's rhythm intact.

Next came breakfast. It was simple. Each filled their stomach with rice porridge, a bit of lentil stew, and buttermilk—typical food enjoyed by those in the Gupta Empire. Everyone ate seated on the floor along the veranda that overlooked the courtyard. Kamala helped her daughter-in-law distribute the bowls, then took her place at the end of the line. She ate last, as custom dictated for widows and elders in many households.

After the bowls were cleared and the younger children shooed away to play, Kamala fetched a small wooden writing board from a shelf. Her grandson, only six, had begun learning his letters. The formal teacher would come later in the week, but she did not mind providing him with daily practice.

"Come and sit, dear one," she said, patting the mat beside her.

He sat cross-legged, eyes following her hand as she traced the first syllable with a reed pen dipped in blackened water. She guided his fingers to follow the strokes. The letters came out crooked and uneven, but Kamala did not scold her grandson.

"Again," she simply said.

As he tried once more, she glanced across the courtyard. Vatsalā was supervising the maid, who was hanging wet clothes along a rope. The younger woman's bracelets jingled faintly. In contrast, Kamala wore nothing around her wrist except for two thin copper bangles. She owned more elaborate jewelry, but she never wore them after her husband's death. Her brightly dyed garments had been put away, too. These days, she only wore *sārīs* that drew no attention: plain, mostly white or pale in color.

Such restraint in dress was common among widows in many respectable urban households of the time. This tradition was shaped by long-standing Brahmanical ideas that linked color and ornament to marital status. But of course, not every widow in Gupta India lived with this degree of austerity. Customs varied depending on the different regions and communities on the subcontinent.

Near midmorning, a neighbor appeared at the doorway, lifting the curtain politely before entering.

"Kamala, have you heard?" she asked after offering a brief greeting. "They say there will be special recitations at the Viṣṇu temple this evening. The priest from the next village is visiting."

Kamala listened, nodding. She asked a few quiet questions, including the exact timing, the offerings needed, and which families had already pledged oil for the lamps. Details mattered in these things. Once the neighbor left, Kamala called her daughter-in-law.

"If you plan to go," she said, "set aside some sesame oil. And ask Devadatta to confirm the hour when he returns from the office. The children should not be taken too late."

Vatsalā nodded, grateful for the clarity. Decisions about temple visits and offerings were technically her husband's to proclaim, but it was Kamala who smoothed them into everyday life.

By late afternoon, Devadatta returned home from his duties. He brought news of a minor tax adjustment and a rumor about an incoming skirmish in a distant province. Kamala listened to her son, but without pressing for details. After all, politics no longer directly concerned her. Still, she knew that news like this was not to be taken lightly. She knew how an empire could change when men spoke in lowered voices and money had to stretch farther than before. The tone in Devadatta's words told her enough.

Suddenly, one of her grandchildren developed a mild cough. Concerned, Kamala quickly sent for the local *vaidya* (physician), who arrived later with a small cloth bag filled with jars and packets. Kamala greeted him respectfully, then stood slightly to one side as he examined the child, listening to his chest and peering at his tongue.

"Thankfully, there is nothing serious," the vaidya said. "The young one spent too much time shouting in the courtyard and not enough resting." He prescribed a simple decoction of herbs and warm water.

Kamala caught his eye. "How often do I feed him this?"

"Twice a day," he replied. "Morning and night, just until the cough settles."

She nodded, committing the instructions to memory. Later, as Vatsalā prepared the remedy, Kamala hovered nearby, checking the quantities and making sure the vessel was clean. She did not take over, but she refused to stand idle.

In the evening, the family began discussing the matter of the recitation about to take place at the Viṣṇu temple. The children were excited to participate, so Devadatta agreed to take them and his wife. Adhering to his mother's request, Devadatta promised to return before it grew too late. Kamala herself chose to stay behind, as she preferred the quieter hours at home now.

After they left, the house felt unusually still. After finishing her chores, the young maid retired to her room. Kamala, on the other hand, still had energy. She walked slowly through the rooms, making sure everything was where it should be, from the grain jars that lined the shelves to the stools in the kitchen and the pots that hung there. She made adjustments where necessary; these small adjustments calmed her more than any long conversation could.

In the courtyard, the light had faded to a deep blue. Kamala picked up a small *dīpa* (oil lamp used for lighting and simple rituals), filled it with a little sesame oil, and adjusted the cotton wick. She lit it from the flame at the household shrine and placed it in the center of the courtyard, then lit two more for the inner rooms. The glow was soft but enough to hold back the darkness.

Then, she lowered herself onto the veranda, knees creaking slightly, and sat with her back against a pillar. For a few moments, she did nothing but simply listened to her surroundings. She could hear the distant murmur of neighbors, the occasional call of a street vendor, and the faint sound of temple bells carried on the evening air. No one called for her, and no decision urgently required her voice, yet she felt content.

When her family finally returned, Kamala immediately stood to receive them. She asked brief, pointed questions about the temple ritual, to which her grandchildren responded with lengthy descriptions. Then, once everyone had eaten and drifted off to their respective rooms, she returned to the courtyard one last time.

She checked that the main *dīpa* still had a little oil, nudged the wick to prolong its life, and adjusted the edge of her *sārī* against the slight night breeze. These actions were nothing remarkable—just one of those small things she did without thinking, keeping the home calm and cared for in ways most people never spoke of but depended on all the same.

Conclusion

You have finally reached the last section of this book, and by now, you should have noticed something: The story of ancient India has way more mysteries than you might ever expect. The deeper you go, the more the ground moves. Answers lead to new questions, and familiar names suddenly gain new details. For a land so old, India surely is full of surprises.

Take the story of the Harappan civilization, for instance. No one was aware of its existence for centuries. Ancient cities lay hidden under soil and riverbeds until archaeologists in the nineteenth century realized that the mounds they had been surveying were more than just ordinary ruins. Planned streets, bead workshops, advanced drainage systems, seals, pottery, a mysterious script—an entire urban area came back into view after thousands of years of silence.

The discoveries have not slowed down. In fact, ancient sites like Rakhigarhi, Dholavira, Bhirrana, and Lothal continue to add something new. Sometimes these discoveries confirm what scholars suspected, and sometimes they overturn almost everything they have confidently confirmed.

The same can also be said of the Mauryan period. Chandragupta, Chanakya, and Ashoka are names that seem familiar. However, the details surrounding these figures keep changing as new interpretations and findings emerge. Ashoka's edicts, scattered across rocks and pillars, continue to be re-read as scholars compare languages, regions, and clues. Archaeologists still debate the exact layout of ancient Mauryan cities and religious centers. Even records of the supposedly well-documented Mauryan state still hold gaps that modern research is trying to fill.

While the Gupta era is celebrated for its beautiful art, literature, and impressive scientific advances, the period also had its own set of uncertainties. Coins, inscriptions, temple remnants, and texts still spark debates among historians and scholars alike. How wealthy were they, really? How stable? How interconnected was the empire with the rest of Asia or the lands beyond the Mediterranean? Each year, new studies adjust our understanding.

Even India's oldest stories behave the same way. Famous epics like the *Mahābhārata* and the *Rāmāyaṇa* are filled with exaggeration, grand battles, impossible weapons, and of course, supernatural beings. Yet, when scholars and archaeologists examine them carefully, some details begin to line up with reality. Ancient place names, descriptions of rivers, references to tribes, hints of migrations—these fragments sometimes match what research uncovers. These epics may not be literal histories, but they also remember.

And that is the real charm of studying ancient India. It refuses to sit still. There are still ruins waiting and inscriptions to be deciphered. And, who knows, maybe the next detail that reshapes what we know about ancient India will come from a place no one thought to look. History, after all, has a habit of surprising us when we least expect it.

Part 2: Ancient China

Discovering Lost Stories from Chinese History

Introduction

Speaking of the world's oldest and earliest civilizations, our minds cannot help but wander to the ancient Egyptians under god-like pharaohs, the battles fought by the Spartans, and of course, the cuneiform and ziggurats once built by the Sumerians. The Chinese civilization, however, began later—about 1,500 years after the rise of Egypt and Sumer. But China also belongs to another category: the world's oldest continuous civilization. For over four thousand years, the Chinese civilization had witnessed the birth of dynasties and their declines, philosophies blossoming and waning, and different inventions that reshaped the world. And yet, it endured. The continuity of its language, traditions, and recorded history distinguishes it from every other ancient culture.

Just like any other civilization's, China's history is layered. At first there were myths and legends that spoke about the civilization's beginnings. These stories include tales of the sage kings (Yao, Shun, and Yu) who were often credited with introducing agriculture to the people, instituting moral rule, and even taming rivers and floods that endangered the land and its inhabitants. Then, the story moved into firmer ground, complete with archaeological evidence and written records. This is when the timeline begins to sharpen.

Both archaeology and contemporary records firmly attest that the Shang dynasty (c. 1600–1046 BCE) is the very first Chinese dynasty. The discovery of the oracle bones, in particular, gives us a glimpse into its world of kingship, warfare, and ancestor worship. Its capital was at Anyang. This was where palaces once stood with the royal tombs telling us much more about the foundations of early Chinese statecraft. After the Shang came the Zhou dynasty (c. 1046-256 BCE), which developed the idea of the Mandate of Heaven. This doctrine justified a ruler's authority as divinely granted. The mandate could be revoked, however, if he governed poorly. This idea would shape Chinese political thought for many centuries to come.

The later periods of Zhou, especially the Spring and Autumn (770-476 BCE) and the Warring States (475-221 BCE) periods, saw thinkers including Confucius, Laozi, and Mozi rise to prominence. Indeed, the Zhou era is remembered as the cradle of Chinese philosophy. But at the same time, it was an age of endless wars and violence. Chaos only ended—at least for a while—when Qin Shi Huang united the states, becoming China's first emperor and kickstarting the Qin dynasty (221-206 BCE).

After the short-lived Qin dynasty came the Han dynasty (206 BCE-220 CE), which took the kingdom to greater heights. It expanded territory, opened the Silk Road to Central Asia, and developed a sophisticated bureaucracy grounded in Confucian ideals. These achievements are preserved in ancient texts such as the *Shiji* (Records of the Grand Historian), and the *Hanshu* (Book of Han), both of which were compiled by great historians of that age. These accounts also provided us with vivid portraits of emperors, generals, scholars, and insights into everyday life. These works, along with later dynastic histories, were undoubtedly crucial sources for reconstructing the past and will often appear in the chapters that follow.

When the Han faltered, China entered a period of fragmentation once more. This long interlude of division only came to an end with the rise of the Sui dynasty (581-618 CE). Succeeding it was none other than the Tang dynasty (618-907 CE), which is often described by historians and scholars as the Golden Age of Chinese civilization. Here, the Chinese empire reached its zenith. Its borders were expanded even more, giving way for the civilization's ideas to spread across Eurasia and Chinese goods to travel along the Silk Road. Even poetry and literature reached greater heights with figures like Li Bai and Du Fu rising to prominence. Though some historians classify the Tang as part of medieval rather than ancient China, its cultural achievements and global influence ensure its place as one of the crowning moments of China's early history.

To cover the entire history of China would probably take endless pages. The civilization's story is so long that many stories within it have been nearly forgotten. And so, this book aims not to retell the parts that are already widely known but rather to focus on the voices and episodes that have slipped through the cracks of grand narratives.

Chapter 1 – Forgotten and Vanished

Some consider the Taklamakan Desert one of the most isolated locations on earth. The desert was known as the place of no return, and this was for a reason. This deadly sea of sand stretches across northwestern China for more than 330,000 square kilometers. Named one of the largest shifting-sand deserts in the world, the region consists of nothing but vast dunes that rise and fall like waves on a frozen ocean. Believe it or not, some can tower as high as three hundred meters! Since the winds reshape the landscape almost constantly, you could easily get lost; the wind would erase your footprints and swallow your paths within hours if not minutes. The desert is even deadlier in the summer months. Surface temperatures can climb to blistering extremes. But winter is no better: the nights are usually ice cold with temperatures dropping well below freezing. Unsurprisingly, water is hard to come by. Those who are brave enough to traverse across it risk death by thirst and disorientation. Even if you survive thirst, the sudden sandstorms could easily bury you alive.

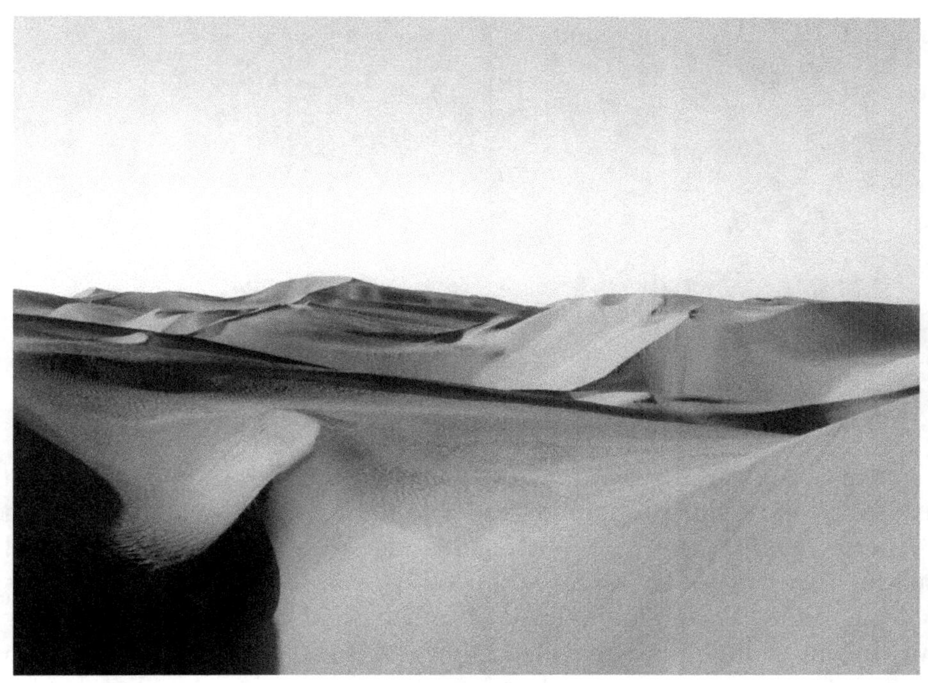

The Tamaklan Desert.[20]

It is no wonder that during ancient times, caravans traveling along the Silk Road preferred to avoid traversing the secluded desert. Typically, ancient merchants would choose one of the two safer paths that would take them around the edges of Taklamakan. The northern route followed the line of the Tianshan Mountains, skirting the desert's rim through a string of oases before heading westward. The southern route, however, required merchants to trace the foothills of the Kunlun Mountains, which would eventually lead them to settlements that clung to rivers flowing down from the highlands. Both routes eventually rejoined on the far side of the Tarim Basin. This allowed the ancient merchants to continue their journey toward Central Asia and beyond.

However, before pressing onward, some would stop at a certain oasis kingdom to replenish their supplies, trade their goods, and rest their animals. Known as Loulan, this fortified city sat on the eastern edge of the Tarim Basin near the salt lake of Lop Nur (also known as Luóbù Pō). Mud-brick houses dotted the city, with fields of millet and barley adorning its landscape. To weary travelers, the sight of this city and its canals carrying water from the Tarim must have appeared like a mirage turned real.

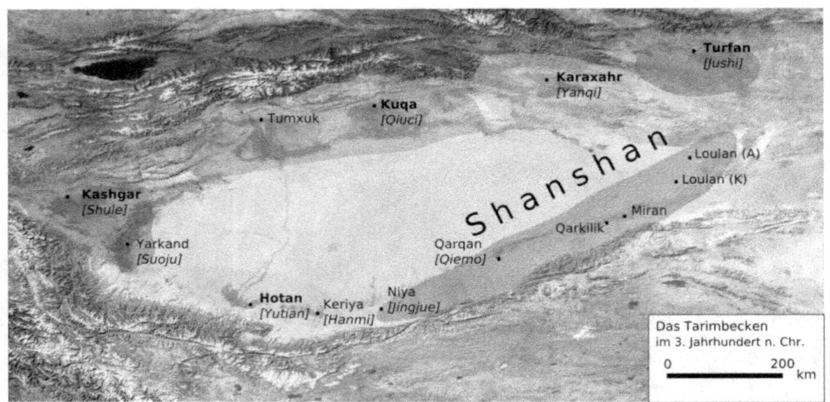

The Tarim Basin and its surrounding areas, circa 3rd century.[21]

One of the earliest mentions of Loulan came from its conquerors. In 126 BCE, the Chanyu, supreme leader of the Xiongnu, wrote to the Han emperor. In his letter, he boasted his victories, claiming that he had subdued an array of territories and people, from the nomadic pastoralists Yuezhi to the Wusun, the Jie, and of course, the Loulan. While the letter was meant to intimidate the Han emperor, the mention of Loulan also placed the city on the pedestal of history, turning it into a political prize that both the Xiongnu and the Han would compete to control in the centuries that followed.

Another mention came from a traveler named Zhang Qian, who was dispatched the same year by the Han dynasty. His mission was to cross the Tarim Basin, initiate transcontinental trade on the Silk Road, and seek alliances in the Western regions to join their fight against the Xiongnu. Zhang Qian passed by Lop Nur and laid eyes on Loulan. According to his description, the city was unlike any other settlement in the desert. Not only did it have walls that guarded the fields and canals that sustained it, but its location was also strategic: Loulan stood at the crossroads of east and west. The reports of his travels were so valuable that even Sima Qian quoted them extensively in his chronicles.

Unfortunately, it was its strategic location that invited chaos. The Han dynasty had its eyes on the city, aiming to turn Loulan into a buffer and staging post for the Silk Road. The Xiongnu, on the other hand, planned to transform it into a forward base against Han advances. Eventually, both sides pressed the city to swear loyalty. The Han, for instance, sent more envoys into the western regions after Zhang Qian returned with his reports. But the desert was relentless, and its inhabitants too were fierce.

Historical records, especially from the Book of Han, recalled how Loulan and its neighbor, Gushi, laid an attack against the Han envoys. When news of the assault reached the Han court, more troops were dispatched, with the goal of subduing Loulan and forcing it to pay tribute. Unable to face such massive and powerful forces, Loulan relented.

Of course, the Xiongnu also refused to remain silent. After all, they had already boasted their grip over the city in a letter to the Han. They, too, demanded tribute. Loulan was forced to hand over grain and livestock to their court, as well. The kingdom was now caught between the two powers. Loulan knew that to defy one of them would certainly bring destruction. Even hostages (princes) were handed to these powers. It was only when a Loulan king died that the hostages were allowed to return home. The new king, however, was required to send his own sons in their place.

Tensions finally broke out when a prince raised in the Xiongnu court ascended as the new king of Loulan. The Han emperor demanded that the new king present himself to demonstrate allegiance. However, the Loulan king refused to do so. This was largely due to the Han breaking their promise: they had failed to return one of the hostages when the new Loulan king ascended the throne. The Loulan also grew bolder and began attacking Han envoys once more.

What followed was violence. The Han emperor sent an emissary named Fu Jiezi to the city. He traveled to Loulan with all sorts of goods, including silk, gold, and fine wine. The king welcomed the envoy with open arms and held a feast for him. Fu Jiezi then presented his fine wine and offered to pour the king a drink, to which he gladly accepted. Fu Jiezi made sure he refilled the king's goblet each time he drank the wine. When the king was finally drunk, Fu Jiezi stabbed him to death. His severed head was then hung from one of Loulan's towers as a warning to those who dared to resist the "Son of Heaven."

This marked the end of Loulan's independence. A new king indeed rose to the Loulan throne—the younger brother of the assassinated king—but he was nothing more than a puppet of the Han. The kingdom also received a new name. Referred to as Shanshan, the kingdom was forever bound to the empire of the east.

Although its sovereignty was a thing of the past, the oasis city was still a hot spot for caravans traveling through the desert. In fact, Loulan remained a vital link in the Silk Road network. Archaeological findings reveal a culture both practical and cosmopolitan. Textiles dyed in reds and blues speak of local skill. Tools, combs, and pottery show everyday adaptation to desert life.

But still, prosperity was not meant to last; it was as fragile as the waters that sustained the city. As centuries passed, the Tarim River shifted its course. It no longer flowed reliably into Lop Nur. With its water supply depleting and its canals slowly cracking into empty ditches, Loulan began to falter. Its decline was also hastened by the raids launched by many nomadic tribes in the region. Then came the shifting of the trade routes, which led to Loulan's further decay. The Buddhist pilgrim, Faxian, who passed through the city during his travels in 399 CE, wrote how the city had become a ghost town, waiting for the sands to eventually swallow it whole.

Loulan was consumed by both the towering sands and time itself. It was only in 1900 that the kingdom resurfaced when a Swedish adventurer named Sven Hedin stumbled across the ruins as he journeyed through the Tarim Basin. There, he found what was left of the once flourishing oasis city: remnants of the sun-dried brick walls that protected the people and their fields thousands of years ago, destroyed watchtowers, and the dry bed of a canal that once fed the oasis.

After Hedin came the Hungarian British archaeologist Aurel Stein, who studied the site and documented it in detail. Excavations revealed a variety of artifacts such as coins, official documents, silk fabrics, lacquerware, wood carvings, and bronze tools. Some of these items even show Greco-Roman influences. These discoveries undoubtedly confirmed Loulan's life as a Silk Road city.

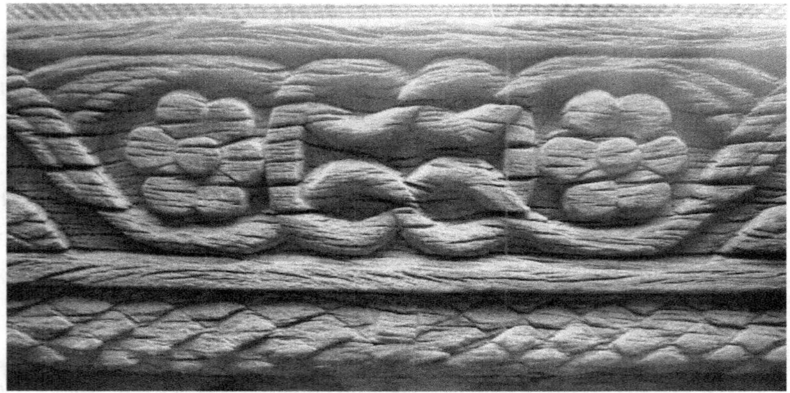

A carved wooden beam recovered from Loulan, which bore patterns influenced by ancient Western civilizations.[23]

One of the two most remarkable discoveries was the underground water channels, which were similar to the *karez* systems still used today by the peoples of the region—particularly the Uyghurs. Relying on differences in altitude and the pull of gravity, these water channels could collect meltwater from distant mountains and guide it toward the oasis. Since the channels were built underground, water was protected from both sandstorms and the desert sun.

Of course, Buddhism too left its mark on the vanished kingdom. Along with modest houses, temples and pagodas were also uncovered from the sands. These structures are evidence of the spread of the Buddhist faith across the desert by the first centuries CE. Scholars suggest that Loulan may have been a rest stop for monks and pilgrims who were traveling between China and India.

The second most remarkable finding was the body of a woman, referred to by historians as the Loulan Beauty. This mummy was discovered in 1980. Although tests showed that she lived nearly four thousand years prior to the kingdom's height, it is hard to dismiss the exceptional state of her body. Preserved perfectly by the desert's temperature and arid air, the mummy still has auburn hair attached to its skull. Even some of her delicate features survived the test of time—as if she was buried only a few decades ago.

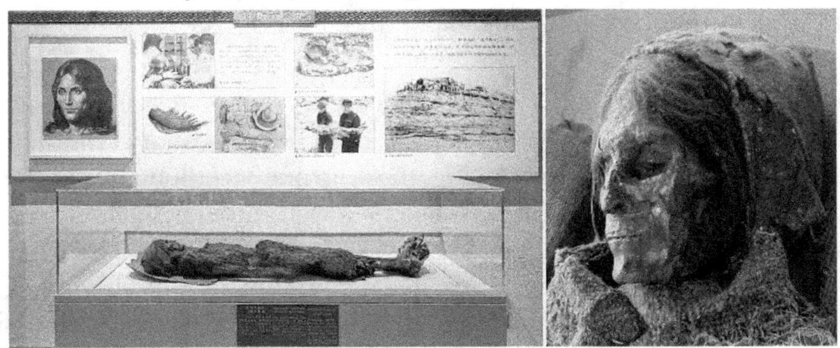

The Beauty of Loulan, now exhibited at Xinjian Museum.[20]

Today, the site of Loulan lies within a restricted military zone. While its ruins are largely inaccessible, its story continues to captivate historians and archaeologists.

A Discovery That Challenged China's Well-Known Past

The *Iliad* is thought to have been composed by Homer in the seventh or eighth century BCE. It narrates the Trojan War, which revolved around the ancient city of Troy. Although the Trojan War became a favorite subject, especially in the history of ancient Greece, many dismissed the city's existence as pure myth. This view, however, changed in the 1870s.

German archaeologist Heinrich Schliemann, convinced that the city was real, embarked on a mission to uncover the truth. Arriving at the hills of Hisarlik in modern-day Turkey, he dug layer by layer until he eventually uncovered the stone walls and artifacts of a city long thought to be imaginary. From then on, Troy was no longer the stuff of poetry alone. It was real, complex, and historical. Its rediscovery undoubtedly reset the way the world thought about ancient Greece.

Then, over a century later, something very similar happened in China. For many years, it was common belief that all Chinese civilization began in a single place—the fertile valley of the Yellow River. It was here that many dynasties rose in sequence, starting from the mysterious Xia to the Shang and Zhou, who each built upon the achievements of the dynasty before. Archaeology confirmed much of this story. The Shang dynasty, which centered at Anyang, left plenty of evidence for our generation to uncover, such as the oracle bones (the earliest Chinese writing, used for divination) and ritual bronzes, which were believed to have been commonly used in ancestor worship. Meanwhile, other regions like Sichuan, Yunnan, or the south were seen as peripheral; they borrowed culture and influence from the Shang and were never considered equal centers of civilization in their own right.

Fast forward to the early twentieth century when historians saw the need to redraw the map of China's past. It all began with a certain farmer named Yan Daochang. In 1929, the farmer accidentally made an astonishing discovery while he was digging a well in his field in Guanghan, Sichuan. As it turns out, beneath his land was a large stash of jade artifacts. Excavations took place for decades following this discovery, but the finds did not cause much of a stir. Jade is indeed valuable, but since the gemstone fit within the broad traditions of Chinese antiquity, these discoveries were not considered unusual.

Another discovery in 1986, however, appeared strange enough that it challenged everything historians thought they knew about the origins of Chinese civilization. Archaeologists had uncovered two enormous sacrificial pits. Expecting yet another cache of jade, they were surprised to learn that beneath the earth was a bronze mask with features they had never seen before. Its almond-shaped eyes bulged outward; the nose was sharp and protruding, while the ears flared wide. These features were utterly unlike anything in the Chinese Bronze Age. This was not the only mask they uncovered. They also found one inlaid with gold foil and a few others that varied in size but were similar in fashion.

As days passed, more artifacts surfaced. One of the most popular was a standing bronze man that measured at least eight feet tall. It featured a long pair of arms that made it appear as if the statue was presenting a gift to the heavens above. Historians suggest it could be plausible that in its glory days, the statue once held a sacred object, perhaps a piece an ornament of jade or ivory.

The same year, hundreds of broken pieces of a bronze tree were uncovered. Upon restoration (which took nearly a decade to complete), the sacred tree appeared rather massive. The trunk itself rose in three tiers, each featuring three branches growing out of it. Curling downward like flowing ribbons, these branches also had flowers at full bloom, complete with small birds perched on top of them. From these larger branches sprouted smaller offshoots, each heavy with fruit. In total, there were twenty-seven

The reconstructed Sanxingdui sacred tree.³⁴

of them, glimmering like a treasure left under the blazing sun. Last but not least, the sacred tree also has a dragon twining around its lower trunk. The artistry was surreal, especially considering it was constructed many thousands of years ago.

Other treasures found buried underneath the earth included elephant tusks, gold scepters, jade blades, cowrie shells, and ritual vessels. To many, these items may look like the refuse of a city, but to well-trained eyes, they could be a part of a massive ritual deposit on a scale unlike anything known from the Shang.

Historians familiar with the culture of the Shang dynasty could easily notice the stark contrast. While the geometrical bronze vessels from the Shang were typically heavy, symmetrical, and decorated with *taotie* motifs, the ones from the Sanxingdui site were completely different; most of them took on fantastical and sculptural forms. It's also possibly their purpose was not the same. While bronzes from the Shang dynasty were linked to ritual feasting and ancestor worship, the ones from Sanxingdui appear to have been part of sacrificial pits. Many Sanxingdui artifacts were deliberately broken or burned before burial, which could suggest a very distinct set of religious beliefs.

Remarkably, the earth had not finished giving up its treasures. Excavations in 2021 resulted in the discovery of six more sacrificial pits, all full of mysterious artifacts. Another bronze mask was uncovered, though this one was larger than the archaeologists had ever seen. Dating to around 1300–1100 BCE, the mask was over seventy centimeters high and 131 centimeters wide. It was so massive that its face, eyes, and ears had been cast separately before being soldered together. It also had openings on the forehead and at the sides that led archaeologists to believe that it was once attached to something else—perhaps a great statue or a wooden effigy. Upon further inspection, archaeologists also found traces of silk near the mask's right eye. The reason for this is still being discussed.

Apart from the big bronze mask, a rather peculiar figure was also uncovered from another one of the pits. Rising to seventy-five centimeters tall, this statue was a hybrid of a tiger and a dragon. It featured a pair of bulging eyes, a set of jutting teeth, and a band-like piece in its mouth. On its base stood a bird.

In light of these discoveries, it is safe to assume that the Sanxingdui culture was not an offshoot of Shang culture but an independent civilization equal in sophistication, with its own worldview.

Soon, archaeologists pointed to the ancient Shu culture, arriving at a plausible conclusion that Sanxingdui was connected to it. Indeed, Shu had been mentioned in later Chinese texts, but its history was murky and often shrouded in legend and myths. Its first king was believed to be an individual named Cancong, who was credited with introducing significant advancements in agriculture and silk production. King Cancong of Shu was also said to have had bulging eyes. Scholars suggest that his unique feature marked him as more than just a mortal king. Perhaps, to his people, he may have been seen as a shaman or even a divine figure. Interestingly, this belief seemed to echo uncannily in the Sanxingdui masks, which often sport the same protruding eyes.

The bronze mask, thought to be a depiction of King Cancong.[25]

For centuries, Shu was considered peripheral to the grand dynasties of the north, if it was considered at all. But Sanxingdui changed that view. What's more, the civilization's discovery also reset assumptions about early China entirely. It was no longer possible to view Chinese civilization as flowing from a single source in the Yellow River Valley. Archaeological evidence proved that China's Bronze Age had multiple centers that flourished in their own ways. The Shang dynasty shone in the north, while Sanxingdui rose in Sichuan.

However, just as suddenly as it appeared, Sanxingdui vanished. The site was abandoned sometime around 1100 BCE, leaving behind zero written texts to explain the reasons. But, of course, theories abound. Geologists suggest that the region was struck by a massive earthquake. This shifted the flow of the Min River, cutting off water to the city.

Without water, life in the Sichuan basin would have been impossible. Hence, the population was left with no other choice but to move. Another theory involves catastrophic flooding, which was hinted at in ancient texts. If this was true, the flood could have drowned the city. The burned artifacts in the pits might have been part of desperate rituals to appease the gods and stop a catastrophic event.

Invasion could also be one of the reasons the culture suddenly vanished. Sanxingdui was rich in gold and bronze, making it a tempting prize for neighboring, power-hungry rivals. If an enemy overran the city, the ritual destruction of sacred objects could have been intended to break the enemy's spiritual power.

A golden mask uncovered from Jinsha, which had details similar to those from Sanxingdui.[26]

The most intriguing theory, however, comes from just forty kilometers away, at the site Jinsha (located in Qinyang, Sichuan). Here, archaeologists had uncovered another collection of artifacts that bore a striking resemblance to those unearthed at Guanghan. This included bronze and gold masks—though they were smaller than the ones found in Guanghan—jade, and ivory. These findings suggest that the Sanxingdui simply relocated, turning Jinsha into their new center. If so, Sanxingdui did not vanish entirely but lived on in a new landscape.

Chapter 2 – Unsung Men of Ancient China

It was 383 CE, and the balance of power in China appeared hopelessly uneven. A battle was about to take place on the banks of the Fei River (located in present-day Anhui Province). On one side stood the forces of the Former Qin, who were fighting for their ambitious ruler, Fu Jian. According to ancient chroniclers, Fu Jian had dispatched nearly 900,000 men, whom he had gathered from every corner of his empire.

Camping across the water were only 80,000 soldiers of the smaller Eastern Jin dynasty. The sight of their enemy must have been overwhelming. The Qin outnumbered them well over ten to one. Their camp stretched as far as the eye could see. When night came, fires from their camp dotted the night sky as if the constellations themselves had come down to earth. The neighing of countless horses, which echoed day and night, added tension to the air. For a time, it looked like the heavenly gods themselves had already decided the victor of the battle.

Yet, the forces of Jin were not so easily deterred. After all, numbers alone do not decide battles. The troops were already arranged in a special, extra-wide formation. Their lines stretched far across the riverbank, giving the impression of an army much larger than it truly was. Morale among the soldiers was also high, especially since they were commanded by a seasoned general named Xie Xuan. However, although the Jin army was fearless and disciplined, Xie Xuan knew that he could not depend on brute strength alone to emerge victorious against such a massive force. And so, after days of stalemate—neither side made a move, each waiting for the other's misstep—Xie Xuan devised a strategy. He sent a messenger to the Qin commander, Fu Rong, with a proposal. Xie Xuan requested that the Qin army pull back slightly from the riverbank so that the Jin could cross and face them on equal ground.

When the request was carried to Fu Jian, he immediately gave his blessing; the Qin ruler was confident that such a small move would not make any difference in the outcome of the battle. With his approval, Fu Rong ordered the front lines to step back, clearing space for their enemy to cross. However, in an army of such immense size, where orders had to ripple through countless ranks and languages, misunderstandings spread easily.

When the front lines began to step back, many misunderstood the movement. They believed that retreat had already begun and defeat was in order. Confusion took over the Qin army, followed by panic. Soldiers jostled and stumbled as the line broke its shape. This was the very moment Xie Xuan had been waiting for. Seizing the opportunity, he ordered his troops to advance. Banners were raised and battle cries rose as they charged across the Fei River. The Qin army, so mighty in appearance, collapsed in an instant. Tens of thousands threw down their weapons and fled, while others trampled one another, desperate to retreat.

The defeat destroyed Fu Jian's ambitions. His empire experienced fracture in the years that followed. The Eastern Jin, on the other hand, successfully preserved its existence against all odds.

It is safe to say that war was not a stranger in ancient China. For many centuries, the land had gone through countless episodes of conflict that scarred and shaped the empire. Kingdoms had risen and fallen in waves of chaos, with their borders constantly shifting after each battle. This was especially visible in the age of the Warring States, when it was common to see armies of hundreds of thousands trampling across not only the battlefield but also the countryside. True, peace existed, but it was more of a pause between battles rather than a lasting condition. Out of this chaotic era came the world's most enduring manual of strategy, *The Art of War.* Authored by Sun Tzu, the famed strategist who served the state of Wu, the writings prove useful even to this day.

The Four Greatest Generals of the Late Warring States are highly revered for their contributions to the world of warfare. The first was Lian

Po of Zhao, whose defense strategies at Changping were so effective that even the Qin could not penetrate the city. When he was pulled into intrigue and replaced, Changping was left exposed. His removal opened the way for another great general, Bai Qi of Qin, to make a move. Also known as the "Human Butcher," he was responsible for bringing Qin to multiple glories, including the annihilation of Zhao forces at the Battle of Changping in 260 BCE. Then there was Li Mu, whose careful planning and deception successfully defeated both steppe nomads and Qin armies. He also managed to delay Zhao's fall for years. Last but not least was Wang Jian, whose campaigns crushed Chu (Qin's strongest rival) and gave way for the unification of China.

Yet the fame of Sun Tzu and the Four Great Generals often eclipses others whose loyalty and brilliance were just as vital to their times. Wu Qi, for instance, was one of the overlooked figures whose reforms transformed armies and brought victories. His end, however, was as tragic as his life was extraordinary.

The General Who Valued Merit

Born in the chaotic fifth century BCE, Wu Qi was already used to living a life where peace was far from reach. Since he belonged to a minor noble family, he was given a good education but not a guaranteed position in high office. If he wished to rise through the ranks, Wu Qi must present his worth and talent rather than strictly his inheritance. And so, he began young. The future general filled his early years with studies of military strategies. His earliest career began in the small state of Lu, which was also his mother's homeland. But there he gained only little recognition.

Later on, he entered the service of Wei, at that time considered one of the strongest of the Warring States. Under Marquess Wen, he was given command against the state's greatest rival, Qin. This was the beginning of his glory; Wu Qi demonstrated his brilliance and always struck his enemies with careful calculation.

His talent in warfare shone especially in 389 BCE, when Wei and Qin clashed for dominance in the west. Under his command, the Wei army succeeded in launching a surprise assault on the Qin camp. They also captured the enemy general, forcing the Qin into a hasty retreat. This victory secured Wei's western frontier. Wei faced Qin several more times and, again, Wu Qi distinguished himself. Many more battles were won, further securing Wei's dominance in the Central Plains. By this time, Wu Qi's name had become known far and wide, his victories spoken with the utmost respect.

What placed him apart from all other war generals, however, was his philosophy of leadership. Wu Qi believed victory began with discipline and shared hardship. Hence, despite being rewarded for his achievements, Wu Qi lived just as his men did. He ate coarse rations, slept under the same conditions as his soldiers, and most remarkable of all, even tended to the wounded himself. This undoubtedly won him the respect of common soldiers who would fight alongside him in a heartbeat. But, while Wu Qi was respected by his men, his influence also made him a target in the eyes of the nobility, especially those who felt like their privileges had been stripped away in favor of merit. He eventually fell out of favor with Wei.

Still, Wu Qi refused to stand back despite looming threats. He was later invited to Chu, where he was made chancellor under King Dao. With his new position, Wu Qi continued to build a name. He always preferred merit rather than inheritance or privileges, often giving promotions to capable men regardless of rank. Those deemed incompetent were dismissed.

He enacted reforms that transformed Chu's military and administration and cut corruption, bringing Chu to new heights. The annual salaries of Chu officials were reduced; the saved money flowed into the military so that Chu could train more professional armies. With a stronger force, Wu Qi went on to launch a campaign against the state of Yue. Victory was achieved, which further expanded Chu's borders and restored its influence. With Wu Qi at the helm, Chu grew ever stronger, to the point that it could rival both Qin and Wei.

Unfortunately, history would repeat for Wu Qi. The only difference was that this time, it cost him his life. Wu Qi's policies indeed benefited the state greatly, but his honesty and reforms threatened the aristocrats who had long grown fat off corruption and privilege. The aristocrats knew that to reassert their power, Wu Qi must go. So, when King Dao of Chu passed, they made their move. Archers were hidden at the king's funeral. It was said that Wu Qi immediately spotted the assassins. The *Shiji* narrates that instead of running for cover, the war general leapt to the king's remains. He tried shielding the king's corpse from arrows even as he was struck dead.

The aristocrats succeeded in killing Wu Qi (though they faced punishment for hurting King Dao's corpse) but failed to erase Wu Qi's legacy. The compilation of his military writings, the *Wu Zi*, stands alongside Sun Tzu's *Art of War* as one of the Seven Military Classics of China.

A Scholar Turned General

If Wu Qi's brilliance lay in reshaping the armies of the Warring States, then Ban Chao's genius was in extending Han power far beyond the empire's heartland. His beginnings, however, were rather humble. Ban Chao grew up in a family of scholars. His sister, Ban Zhao, would soon become one of China's most famous female historians. It looked as if the path had been laid for him. Ban Chao was expected to live a quiet life, especially considering he was nothing more than a mere clerk in the Eastern Han court during the first century CE. Instead of riding through battlefields with a sword in hand, he filled his days copying official documents. But, over time, Ban Chao realized that he must pursue another path.

His dreams soon came to reality in 73 CE when the Han launched a major campaign against the Xiongnu. Alongside a military campaign, the Han court also sent smaller envoys on missions into the Western Regions (Tarim Basin) to secure allies and re-establish Han influence over the oasis kingdoms, including the Shanshan, Khotan, and Kashgar. Ancient sources record that Ban Chao was assigned to join this very military expedition as an assistant. This opportunity was possibly given to him because of his family's reputation as respected scholars (especially his father, Ban Biao, and his brother, Ban Gu).

Things changed when the Han envoys arrived at Shanshan. The king of the kingdom appeared hesitant to pledge allegiance to the Han. It also did not help that envoys of Xiongnu had likewise arrived in the region, hoping they could earn the Shanshan king's allegiance. Seeing that the survival of Han influence in Shanshan hung in the balance, Ban Chao chose to make a daring move. With only thirty-six men supporting him, Ban Chao led an attack. Under the cover of the night sky, he and his little band snuck into the Xiongnu camp. The envoys had their guard down, as they did not expect an attack by such a small force of Han envoys. When a blade slashed its first victim, who was sleeping soundly, panic immediately ensued. The Han party cut down its enemy one by one. Ban Chao then presented the severed heads of the envoys to the king of Shanshan. Both stunned and intimidated, the king pledged loyalty to the Han.

From then on, Ban Chao's reputation grew. He moved from oasis to oasis, persuading, intimidating, or defeating local rulers into alliance with the Han. At Khotan and Kashgar, he secured key Silk Road states by playing diplomacy and force in equal measure. Then, in 94 CE, he led campaigns that subdued Kucha and Turfan. By 97 CE, more than fifty states of the Western Regions had acknowledged Han supremacy.

A statue of Ban Chao in Kashgar.[27]

In recognition of his achievements, Ban Chao was appointed protector general of the Western Regions, the highest Han authority in Central Asia. He held the position for more than thirty years, ensuring that the Silk Road remained in Han's control. Ban Chao was also credited with sending an envoy named Gan Ying beyond the borders of China to learn more about the Roman Empire. Gan Ying never reached Rome, but he did set foot on either the eastern coast of the Mediterranean Sea, the Black Sea, or the Parthian coast of the Persian Gulf. Although he failed to establish direct contact with the Romans, Gan Ying returned with a detailed report that expanded Chinese knowledge of the West.

As for Ban Chao, the deserts and mountains of the west became his home as his duty was tied to the Western Regions. He was relieved of his duty in 102 CE because of his worsening health condition. Ban Chao returned to Luoyang and died of his illness in the same year.

A Reputable General Cut Down By the Emperor

Tan Daoji was a respectable general of the Liu Song dynasty, serving under Emperor Wen. He was active in the first half of the fifth century CE, when the states of Liu Song in the south and Northern Wei in the north were constantly at each other's throats. Though his name is less remembered today, it is hard to dismiss that his campaigns succeeded in preserving the south from northern conquest. The story of his death, however, revealed the perils of loyalty in a world where emperors tend to trust intrigue more than their best generals.

A portrait of Tan Daoji.[28]

When Daoji was born, China was already fragmented. The north had fallen into the hands of non-Han dynasties, while the south was held by the Liu Song. Tan Daoji did not have a slow start to his career. Able to distinguish himself as a soldier with both talent and courage, he grew his reputation rapidly. He was known among his troops for fighting with not only skill but also a sense of fairness and discipline.

His reputation grew even more during the campaigns against the northern states, particularly the Northern Wei. When the north advanced southward, it was Tan Daoji who became the very shield of Liu Song. Of course, this was not the last of his campaigns. Later, Tan Daoji mounted many more counterattacks that left a deep mark on the enemy. This further cemented his reputation and earned him the ultimate devotion of his troops. Even contemporary records praise him as one of the dynasty's most capable commanders. He was described as a man whose leadership allowed the Liu Song to hold its ground against a stronger foe.

But regardless of his enormous contributions to the state, Tan Daoji was not shielded from envious nobles. Like many Chinese generals before him, his growing fame made him a target for intrigue. However, unlike Wu Qi, who faced jealous aristocrats, Tan Daoji was targeted by the emperor himself. Emperor Wen of Liu Song, though a capable ruler, had grown uneasy about Tan Daoji's popularity with the army. Whispers at court also made it worse for the general. Some quietly warned the emperor that the general would soon pose a threat to the dragon throne. Others spoke of the army's devotion to Tan Daoji, suggesting that with such support, the general could usurp the throne by force. In the end, these whispers kept the emperor awake at night. He was certain that Tan Daoji was a man too powerful to be left unchecked.

And so, the general's fate was sealed. The emperor moved against him in 436 CE. Tan Daoji was summoned to court under false pretenses, accused of treason, and arrested. Although the charge was baseless, Tan Daoji was executed. Even two of his most trusted comrades were entangled in the situation and put to death. This brought dire consequences. His loyal soldiers had been left leaderless, and morale collapsed in an instant. Meanwhile, when news of Tan Daoji's death reached Northern Wei, they were said to have rejoiced. Taking advantage of the situation, they advance into Liu Song, wreaking havoc across six provinces. Ancient sources record that Emperor Wen regretted his decision, lamenting that Liu Song would never have faced such destruction if Tan Daoji were alive.

Zhang Heng and Cai Lun

Of course not all of China's great figures left a mark on the battlefield. For every general who defended frontiers or won dynasties, there were men whose genius lay in invention, science, and culture. Take Zhang Heng, for instance. Born in Nanyang (located in present-day Henan Province) during the Eastern Han dynasty, Zhang Heng was known to have displayed his curiosity at an early age. Unlike many of his contemporaries who focused only on Confucian classics, he preferred to dive into the realms of mathematics, astronomy, and mechanics.

As a member of a distinguished family, Zhang Heng unsurprisingly managed to obtain several positions in the court of the Eastern Han. He was even offered a promotion to the role of an imperial secretary. Although this was a high office close to the emperor, Zhang Heng humbly declined the offer. As a man of honesty and principle, he wished to not involve himself in the factional struggles and corruption that often plagued the court. He knew that accepting the position would soon force him into constant conflict with powerful figures. After all, Zhang Heng was far more devoted to astronomy, mathematics, and invention than bureaucratic duties. Instead, he requested to serve as the prefect of Henan. This was a less prominent role, but it allowed him to continue his astronomical studies and inventions.

His greatest achievement came in 132 CE. For years, Zhang Heng had been studying the earth. China was no stranger to earthquakes; thus, he made it his ultimate goal to detect them as they happened, even at great distances. He eventually came up with the device known as the seismoscope. This large bronze vessel was shaped like a barrel. Eight dragons adorned it. Their heads pointed in different directions, and each held a bronze ball in its mouth. Each of these dragons was also accompanied by a bronze toad beneath it. Inside the vessel, Zhang Heng installed a system of levers and pendulums. When an earthquake struck, even one too faint to be felt locally, the mechanism would be activated, causing one dragon to release its bronze ball into the mouth of the waiting toad below. This indicated the direction of the quake. According to historical records, the seismoscope once signaled a quake to the west. Interestingly, messengers arrived at the capital days later, confirming that the device was right: an earthquake had shaken the distant as Zhang Heng's device had indicated.

A replica of Zhang Heng's seismoscope.[29]

Zhang Heng studied not only the earth but also the heavens. He improved the armillary sphere, a device for mapping the stars, and created more accurate calendars by observing celestial movements.

While Zhang Heng measured the earth and heavens, Cai Lun gave us paper. Born in Guiyang (modern-day Hunan), Cai Lun initially entered the palace as a eunuch, possibly in 75 CE, serving Emperor Ming at the end of his reign. He remained a eunuch well until the rise of Emperor He of Han. Details of his early years have been lost to time, but in 105 CE, he made a breakthrough that almost immediately changed the world.

The ancient Egyptians had been writing on papyrus, which was made from the stalks of papyrus reed pressed and dried into sheets. It served well enough along the Nile, but it was fragile, costly to transport, and ill-suited to the needs of a vast empire like Han China. Instead, before Cai Lun presented his idea, the Chinese wrote on bamboo strips, wooden tablets, or in some cases, silk. However, these materials were not suitable in the long run—they were either heavy, cumbersome, or extremely expensive.

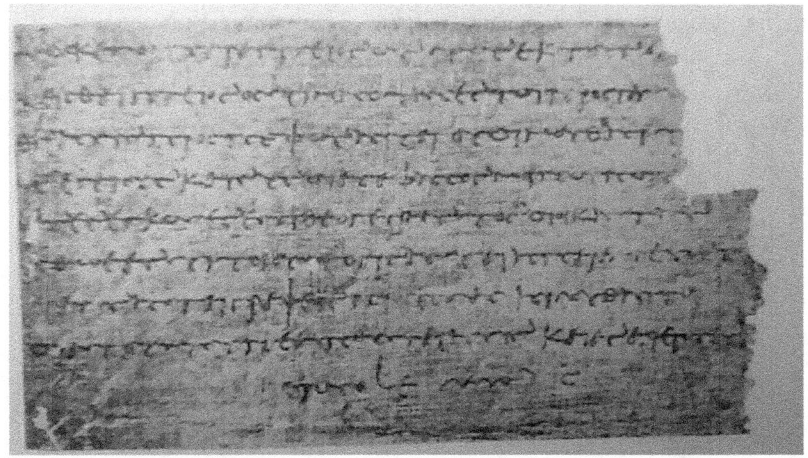

A letter written on papyrus, dating to the 3rd century BCE.[80]

Cai Lun, however, introduced a more refined method of creating paper, which he presented to Emperor He. He devised a process of pulping tree bark, hemp, old rags, and fishing nets. The mixture was then strained through a fine screen before being pressed and dried into thin sheets. The result was not only light but also durable and cost effective. This new form of paper undoubtedly revolutionized administration; governments and scholars could record and copy texts way more than before, merchants could keep accounts more efficiently, and ideas could spread more widely than ever.

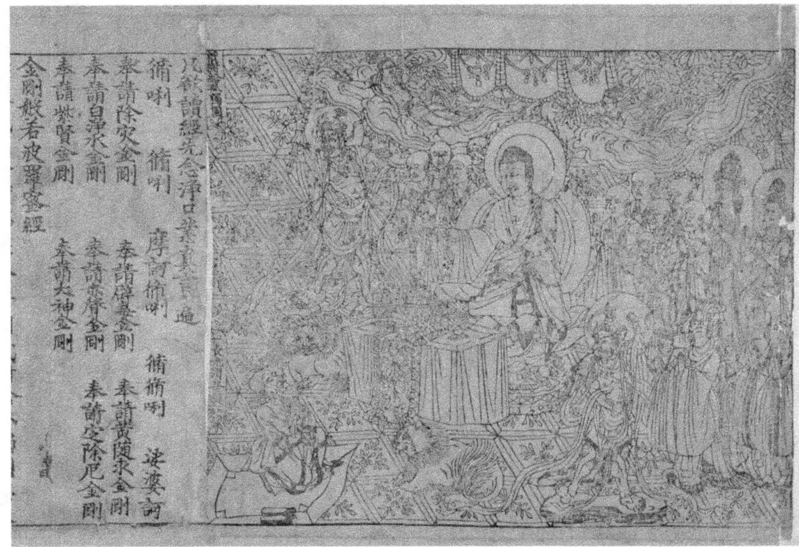

The Diamond Sutra, known as the earliest printed book.[81]

This invention won Cai Lun positions in court and rewards in the form of land. Despite his contributions, Cai Lun was fated to have a rather grim end. When palace politics turned against his faction, he lost imperial favor. Facing disgrace, Cai Lun took his own life by drinking poison in 121 CE.

Chapter 3 – Women Who Defied All Odds

Scanning through the pages of China's early histories, it is easy to notice that most of the stories are crowded with the names of emperors, generals, and ministers. These men were the ones often featured in the annals. Their achievements in grand battles were the ones often recorded with as much detail as possible, along with their edicts, rise, and fall. Names of women, however, are far less visible. When they do appear, it is often in the margins; their names are often accompanied by descriptions like "mother of kings" or "an emperor's favorite" or themes like virtue and caution.

This is not surprising, since from the earliest dynasties, social order was shaped by patriarchal ideals. The ancient Chinese were well acquainted with the doctrine of the Three Obediences. According to Confucius, who taught this doctrine, women were expected to obey their fathers before marriage, their husbands after marriage, and their sons if they were ever widowed. Although this principle was widely accepted in that era, it limited women's independence. Most of the time, a woman was confined to the roles of a daughter, a wife, and a mother. Her virtue was measured by loyalty and modesty within the household rather than personal ambition.

True, there were stark contrasts between the daily lives of female commoners and the elites. Those without prestige typically filled their days weaving, raising children, and managing other household affairs.

Some, especially those in poorer families, also labored in the fields and markets. Among the elites, women did no such thing. More often than not, these mundane chores were assigned to servants while the women enjoy refinement in music, poetry, and calligraphy. However, their talents were meant to polish their husbands' already existing prestige rather than to secure their own. No matter their status, the lives of women in ancient China had boundaries. Legal codes also leaned more toward men, granting them authority over property, marriage, and divorce.

But there were always cracks in the system, allowing a few fortunate women to make a name for themselves—though often, history forgets them. Marriage alliances were one of the ways. Through this small opportunity, women (of noble class, of course) could become imperial consorts or even empresses. They could wield influence, though often precariously, at the side of emperors. In some instances, empress dowagers ruled as regents, at least until the future emperor came of age. There were also times when the imperial concubines altered the balance of power at court.

Meanwhile, outside the palace, there were women who carved their paths as poets and scholars. Some gained authority through religion, particularly Daoism and later Buddhism. This allowed women to step up as priestesses and nuns. And in rare, extraordinary cases, women donned armor, raised banners, and took to the battlefield.

These moments clearly displayed how women were not simply silent figures behind the scenes of history. Despite restrictions, some succeeded in defying the odds, though most of their stories are nearly forgotten. Some were purposely erased, since their narratives did not fit the norm of a patriarchal society. But some of their names appeared in oracle bone inscriptions, and some of their stories survived in fragments of funerary stelae, poems, or the records of reluctant male historians.

One of the findings that sheds more light on women figures of ancient China was made in 1976. Archaeologists were excavating at Yinxu, the ancient Shang capital near Anyang, when they made a surprising discovery. They found a tomb, sealed and undisturbed beneath the layers of earth for over three thousand years. When opened, the tomb revealed an array of precious treasures and artifacts, including over a thousand bronze and jade objects, hundreds of bone implements, and most interesting of all, a variety of weapons.

Fu Hao's burial pit.[32]

In ancient times, not everyone was buried with weapons; they were typically found in tombs belonging to warriors and generals. So, this meant only one thing: the resident of the tomb was known for her martial prowess and involvement in battles and wars. Among other things, they discovered a set of oracle bones. Some of them spoke of a time when six hundred women filled the ranks of the military. Many others had a certain name inscribed on them: Fu Hao.

According to ancient sources, Fu Hao was one of the most extraordinary women in early Chinese history. She lived during the late Shang dynasty, sometime around the thirteenth century BCE. Details of her early life are rather obscure, but evidence suggests that Fu Hao was a high-born princess of a vassal state of the Shang dynasty—possibly a state on the border or the steppe. Given this status, she was bestowed with great education and wealth. When she was only a teenager, Fu Hao found her destiny entangled with that of King Wu Ding of Shang. All those years, the king had been strengthening his position, and one of the ways was to marry a woman from each neighboring tribe. Fu Hao became one of his sixty-four wives, though later she would climb through the ranks, becoming one of the king's three consorts.

However, she lived during a time of war. Seeing that the struggle between Shang and its enemy, the Tufang tribe, had stretched across generations, Fu Hao decided to take bold action. She recommended herself as the general of the Shang army. At first, the king was hesitant, especially when his wife was but a teenage girl. But, since the war had lasted for far too long and his generals seldom returned with news of victory, King Wu Ding reluctantly agreed. The young Fu Hao was sent to the battlefield. Much to everyone's surprise, good news soon arrived at the capital. Their enemy had finally been defeated in a single decisive battle, and Fu Hao was the one who commanded the troops. This was the beginning of her impressive career in the military.

From then on, Fu Hao earned the respect of many, and her achievements continued. Along with her dear husband, Lady Fu Hao succeeded in extending Shang's borders. Campaigns were launched against the neighboring Yi and Qiang. Her most impressive military achievement was when she went against the state of Ba. Backed by two other generals named Xi Li Zhi and Hou Gao, Lady Fu Hao led a force of 13,000 warriors in an ambush against the enemy. This event, inscribed on bones and tortoise shells buried in her tomb, is remembered as one of the earliest large-scale ambushes in the history of China.

Fu Hao did not have her entire attention on military campaigns. She was also a high priestess in charge of the Shang's grand religious ceremonies and sacrificial rituals. Of course, despite having built a name of her own, Fu Hao was also described as a loyal wife to King Wu Ding. The king himself appreciated her so much that stories claim he would wait for his wife's return from war outside the capital city. Once reunited, the two would dismiss their guards so they could spend time together uninterrupted. King Wu Ding also rewarded her greatly for her contributions. The lady was given not only wealth in the form of jewelry, gems, and exquisite silk but also her own land, along with three thousand soldiers for her to command to her liking.

But, unfortunately, Lady Fu Hao did not enjoy a long life. She left the world of the living at the age of thirty-three. Some say she died during childbirth, while others claim she departed due to a lethal wound obtained in a war. King Wu Ding was so saddened by her departure that even in her death, he bestowed a new title upon her. Her posthumous temple name was Mu Xin. The king had two more queens after her death, though these were merely political alliances. Fu Hao, however, was remembered, especially during times of war. The king would invoke her name in official ritualistic ceremonies, seeking her blessings.

Yet unlike most royals, Fu Hao was not buried in the grand royal cemetery. Instead, Wu Ding placed her tomb close to the sacred precinct of Yinxu, perhaps to ensure her spirit remained near the center of ritual life. Because her grave was apart from the usual cluster of royal burials, archaeologists did not find it earlier. Hence, her story remained forgotten until its rediscovery in 1976.

First Female Historian in Chinese History

Ban Zhao was born sometime in 45 CE into a family of scholars. Her father was none other than Ban Biao, a prominent historian during the Han dynasty. Growing up in such a household, Ban Zhao was fortunate to have received a great education and access to valuable books and rare palace manuscripts usually inaccessible for most people. Ban Zhou herself was a lover of knowledge. Ever since she was young, she could often be found surrounded by books and scrolls day and night or involved in debates of history and philosophy with her brothers.

Like most women of her time, Ban Zhao entered married life at an early age—she was only fourteen years old. But not long afterward, her husband died. She never remarried but chose to focus solely on studying literature. Then, another tragedy struck her life, though this one would give her the role that would define her life. Her brother, Ban Gu, was deeply involved in court politics. He was close to Dou Xian, the brother of Empress Dowager Dou. So, when Emperor He launched a coup against Dou Xian in 92 CE, Ban Gu too was dragged down. He was arrested and died in prison the same year. This left the *Book of Han*, initially begun by Ban Biao, incomplete.

The court then requested Ban Zhao, who was already in her forties at that time, to continue the project. She focused especially on the astronomical, ritual, and chronological sections, all of which required scholarly precision. In addition to drafting these sections, Ban Zhao also served as editor for Ban Gu's earlier drafts, ensuring that the document was ready for official presentation. The *Book of Han* was essentially completed around the early 100s CE and later became one of the great official histories of China.

A depiction of Ban Zhao.[88]

Ban Zhao's hands were crucial to the completion of the book, but her accomplishments did not end there. She was also made a tutor, ordered to share her vast knowledge with Empress Deng Sui and the court ladies. She tutored them in literature, history, and etiquette. Because of this, Ban Zhou gained political influence. She was even given the title "Gifted One," and the empress appointed her as a lady-in-waiting. Her wisdom was so precious that the empress consistently sought her advice, even as she became regent for the infant Empress Shang of Han. In gratitude, the empress gave both Ban Zhao's sons appointments as officials.

It was also during this time that Ban Zhao wrote her most famous work, known as *Nü Jie* (Lessons for Women). To modern readers, her work may appear backward or even unreasonable. In her writing, Ban Zhao appeared to have reinforced Confucian ideals of female submission. She emphasized humility, obedience, and advising a woman to yield and be compliant to her husband. This may sound suffocating, especially when we are living in an age that values independence and equality above all. But still, it is hard to dismiss that in the context of the Eastern Han, her work was groundbreaking. She did not instruct a woman to blindly submit to her husband. Instead, she argued that women must receive education, for without it, they would not be able to properly fulfill their roles as wives and mothers. For this reason, some say that her writings were not only extremely influential in her time but also continued to shape ideals of womanhood for centuries. Some scholars even argue that Ban Zhao's work still holds practical applications. Beyond submission, her work also emphasized harmony within households, self-discipline, and the cultivation of moral character—traits that many would agree transcend eras. In this way, her text can be read both as a reflection of Confucian patriarchy and a manual on how women could navigate and survive within its confines.

Ban Zhao died around 116 CE, leaving behind all of her work. Her daughter-in-law, née Ding, collected her works, compiling them into three different volumes known simply as "Collected Works of Ban Zhao." Unfortunately, most of them have been lost to time.

The Princess Who Raised an Army

The Sui dynasty was on the verge of destruction. Famine had swept across the land. Harvests failed, and taxes were as high as the sky itself. The armies had no rest, as they were ordered to march endlessly, building canals, repairing walls, and fighting wars on distant frontiers. Villages were stripped bare; capable men were conscripted, leaving women and children to scrape survival from their barren fields.

Having seen enough chaos, Li Yuan, the commander of the northern frontiers, chose to revolt against Emperor Yang of Sui in 617 CE. He then sent messengers to his daughter, Pingyang, and her husband, General Chai Shao, to join his cause in Taiyuan. However, since they were still in the Sui capital, Chang'an, Chai Shao was worried that it would be impossible for them both to escape without alerting anyone. So, Pingyang advised her husband to depart alone while she figured out another way to quietly leave the city. Chai Shao eventually united with Li Yuan later that year.

Pingyang, on the other hand, went into hiding before she finally left the city in secret. Once out of the city walls, she sought refuge with her relatives across the Yellow River. Knowing that it was unwise for her to remain in hiding while her father and husband instigated a rebellion, Pingyang chose to act. She sold her possessions and distributed her wealth to those who agreed to join the rebellion. Her servants were sent to persuade a few rebel leaders who almost immediately agreed to join arms. She also offered grain to farmers and, according to some sources, even bandits, promising them protection and relief should they choose to join the cause.

With enough numbers, Pingyang began to move. She imposed strict rules of no looting, no harming civilians, and fair trade for supplies. Her discipline distinguished her followers from predatory rebels. As a result, many more flocked to her banner. Her followers, referred to as the Army of the Lady, numbered tens of thousands. One town after another opened its gates, granaries were seized intact, and the roads leading to Chang'an, the Sui capital, were slowly cut away. Couriers no longer dared to ride, and magistrates who resisted were swiftly brought to heel. When her father began marching west, he did so with confidence, knowing that Pingyang had already secured the ground.

Pingyang and her forces provided the support that Li Yuan needed, and he successfully captured Chang'an in November 617 CE. He first installed Emperor Yang's grandson as a puppet ruler. It was only after the emperor's death the following spring that Li Yuan declared himself the new ruler, taking the name Emperor Gaozu. Thus began the era of the Tang dynasty.

As for Pingyang, she lived only for several more years. Her life came to an end in 623 CE when she was only in her twenties. The assumed reason for her death varies, with some claiming she died at childbirth. Others suggest that Pingyang sustained a wound during the rebellion, which later developed into a more serious health implication. Not forgetting her massive contributions to the rebellion, Emperor Gaozu ordered a funeral fit for a war general, complete with music bands. At first, his ministers protested the idea, but the emperor was quick to silence them, exclaiming that the Tang dynasty would have never existed without the help of Pingyang.

The Sorrowful Poet

They were coming for her. Cai Yan, better known by her courtesy name Wenji, was the daughter of Cai Yong, one of the most respected scholars of the late Han dynasty. As a girl born into privilege, all she ever loved was poetry. Cai Yan was married, but not for long; her husband died shortly after their union. She also had no children. Hence, day and night, she would spend her time reading and practicing calligraphy. It was as if she could not live a day without having a brush in her hand. However, no amount of poetry could save her when her town was visited by unwanted guests in 194 CE.

This was a period of turmoil. The Xiongnu had been actively intruding Han territories, causing havoc. One day, these Xiongnu horsemen decided to raid the town where Cai Yan resided. She was kidnapped and taken north, dragged against her will into the untamed steppe and beyond the region she was familiar with. At this point, Cai Yan was certain that her life would soon end. After all, the ancient Chinese had always viewed those from the northern regions as barbarians who preferred the language of violence rather than the ways of civilization.

But the Xiongnu kept her well and alive, albeit as a prisoner. The Xiongnu chief was said to have taken a liking to her, and he eventually claimed her as his wife. From then on, she was treated with the rights due to a consort. She remained with the Xiongnu for twelve long years and even bore the chief two sons. Despite the great treatment she received, Cai Yan never felt at home. There were times when she wept quietly late at night, her heart longing for the life she once had.

Little did she know her time with the Xiongnu was almost over. Back in China, the warlord Cao Cao had already risen to power. Having consolidated the fractured Han empire, he soon moved to rescue Cai Yan. The reason behind his decision is never confirmed, but scholars suggest that he knew her father, Cai Yong. To honor the family, he chose to bring Cai Yan back. She was also the only one left of her clan.

Cao Cao negotiated with the Xiongnu chieftain. After he paid a large sum, Cai Yan's release was finally secured. Although she could finally return, just as she had always wished every night, Cai Yan departed with a heavy heart. According to Xiongnu tradition, children must remain with their father. Therefore, Cai Yan was forced to leave her sons behind.

A drawing of Cai Yan drafting her poetry.[54]

Upon returning to the land she once called home, Cai Yan was married to a government official named Dong Si. She had regained her freedom, yet the memory of her life far from the borders never left her. And so, she picked up a brush and began pouring out her thoughts and feelings. She composed works that captured both her grief and resilience. Known as the "Eighteen Songs of a Nomad Flute," her writings were remembered especially for their sorrowful tones. The verses spoke of life on the frontier, the endless winds of the steppe, the ache of separation, and the loneliness of a woman caught between two worlds.

Her story is unusual not only for its tragedy but also for its survival. While countless women endured captivity and loss during the fall of the Han, Cai Yan's voice is one of the few that still reaches us, carried in poems attributed to her and in the stories retold by later historians.

The Female Minister

You may have heard of Wu Zetian. She was known to be the only woman in ancient China to ever sit on the throne, ruling in her own right. Her name is often included in books as a symbol of female power in a world that rarely allowed it. Not so many, however, remember the name Shangguan Wan'er, whose influence grew at the same time Wu Zetian was carving her destiny.

In contrast to Cai Yan, whose story began with peace, Wan'er's began in blood. Her grandfather, Shangguan Yi, was once a high-ranking minister. Things took a darker turn, however, when he fell out of favor with the empress. It is said that Shangguan Yi grew so discontent with the empress's controlling behavior that he proposed to Emperor Gaozong that the empress be deposed. Empress Wu eventually learned this and immediately planned for his removal. She accused the minister of treason, resulting in the execution of Shangguan Yi and much of his family. Wan'er, who was only a child at that time, was spared but was condemned to palace servitude.

But Wan'er had a gift for words. She could compose elegant poetry and draft documents with both precision and grace. Her talent soon attracted the attention of those in the palace, including Wu Zetian herself. Recognizing her brilliance, the empress chose to bury the hatchet and took Wan'er into her inner court. From then on, her influence soared. Wan'er became Wu Zetian's secretary and eventually her voice. Her words mattered most, second only to the empress. From crafting verses, Shangguan Wan'er's responsibilities grew to include polishing proclamations, drafting imperial edicts, and advising the empress on state matters.

Of course, she was more than just a mere scribe. Wan'er knew that relationships with the other court officials were important if she were to survive the world of politics. Consequently, she never shied away from mingling with scholars and officials, often hosting gatherings where poetry and politics were discussed. Some say she could match wits with even the empire's greatest minds, and her literary salons gave her influence beyond the written page. Chroniclers also note that when disputes arose, many waited to see how Shangguan Wan'er would phrase the matter, for her words could tip the balance of interpretation. Her role in the court was so important that contemporaries refer to her as the "female prime minister." It is safe to say that only a few women in Chinese history ever wielded such recognized, practical authority without sitting on the throne.

Her influence did not disappear even after Wu Zetian died in 705 CE. When Emperor Zhongzong rose to the throne, Wan'er became one of his concubines. Aware of her experience and abilities, he entrusted Wan'er with matters of the state, especially in drafting edicts. She also became the confidant of the emperor's wife, Empress Wei. This, however, was the beginning of her fall.

Empress Wei dreamed of following the footsteps of Wu Zetian. Thus, when Emperor Zhongzong died in 710 CE, she was quick to make a move. The empress persuaded Wan'er to assist her: she was tasked with drafting a fake pre-dated will detailing the late emperor's wish to pass the throne to his son and the regency to the empress. But, a coup soon erupted, led by a rival to the throne, Li Longji (the son of Emperor Taizong), who allied with his aunt, Princess Taiping. Li Longji killed Empress Wei, along with her clan members. Li Longji and his men then made their way to the pavilion where Shangguan Wan'er lived. Sources described how Wan'er stepped out of the pavilion to greet Li Longji. She hoped to be spared from the bloodshed, but Li Longji had already made up his mind. In the end, Shangguan Wan'er was beheaded.

Chapter 4 – Kill or Be Killed

The forces of Qin under King Zheng were unstoppable. By the late third century BCE, they had already emerged victorious over two rivals: Han, the weakest of the seven states, and Zhao, the more formidable one. With the fall of these two states, the Qin looked no further to secure yet another victory. This time around, they turned their gaze to Yan, a northeastern kingdom of mountains and river valleys.

Of course, Qin's advances toward the state were not a secret. King Xi of Yan himself knew that his state did not stand a chance against the powerful Qin. Therefore, to preserve peace, he offered his son, Crown Prince Dan, as a diplomatic hostage to Qin. Such hostage arrangements were common, especially in the ancient world. (Rome would later take sons of conquered kings to ensure loyalty, just as the Greeks once held prominent figures as hostages to guarantee alliances.)

Diplomatic hostages like Prince Dan were not supposed to be treated like any other lowly hostages put in shackles following a battle. However, records suggest that, despite starting off well, King Zheng eventually began treating the crown prince poorly. This filled Prince Dan with resentment. Humiliated that he was seen as a pawn rather than a prince, he began to plan an attempt many deemed impossible: assassinate King Zheng and save the state of Yan from the upcoming grasp of Qin.

Following his return to Yan, Prince Dan wasted no time in planning his mission. In hopes of securing a higher chance of succeeding, he began searching for a man of rare courage. As if the heavenly gods were on his side, the prince found the individual through his friend, Tian Guang.

"I may have the exact man who could defy the odds and ensure the success of your mission," Tian Guang likely said to Prince Dan.

The man was known as Jing Ke. Born in the minor state of Wey, he was far more than just an ordinary retainer. Jing Ke was not only given good education in his younger years but also well versed in martial arts; he was especially skilled in swordsmanship. Jing Ke was said to have remained in his homeland of Wey until the state was annexed by Qin in 239 BCE. From then on he fled, eventually arriving in Yan, where his disdain for Qin aligned with that of the crown prince.

Having found someone to carry out the mission, Prince Dan began concocting the assassination. The plan was to strike the king of Qin with a poisoned dagger. Procuring the sharpest dagger available and lining it with poison was a walk in the park. Approaching the king with the weapon, however, required a smart scheme. Jing Ke proposed to mask the assassination with an audience of surrender. He planned to get the king's attention by offering him two tokens of loyalty: the severed head of the man who betrayed Qin and a map of Dukang, the first region of Yan that Qin desired.

The first token required a sacrifice. The story goes that Jing Ke himself traveled to meet the traitor. Known as Fan Yuqi (identified in some accounts as Huan Yi), he was once a loyal Qin general. He had fallen out of favor with the king of Qin, who was said to have placed a bounty of one thousand gold pieces on his head. Jing Ke knew that Fan Yuqi harbored resentment and would not hesitate to exact revenge on King Zheng. So, when the plan for assassinating the king was laid before him, the former Qin general immediately agreed to get his hands dirty, although he would not be able to witness the downfall of the king. He took his own life so that his severed head could be offered as a prize to King Zheng.

With the first gift successfully in his hands, Jing Ke then prepared the second one. He rolled the silk map of Dukang with care. Within it concealed the poisoned dagger, which he would use to end the life of the merciless king.

Jing Ke was not to travel alone. Prince Dan had already assigned a youth named Qin Wuyang to assist Jing Ke in his mission. Qin Wuyang was not a nobody; he was infamously known for having committed murder at the young age of thirteen. While Jing Ke bore the map, Qin Wuyang carried the head of Fan Yuqi.

The two entered the capital of Qin, Xianyang, in 227 BCE. The court officials marveled at the grisly display of Fan Yuqi's severed head. They were confident that Jing Ke, who had arrived under the guise of an ambassador of Yan, meant no harm and was only pleading for the king's mercy. The next move was to present the map to the king.

But tension made its first appearance in the episode when Qin Wuyang found himself frozen. He faltered as he approached the throne, completely struck by fear in the presence of the Son of Heaven. Jing Ke was quick to cover the situation. He apologized for his companion's sudden paralysis, excusing it as the common reaction of a youth awed by the splendor of the royal court. Still, the guards intervened. They barred Qin Wuyang from taking a step further and ordered Jing Ke to proceed alone.

As if he had practiced the scene multiple times, Jing Ke approached King Zheng and presented the map. The king unrolled the scroll while the courtiers leaned forward to get a clearer view. The very moment the dagger was revealed, Jing Ke snatched it without hesitation. He seized the king's sleeve and thrust in the poisoned dagger. But King Zheng managed to dodge the strike, ripping his sleeve in the process.

A mural depicting the assassination attempt.[85]

The king desperately tried to unsheathe the long ceremonial sword that hung at his side, but it proved too cumbersome to draw while running. At this point, it looked as if his fate had been sealed. No minister near him was armed since it was customary for them to leave their weapons outside during royal ceremonies, and the guards were stationed outside the hall. Suddenly, a physician named Xia Wuju intervened. He threw his medicine bag at Jing Ke, who stumbled for a few seconds. This was enough time for the king to gain more distance from his assassin and finally unsheathe his sword.

Now armed, King Zheng struck at Jing Ke, running his blade across the assassin's thigh. Jing Ke, refusing to surrender that easily despite bleeding heavily, hurled the dagger toward the king. But, instead of hitting King Zheng, the dagger accidentally landed on a pillar. Seizing the opportunity, the king drove his long ceremonial sword into Jing Ke again and again, stabbing him a total of eight times.

Jing Ke collapsed, but using the last of his strength, he sat upright with his legs splayed. This was a posture considered gravely rude. He then threw curses at the king. Guards, having finally stormed into the chamber, finished him off. Qin Wuyang was said to have attempted to flee the palace grounds but was unfortunately cut down by the royal guards.

Silence soon filled the air. Only the ragged breath of the king could be heard. He slowly returned to his throne and was said to have sat there motionless while still clutching his bloodied sword. When he finally caught his breath, King Zheng turned to the physician Xia Wuju and thanked him for his desperate act that slowed Jing Ke's movement.

The state of Yan would face Qin's wrath. Prince Dan sent his army to put up a fight, yet all was already written: Yan must fall under Qin. King Xi of Yan again tried to appease the King of Qin by ordering the death of his own son. Yet, this did not accomplish anything. His state was annexed and destroyed.

With Yan subdued, the rest of China soon followed. By 221 BCE, King Zheng of Qin succeeded in uniting the lands. He rose as Qin Shi Huang, the first emperor of unified China. It was the start of a new age.

The Burning of Books and Burying of Scholars under Qin Shi Huang

Of course, wars and battles were not the only things the emperor had to deal with to ensure the stability of his newly founded empire. He also had to reshape the thoughts of his people.

The emperor's chosen ideology was Legalism, which demanded strict laws, severe punishments, and absolute obedience. But this doctrine was not welcomed by all, especially Confucian scholars. For generations, they served as moral critics of kings and advisors in courtly ethics. Their teachings spoke of the virtue of rulers, the Mandate of Heaven, and of course, the importance of tradition. Basically, Confucianism suggested that a ruler's legitimacy depended upon benevolence and moral example, an idea that conflicted with the Legalist doctrine that Qin Shi Huang greatly championed.

The clash came to a head in 213 BCE. Scholars had been increasingly and openly criticizing imperial policies. When Qin Shi Huang finally had enough, the king ordered what became known as the "burning of books." Texts that did not serve the regime's practical purposes were thrown into the flames. These texts—particularly the classics of poetry, history, and Confucian ritual—included the Book of Documents, the Book of Songs, and histories of rival states. The government only saved works on medicine, agriculture, and divination.

This erasure of knowledge and memory did not stop there. The following year, the emperor unleashed yet another violent order. According to the *Shiji*, the emperor proclaimed hundreds of scholars guilty for sowing discord just because they clung to the old ways. They were ordered to be buried alive. But this gruesome event has always been a matter of dispute. Some scholars suggest it may not have occurred as described, while others agree that it happened but might have been a smaller, more targeted event or perhaps a misinterpretation of other punishments.

The Xuanwu Gate Incident

The Xuanwu Gate Incident is a story of brotherly rivalry. It all began when Emperor Gaozu of the Tang dynasty named his eldest son, Li Jiancheng as crown prince. This, of course, did not sit well with a few others in the empire. Some whispered that despite being the first born, it was not Li Jiancheng who should succeed Gaozu, but the younger Li Shimin. This was not surprising since Li Shimin had already proven himself on the battlefield, especially when the Tang dynasty was still struggling to climb its way to supremacy. Li Shimin had led his forces against multiple formidable adversaries; he defeated the warlord Dou Jiande, who controlled much of Hebei, and crushed Wang Shichong, who once dared to declare himself emperor in Luoyang. Through these major victories, Li Shimin's influence grew tremendously. Soldiers hailed him as a respected commander, and scholars viewed him as the right fit for the throne.

Li Jiancheng, on the other hand, was not bestowed with the same opportunities as his younger brother. He was stationed along the northern frontier, where he was responsible for protecting the empire from the Tujue (powerful Turkic nomads of the steppe). Although this was indeed an important assignment, his position far from Chang'an (the capital of the Tang dynasty) made it difficult for the crown prince to outshine Li Shimin.

It also did not help when Emperor Gaozu himself acknowledged Li Shimin's growing influence. Perhaps seeing the potential in his son, the emperor gave him control over the civil and military administration of the eastern plain, based in Luoyang (the old imperial capital). This allowed Li Shimin to establish a second court of his own, which he filled with fifty handpicked civil and military officials. The prince even established the College of Literary Studies and appointed eighteen scholars who also constantly advised him on matters of state. This stirred discontent within Li Jiancheng. He was afraid that his brother would soon be ambitious enough to go for the throne. He shared this view with his other younger brother, Li Yuanji.

By the early 620s, the relationship between the brothers had turned extremely sour; it eventually hardened into suspicion and venom. At the beginning of their rivalry, it was hard to predict the ending. Li Jiancheng had the title, chosen by the emperor himself, and the strong support of Li Yuanji. On the other side of the ring, Li Shimin had influence, fame, and loyal allies from the capital.

They did not fight each other with swords on the battlefield. Some said Li Jiancheng and Li Yuanji once tried to slip poison into Li Shimin's cup. Whether this was true or just a rumor remains unconfirmed. What is certain, however, is that the rivalry between the brothers also dragged others down. There was a time when Li Jiancheng and Li Yuanji pointed their fingers to Li Shimin's most trusted advisors, Fan Xuanling and Du Ruhui. The princes lobbied against them, resulting in their dismissal from service. They also once attempted an assassination on Li Shimin's most loyal general, Yuchi Jingde. When this failed, the two slandered Yuchi Jingde at court, which would certainly have cost his life if Li Shimin himself had not intervened in the matter.

Li Shimin was not always a favorite among the officials behind the walls of Chang'an, especially when he was frequently away on campaigns. This created an opportunity for Li Jiancheng and Li Yuanji to elevate their influence. They stayed close to the emperor and enjoyed the support of Gaozu's favored consorts.

But Li Shimin was a clever prince. He knew that to defeat those who played dirty, he must not remain silent. It was better to strike than to be struck. He chose to end everything once and for all at Xuanwu Gate, the northern entrance to the imperial palace. It was heavily guarded and narrow, making it feasible for Li Shimin to trap his brothers. Most importantly, the prince also had an ally stationed there.

"I need your loyalty, Chang He," Li Shimin may have said to his ally.

Years prior, Chang He served under the prince as an officer. In 624 CE, he was reassigned to command the troops at the Xuanwu Gate. Li Shimin bribed his ally and gave a simple order: when the moment came, Chang He and his soldiers were to obey Li Shimin rather than the crown prince.

Next was to think of a way to lure his brothers to the gate. This was when Li Shimin played his boldest card. He submitted a memorial to Emperor Gaozu, accusing his two brothers of illicit affairs with several of the emperor's consorts. It is plausible that many found the claim scandalous and hard to believe. Yet, Gaozu could not ignore it, especially coming from his son, who had given the empire many victories. Therefore, he summoned Li Shimin for an audience the following morning.

News of the accusation spread, eventually reaching the ears of one of the emperor's consorts, Zhang. With haste, the consort sent words to Li Jiancheng, informing the crown prince of the accusations made by his ambitious younger brother. With forces ready, Li Jiancheng and his loyal brother, Li Yuanji, rode toward the palace, hoping they could consult the emperor personally.

Little did the brothers know they were heading directly into a trap. They entered Xuanwu Gate and, almost immediately, could feel a sense of heavy tension. Li Shimin, knowing that his brothers were about to turn back, spurred his horse forward.

"Stay, my brothers!" Li Shimin said.

Li Yuanji reacted by drawing his bow, hoping he could cut down his brother before the ambush could take place. Yet, his hands betrayed him. The bowstring slipped, and he failed to take the shot. Seizing the chance, Li Shimin immediately shot an arrow, which went through the crown prince. Li Jiancheng fell off his horse, lifeless.

Panic undoubtedly ensued afterward. Li Yuanji escaped the scene with Yuchi Jingde and seventy of his horsemen pursuing him. Arrows were let loose. and one struck true. Li Yuanji fell from his horse, but this was not yet the end of the prince. Li Shimin, determined to eliminate his brother, gave chase. However, as he entered the woods, his horse went out of control. Its reins snagged on the branches, and Li Shimin was thrown to the ground. Seeing a chance to survive, Li Yuanji scrambled to his brother's side. Seizing Li Shimin's own bow, he pressed the weapon against his brother's throat. Fortunately for Li Shimin, his loyal general, Yuchi Jingde, was on his way.

Hearing the distant sounds of hooves, Li Yuanji quickly moved away from his brother. Desperate, the prince fled on foot toward Wude Hall, his residence within the eastern section of the palace. However, death was ready for him. Yuchi Jingde eventually caught up with Li Yuanji before the prince could reach the gates. Like Li Jiancheng, an arrow found a target in Li Yuanji. His flesh was pierced, and he laid dead.

The heads of both princes were then severed and carried back to Xuanwu Gate, where a fight was taking place between the forces of Li Jiancheng and Li Shimin (led by Chang He). Upon witnessing the severed heads of the princes, the fight immediately stopped.

The emperor, on the other hand, was completely unaware of the bloodshed. According to the *Jiu Tangshu* (Old Book of Tang, a tenth-century official history of the dynasty) and the *Zizhi Tongjian* (Comprehensive Mirror to Aid in Government, an eleventh-century chronicle by Sima Guang), Emperor Gaozu was sailing leisurely on a lake within the palace city when the coup erupted. Li Shimin, knowing that it was wise to report the event to the emperor, sent Yuchi Jingde to deliver the news. Startled, the emperor threw questions to Yuchi Jingde; he demanded to know the reason behind the chaos and the names of those who dared to disturb the peace. Yuchi Jingde calmly reported the outcome of the incident. He explained that the deaths of the two princes were necessary for the preservation of order and claimed that the two brothers were indeed a disturbance of peace.

Sources suggest that although he accepted the explanation, Emperor Gaozu was puzzled and uncertain of what should be done. Hence, he turned to his officials. Not long after, two courtiers stepped forward to voice their opinion. They exonerated Li Shimin completely, praising his past victories. They claimed that killings of Li Jiancheng and Li Yuanji were nothing more than a righteous punishment. From this point on, it was clear that the court supported Li Shimin as the new crown prince.

Despite being a step closer to the throne, Li Shimin refused to lay low. Loyalists of Li Jiancheng and Li Yuanji still existed, scattered through the capital. And so, Li Shimin relied once more on Yuchi Jingde, who successfully urged Gaozu to issue an imperial edict ordering all resistance to cease and commanding the remaining troops to submit to the victorious prince.

Three days later, the emperor officially announced Li Shimin as the new heir apparent. Li Shimin enjoyed this new title for only a few weeks. Gaozu soon abdicated the throne, giving way for Li Shimin to rise as Emperor Taizong of Tang.

The Lü Clan Purge

In 195 BCE, Emperor Gaozu of Han (not to be confused with the later Gaozu of Tang) lay on his deathbed. He was suffering from a wound obtained during one of his military campaigns. Of course, whenever a ruler came close to his demise, the same question lingered: who would soon sit on the throne?

The most obvious answer to this question was the crown prince, Liu Ying, the son of the emperor with his wife, Lü Zhi. However, conflict soon came when Gaozu displayed affection for Lady Qi, who eventually became known as his most favored concubine. Together, they had a son named Liu Ruyi. Rumors had been going around claiming that the emperor himself desired to see Liu Ruyi named heir in place of his son with Lü Zhi. In Gaozu's eyes, Liu Ruyi was more spirited and capable, while Crown Prince Liu Ying was considered gentle, perhaps too meek for the throne.

This favoritism undoubtedly planted the seed of bitterness, which over time would grow into violence. Lü Zhi not only hated Lady Qi for securing the emperor's affection, but she also resented her for giving birth to a son who posed a threat to Liu Ying's future. Still, she concealed her resentment while Gaozu lived. But when the emperor finally let out his final breath, the empress knew it was high time to show her true colors.

Gaozu was succeeded by Liu Ying, who ruled as Emperor Hui of Han. His mother became empress dowager. The new emperor was kind-hearted but, at the same time, a tad pliable. In just a short time, he fell into his mother's hands. Empress Dowager Lü Zhi wasted no time in securing her position—after all, this was the time she had long been waiting for. She sidelined ministers she distrusted and elevated her own relatives to key posts. Although Emperor Hui was positioned on top of the hierarchy, behind the scenes, it was his mother who moved the chess pieces.

Of course, Lady Qi would soon face the wrath of the empress dowager. With her husband gone, the empress was free to exact her revenge. She had Lady Qi stripped of favor and thrown into a dungeon. This, however, was not the worst of her punishment for being the object of the former emperor's affection. Lady Qi was also heavily mutilated. First, Lü Zhi had the poor concubine's hair shaved clean. Then, she moved to features that may have once been the favorites of Emperor Gaozu. Lady Qi's eyes were gouged and her ears severed. She was also forced to drink a type of potion that rendered her mute. As if this wasn't enough, the empress dowager also had the concubine's limbs chopped off before throwing her into a latrine and later a pigsty. It took a while before Lady Qi died. To ensure she remained alive to taste the agonizing torture, Lü Zhi force-fed her.

It was said that the empress dowager presented the terrifying state of the concubine to her son. Emperor Hui was left horrified. Legend has it that the sight of Lady Qi scarred him deeply and broke his spirit to the point that he chose wine drinking rather than active governance. His withdrawal from government opened the door for his mother to wield power unchallenged.

Emperor Hui died at the young age of twenty-two in 188 BCE. The crown was then passed to his young son, who was enthroned as Emperor Qianshao of Han. Like his late father, Qianshao was also reduced to the status of a figurehead. It was still Empress Dowager Lü Zhi who dictated the workings of the empire.

Some would say that, on one hand, she presided over an era of relative stability. Taxes remained moderate, and the empire did not face the same crushing levies that had characterized the Qin. The harshness of Legalist rule was softened, and agriculture thrived. Yet for all these policies, discontent simmered in court, especially when it was clear that Lü Zhi gave her full attention to staffing the government with her own kin. Years prior, Emperor Gaozu—with Lü Zhi's advice—had issued a ruling that only members of the imperial Liu clan could obtain high offices. The decree was intended to secure the dynasty's legitimacy by preventing the rise of rival houses. But, ironically, it was Lü Zhi herself who maneuvered to undo this.

She elevated her relatives to high offices. Brothers, nephews, and cousins of the Lü clan were granted the titles of kings and marquises, privileges reserved for the emperor's bloodline. Entire fiefdoms were carved out for her family, often at the expense of the Liu clan's own power. Zhe Lü's careful appointments ensured that the most critical posts were dominated by her kin. Eventually, it was as if a parallel dynasty of Lü was being established within the Han itself.

But few dared to challenge her openly. Things only changed in 180 CE, when the power-hungry empress died. With the only shield protecting the Lü clan off the surface of the earth, resentment that had smoldered for years erupted. The purge began almost immediately. It was orchestrated by senior ministers who had once served Emperor Gaozu and remained loyal to the Liu imperial line. With the support of imperial princes, they struck at the Lü clan before it could rally.

It was merciless. Lü family members were seized from their posts, stripped of their titles, and executed. Some were forced to take their own lives, while others were slaughtered outright. Entire households, including women and children, regardless of their age, were obliterated to prevent any future threat. Within days, the once-dominant Lü clan was reduced to corpses and ashes. It is safe to say that they were erased from political life.

With the clan extinguished, the ministers restored the balance of power to the Liu family. The throne was eventually passed to benevolent Emperor Wen, a distant son of Gaozu, whose reign welcomed a new era of prosperity.

Chapter 5 – Legends That May Have Some Truth in Them

The rivers refused to rest. Seasons passed, yet the waters swelled beyond their banks, drowning fields, homes, and sweeping away entire villages. What should have been fertile plains became dangerous lakes, forcing families to cling to whatever patches of dry earth remained. In contrast to the ancient Egyptians, who viewed the predictable inundation of the Nile as a blessing from their gods, the Chinese faced a different kind of deluge. While the Nile flooding revitalized the many crops of Egypt, in China, the floods looked as if they were threatening to undo a civilization. They came like an uninvited storm—chaotic and destructive.

The misery of his people was getting louder. The ruling emperor at that time, Emperor Yao (one of the legendary sage-kings) began to desperately look for a way to tame the disaster. His attention was eventually brought to a man named Gun. He summoned the man to his palace and entrusted him with the important task of stopping the flood. It was indeed a tough mission; going against mother nature always ended with more destruction. But still, Gun was determined. He came up with a rather bold strategy that included building massive dikes to confine the waters. He envisioned barriers so strong and high that the rivers would be forced back into their channels, subdued by the will of man.

Of course, realizing such a project would take years, and it demanded both labor and sacrifice from countless communities. But it must be done. So, the emperor supplied Gun with dozens of people from all over the land, tasked with heaping earth and stone into towering walls. Villagers who had once farmed their fields now carried baskets of soil on their backs, marching in long lines to raise defenses against the waters. They toiled for months with little rest. At last, walls of earth rose where rivers had once surged freely. The people rejoiced, convinced that the days of turmoil had finally come to an end. They watched as the floodwaters gathered behind the dykes they had successfully built. But over time, the people grew worried once more, especially when it was clear that the rivers remained restless.

Each day, the rivers pressed harder against the walls, heightening the anxiety of the people. When the embankments finally gave way, the destruction that followed was undoubtedly catastrophic. In just moments, the fields drowned completely, and villages were carried away. Many lives were lost. All those years of labor went to waste, for the flood refused to be tamed. Gun had failed.

Interestingly, later tradition added a more mythical reason for his failure. The story goes that Gun had wronged the gods by stealing a magical substance known as *xi rang*. With the celestial self-expanding soil in his possession, Gun placed it upon the earth, causing it to grow endlessly into towering dikes; whenever the water rose, so did the dike. However, his theft did not go unnoticed. Angered, the gods cursed his construction.

Whether the failure was a direct result of the gods' wrath or simply caused by human miscalculation, Gun's effort ended in total disaster, to the point that he, too, met a rather grim end. Some recalled Gun being executed under the order of the new ruler, Emperor Shun, while others claimed he committed suicide by leaping into an abyss. There were also those who talked about Gun being cursed and turned into an animal.

While Gun's demise and failure is often shrouded in myth, many agreed that before he died, Gun passed the responsibility of building the dykes to his son named Yu. At first, many doubted Yu could do any better. They believed that they were doomed to the flood and none could change that. Emperor Shun, however, saw something in Yu that others overlooked. He sensed a quiet determination in him. He knew that Yu was the key to freeing his people from these years of agony. This came to be true because Yu understood the flood differently. While Gun had sought to conquer the waters with force, Yu believed that mastery would come only through respect.

So, he did not begin his task by building walls that could reach the heavens. Instead, he began with observation. For a few years, he traveled across the land, hoping he could trace the restless Yellow River from its upper reaches in the west to its swollen belly in the Central Plains. He studied the valleys, the mountains, the floodplains, and the natural courses through which the waters longed to run. Where Gun had seen only an enemy to be resisted, Yu saw a partner to be guided.

His solution was to channel rather than block. Again, thousands of laborers were gathered to work on the project. However, instead of relying on dykes, Yu planned to cut trenches and open canals. This way, he could carve new pathways through the earth. Without wasting any more precious time, the workers dug great channels to link the swollen rivers to lakes and marshes that could bear the excess. In some places, Gu widened the existing streams. In others, he ordered that new courses be carved entirely, allowing the water to escape toward the distant sea. The plan seemed to be going so well that villagers who had once fled the waters joined in the effort. In time, the floods that once drowned the fields and took the lives of many began to flow and spread more evenly.

Of course, a lot of time was spent to ensure the success of the project. Even Yu partook in the project with his own hands rather than merely standing and giving out orders. According to legend, Yu labored for thirteen years without rest. He dragged himself across provinces and mountain ranges, equipped only with a rough mat to sleep on under the dark night sky. He was so dedicated to saving his people that did not even meet his family. It is said that he passed by his home three times during the mission. Each time, his family, particularly his son, called for him to stop by and rest. Yet, he continued walking, refusing to even turn to his family for a smile. In his mind, to pause, even for a moment of comfort, was to neglect the burden of his duty. True, the story may be exaggerated, but the point is clear: Yu was a man who placed the well-being of his people above all else.

His effort proved fruitful. Fields and crops that were once consumed by the relentless flood were restored to farmers. Roads and villages that were destroyed were rebuilt, allowing the people to thrive once more. Indeed, the Yellow River was still unpredictable, but it was at least manageable.

Emperor Shun was impressed by Yu's strategy and effort, to the point that he raised him to the highest honors. Yu continued to serve the court, displaying his bright mind and talent. He was eventually appointed to command the imperial armies, in charge of defending the southern frontiers from the Sanmiao people. This unruly tribe had been a thorn to the kingdom, especially when it had taken advantage of the floods to raid vulnerable villages.

It is not surprising to learn that Yu led his men against the enemy with the same perseverance he had shown against the waters. Not once did he ever strike before thinking; he was said to be an excellent commander who often studied the land and turned it to his advantage. The campaign against the Sanmiao was undoubtedly fierce, but Yu emerged victorious, driving them away from the borders. Peace was restored to the kingdom, and the people praised him for protecting them not only from nature but also from human enemies.

Then, when it was high time for the emperor to choose a successor, Yu made it to the top of the list. This was a time when rulers were chosen by merit rather than bloodline. Emperor Shun himself was not the son of the previous emperor, Yao. But his capabilities and achievements made him visible to his predecessor, and when the time came, he was the one to wear the crown. Now, Emperor Shun did the same. He elevated Yu above others, including his own bloodline, because of his great deeds, achievements, and character.

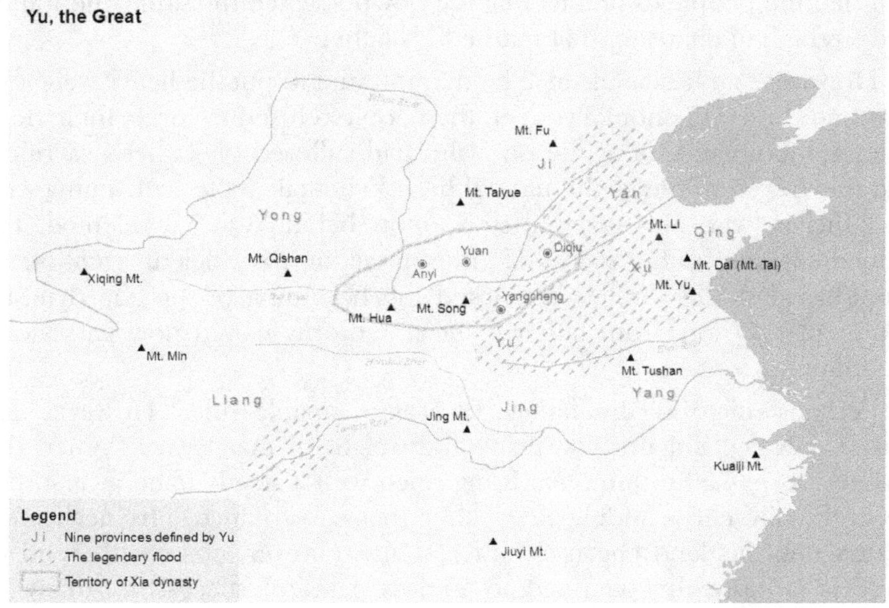

Possible location of the Xia dynasty and the nine provinces established by Yu.[56]

According to tradition, Yu rose to the throne sometime in 2070 BCE. He was an active ruler, traveling constantly across his kingdom and holding audiences with his ministers to discuss matters of the land and things that troubled his subjects. It is safe to say that his reign marked a turning point. He was also responsible for dividing the kingdom into nine provinces. Tribute systems were introduced, and each province was expected to pay in bronze. This bronze was then forged into the Nine Tripod Cauldrons, which are among the most famous legendary artifacts in Chinese tradition. Among Yu's first acts after receiving the Mandate of Heaven, these cauldrons were meant to show the unification of the different regions under Yu's rule. The cauldrons were then passed down as symbols of legitimacy from dynasty to dynasty, much like the crown jewels in later European monarchies. Unfortunately, the Nine Tripod Cauldrons disappeared during the late Zhou. Some said they sank deep into the Si River, never to be recovered again.

Despite being a capable ruler, Yu was but a mortal man; he too could not escape death. As the years of his reign waned, Yu knew it was time to choose a successor. The story goes that he at first intended to pass the throne to his trusted minister. However, the people favored his son, Qi, who as a boy had lived through the troubling time of the flood. The boy endured his father's absence without lamenting or complaining about it. This led the people to predict that the boy possessed the same endurance and strength of character that marked his father.

However, Yu hesitated since he did not want to put the heavy weight of rule onto his son's shoulders. Yet, the people refused to forget their view. They remembered Qi as the one who had suffered his father's sacrifice, and they revered him as the natural heir. Eventually, after convening with his officials, who also threw their support behind Qi, Yu relented. He named his son as his successor, thus breaking the ancient tradition of merit-based succession. This marked the beginning of the Xia dynasty. From ruler to son, from father to heir, authority would now pass along bloodlines.

Perhaps mirroring his father, Qi was a capable ruler. However, his son, Tai Kang, did not live up to the weight of that legacy. When the throne was passed to him, Tai Kang ruled with a steady hand at first, but he eventually chose indulgence rather than governance. His negligence soared until his land began to suffer. This, however, was not the end of the Xia dynasty. It continued to witness a set of successors, many of whom were said to have been highly skilled.

The sixth ruler was named Shao Kang, who, according to tradition, was thought to be the restorer of the kingdom. Before he rose, ancient China was fraught with peril. His own father was a victim of civil strife. When his father died, Shao Kang lived in obscurity until he grew strong enough to return and reclaim his inheritance. To his people, he was a hero; he fought rebellions, revived order, and brought dignity to the house of Xia once more.

But the Xia dynasty was not meant to linger in ancient China for long. Centuries later, under Kong Jia, who reigned circa 1789 BCE, the dynasty began to see the beginning of its end. Kong Jia was often depicted as a heavy drinker, often forgetting his responsibilities. His successors, Gao and Fa, were also remembered for neglecting their subjects. The final ruler from the Xia dynasty was Jie (traditionally dated from 1728 BCE to 1675 BCE). A tyrant whose cruelty pushed away both his allies and subjects, Jie was eventually left with no choice but to face a rebellion near the end of his rule. The uprising was led by a certain Tang of Shang, who overthrew Jie and ended the Xia dynasty by establishing the Shang dynasty.

Now, the question remains: did the Xia truly exist? Unlike the Shang and Zhou, whose inscriptions and records survived the test of time, the Xia left us with no contemporary writings. In fact, the story of Yu taming the floods, founding the dynasty, and passing the throne to his son carries the unmistakable shape of myth. Some viewed this narrative as an origin story that embodies virtue and order rather than a precise chronicle of events.

Archaeology complicates the tale further. Excavations at Erlitou, in Henan province, reveal a thriving Bronze Age culture dated roughly between 1900 and 1500 BCE. Palaces once stood there, bronze casting flourished, and a stratified society wielded significant power. This led scholars to suggest that Erlitou was once the very capital of the Xia dynasty. However, this was a matter of debate. Some scholars disagree with the suggestion, especially when no inscriptions or text have been found that connect the city to the Xia.

These scholars argue that Xia may be a later invention created by historians during the Zhou and Han dynasties, who sought to legitimize dynastic succession and the Mandate of Heaven. By creating a "first dynasty" to precede the Shang, they could frame their own rule as part of an unbroken chain of heaven's chosen rulers. The pro-historic view, however, suggests that the Xia dynasty was real, corresponding to Erlitou or a similar early state but lost to us in the absence of direct inscriptions.

There is no exact answer to this question. The existence of the Xia dynasty is neither a confirmed myth, like the underwater city of Atlantis, nor confirmed history like the Shang and Zhou. It rests instead in the gray zone between memory and archaeology, legend and fact: perhaps a real Bronze Age kingdom, perhaps a story shaped to fit the needs of later generations.

The Expedition for Immortality

With the entirety of China in his hands, Qin Shi Huang was left with one last adversary that he could neither conquer nor bend to his will. This enemy was none other than death itself.

Each day, the emperor wrestled with the thought that, despite having conquered even the fiercest kingdom of all, he too would soon be a victim of death. He had already survived two murder attempts; sooner or later, his luck would certainly run out. So, he consulted his trusted advisors, ministers, and generals about immortality, yet none had the knowledge. He then turned to his physicians and alchemists, all of whom were well versed in the realm of health and medicine. Under the emperor's order, these men of science began experiments. They spent day and night in their laboratories, mixing strange minerals into potions. They experimented with various rare herbs, yet none of these human-made concoctions could loosen death's grip.

Then, the emperor heard rumors of a place believed to be the answer to his trouble. They spoke of three islands that lay hidden somewhere in the eastern seas. These lands were named Penglai, Fangzhang, and Yingzhou and were described as an enchanted paradise where immortals roamed. One of these immortals was named Anqi Sheng. He lived on Mount Penglai and, according to legend, was nearing a thousand years old by the time Qin Shi Huang rose as emperor. On Penglai, one could also find a type of fruit whispered to have the ability to cure any ailment and grant eternal youth to those who consumed it. Some even claimed it could restore life to the dead.

To an emperor who was unwilling to yield to time, it was a must to uncover whether the island existed. Without wasting a moment, Qin Shi Huang launched an expedition eastward, hoping his subjects could return with the enchanted fruit or perhaps an elixir of immortality.

The said expedition was spearheaded by the emperor's court alchemist, Xu Fu. He left the empire sometime in 219 BCE, crossing the relentless ocean and battling through unpredictable weather. Qin Shi Huang made it clear that failure was not an option. Yet, the expedition unfortunately ended in disappointment. Whether beaten back by storms or simply unable to locate the island, Xu Fu had no other choice but to return empty-handed. When questioned by the emperor, he knew that he should not speak the truth. Otherwise, his life would be on the line.

Therefore, the alchemist conjured a story, one involving a sea beast prowling the ocean. He spoke of how the expedition was forced to halt because they were unable to cross without alerting the beast. Shi Huang Di then dispatched his archers to eliminate the creature. When they returned, claiming that they had succeeded in clearing the way, Xu Fu was ordered to embark on a second expedition to the mysterious island.

A Japanese illustration of Xu Fu's voyage.[87]

Another version—rather high in myth—told a different story in which Xu Fu did find the island during his first expedition. When he asked the guardian of the island for the elixir of life, the mysterious immortal told him to come back with offerings.

"Bring me the sons of good families and beautiful maidens," the guardian may have instructed Xu Fu, "along with the products of your various craftsmen. Then only will I permit you to bring the elixir to your master!"

Exaggerations and legends aside, Xu Fu set out on the second expedition on a larger scale. The alchemist brought a total of three thousand men, women, and children on board along with many provisions, seeds, silks, and supplies. However, like his first expedition, Xu Fu failed to find the mystical island. He knew that to return to the empire meant certain death since the emperor would never tolerate failure, especially when it came to his obsession with immortality. Therefore, Xu Fu chose to disappear. The famed alchemist never returned, and that was the last time anyone had ever heard of him and his entire crew.

While it is uncertain where exactly he went, there are suspicions that Xu Fu eventually found Mount Penglai, though to us it is known as Mount Fuji, Japan. Here, the alchemist and the rest of his crew made themselves at home. They introduced new skills to the local people. Among this knowledge was none other than the cultivation of rice, which later became the backbone of Japanese agriculture.

Coincidentally, this legend aligns with what we know from Japanese history. Archaeological evidence places the spread of wet rice cultivation into Japan around the same period, brought over from the Asian mainland during the late Yayoi era. Interestingly, the Japanese themselves came to hold Xu Fu in high regard. In some regions, he was revered as a culture-bringer, a wise sage from across the sea who brought not only the techniques of rice cultivation but also valuable knowledge of medicine, sericulture (silk farming), and new tools. The Japanese even erected shrines, and his statue can be found to this day at Jofuku Park. While we cannot say with certainty that Xu Fu himself was responsible for spreading this knowledge, the timing is close enough to make us think the story may hold at least a few grains of truth.

Chapter 6 – Tragedies of Injustice

Justice in ancient China was never a matter taken lightly. From the earliest days of the Zhou dynasty, the law was viewed not merely as a human system but as an extension of cosmic order. To disturb harmony within the family or the state was to disturb the balance of heaven itself. Legal codes were already strict, and punishments could be harsh. Records tell of a Zhou noble punished severely for a crime that today might seem trivial: he allowed his employees to mistreat peasants under his watch. The court ruled that because he had failed in his duty to protect the weak, his own life was forfeited. Such cases showed how justice was often more about preserving hierarchy and stability than about fairness to the individual.

Then came the Qin and Han dynasties. With their Legalist ideas, this principle was strengthened. Laws were codified and punishments standardized. Often, officials ruled through fear as much as reason. In theory, this created an orderly society where crime was deterred. But, in practice, the weight of the law often fell unevenly. A wealthy merchant could walk free after bribing the right people, while a poor farmer could face the cruelest punishment for petty crimes.

This gave rise to some of the most tragic stories in Chinese history. These were moments when justice did not prevail. These were episodes when innocence was punished and guilt went unscathed. They were tales that horrified contemporaries and have since been remembered for centuries, passed down as warnings of the dangers of unchecked authority.

The Exiled Advisor

There was once a man named Qu Yuan who lived in the state of Chu sometime during the fourth century BCE when China was still struggling through the Warring States period. Born into a noble family, Qu Yuan enjoyed privilege. He rose to prominence as a minister in his twenties, and his main responsibility was advising King Huai of Chu.

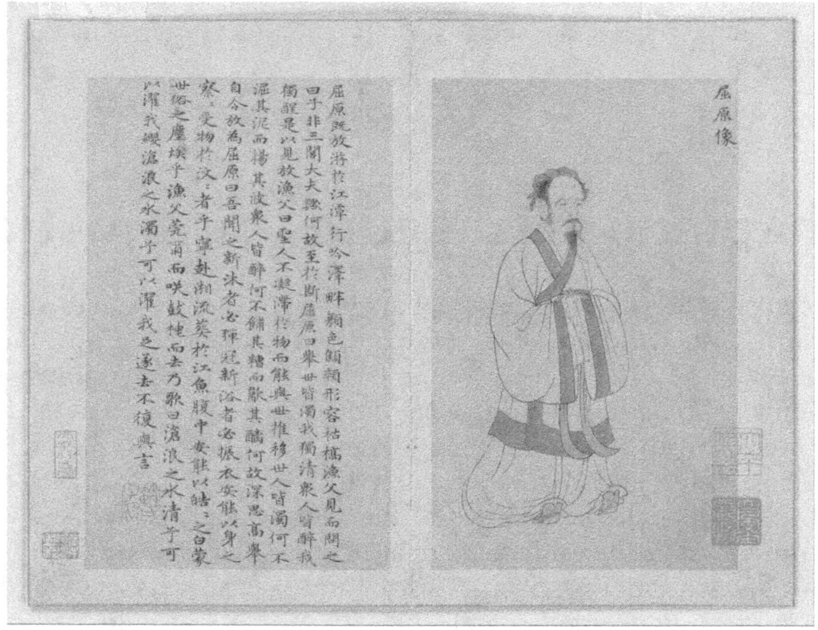

Qu Yuan, depicted in the Nine Songs (an ancient set of poems).[88]

Qu Yuan deserved the position. He was not like the other courtiers. He was well educated, eloquent, and cunning. He was always a step ahead, constantly strategizing for the benefit of his homeland. And so, Qu Yuan was quick to notice the danger that the state of Qin would soon bring, especially as it was rapidly growing. He knew that division and mistrust between the other states would invite total destruction once Qin chose to advance more boldly. Thus, Qu Yuan did not hesitate to urge King Huai to form alliances with other kingdoms like Qi, Han, and Zhao to effectively counterbalance Qin's aggression.

He also pressed for reforms within Chu, advising the king to strengthen the state's administration. As someone who saw the importance of peace and prosperity among not only the nobles but also the common folk, Qu Yuan also worked to ensure the common people were treated fairly.

But the royal court was a dangerous field full of betrayal and dishonesty. Certainly, the king valued him. His ideals and integrity initially made him a favorite, and he was entrusted with drafting decrees and shaping policies. But his virtues did not sit well with everyone. Many, especially those who thrived on flattery and intrigue, were envious of his position and achievement. They detested his honesty. Seeking to enrich themselves, these jealous ministers soon began to plot.

Exactly what the ministers said was never disclosed, but it is safe to assume that their slander included the claim that Qu Yuan was growing too proud and that his insistence on moral uprightness was twisted into arrogance. They may have also suggested how Qu Yuan often looked down on the king's judgment, implying that he, the advisor, thought himself wiser than his sovereign. They also spoke of fear, claiming that Qu Yuan was so dangerously close to the common people that this could turn into a rival power base that challenged the king's authority.

King Huai eventually fell for the slander. This marked the beginning of Qu Yuan's fall. He was later stripped of his office, pushed away from court, and finally exiled from the capital of Chu. Despite giving his life to service, Qu Yuan was thrown out in the blink of an eye. This betrayal cut deep, yet he continued to live—at least for a while. He wandered the countryside and was only allowed to watch from afar as the kingdom he loved slowly journeyed toward its destruction under poor counsel.

It was during this time of exile that Qu Yuan turned to literature. He lamented his fate in his most famous work, called *Li Sao.* He wrote of his dream and despair, expressing both his devotion to the kingdom and his sorrow at its corruption. He likened himself to a fragrant herb in a field of weeds, clinging to integrity while others thrived through deceit.

A few years later, his nightmare turned into reality. Qin's strength had grown tremendously. Its armies were beyond disciplined and would stop at nothing until their king could have every land in his grasp. The state of Chu, on the other hand, was on the brink of collapse. Its alliances had faltered, and the court was panicking. King Huai himself was captured in 299 BCE after being tricked into attending a conference in Qin. He escaped two years later, only to be recaptured once more. He died in 296 BCE, still in the captivity of Qin. Chu was then put under the helm of his son, King Qingxiang, though he fared no better. The king continued to heed corrupt voices and dismissed those who would have saved the kingdom.

It was said that Qu Yuan shouted warnings once more, but as expected, they went unheeded. Overwhelmed with despair, he wandered to the banks of the Miluo River. Losing purpose in life, knowing that he could no longer serve his homeland, Qu Yuan threw himself into the river.

Word of his drowning shocked the people, who wept for his fate. The story goes that fishermen in the area immediately abandoned their catch and rowed their boats toward the place where Qu Yuan had drowned. They rowed back and forth as they beat drums, splashing their oars to frighten fish and evil spirits away, but they never discovered his remains. Over the centuries, this grief transformed into tradition. The dragon boat races held every year on the fifth day of the fifth lunar month mirror the episode when the people of Chu scoured the river for Qu Yuan's body.

Pursued, Celebrated, and Condemned All Over Again

Wu Zixu too was born into the state of Chu, though he lived during the restless years of the Spring and Autumn period, centuries before Qu Yuan. He belonged to a noble family, where his father, Wu She, served as a minister. His life changed when a minister named Fei Wuji slandered his father and elder brother, accusing them of disloyalty. As a result, they were sentenced to death. Wu Zixu, who was still young at the time, fled the kingdom, as the king had dispatched soldiers to eradicate his entire family.

Branded as the son of a traitor, Wu Zixu was left alone and hunted. He made his way to the west, never once revealing his real name to anyone he encountered. He crossed rivers, living on scraps, and spent his nights awake, fearing capture. A certain legend spoke of the time when he was nearly captured by his pursuers. When he reached the Huai River, Wu Zixu hid among the reeds. He was then discovered by a certain fisherman who asked his name. He never answered, but the fisherman guessed his identity. Claiming that Wu Zixu's destiny was not yet complete, the fisherman assisted his escape.

His destiny brought him to the kingdom of Wu, where he managed to secure a position under Prince Guang—later known as King Helü of Wu. Perhaps knowing that it was better to remain honest, Wu Zixu informed the prince of his past. He even included the part where he sought vengeance against the king of Chu for murdering his family.

A copy of Sun Tzu's Art of War, written on bamboo.[39]

When the prince seized the throne, Wu Zixu remained loyal. He became the king's most trusted counselor. Together with the famed strategist, Sun Tzu (known best as the author of *The Art of War*), Wu Zixu played a hand in pushing the kingdom into its golden age of military power. Wu Zixu's knowledge of Chu's terrain and politics also made him invaluable. For years, he bided his time, waiting for the right moment to strike at the state that had once wronged his family.

That time came in 506 BCE, when King Helü, urged by both Wu Zixu and Sun Tzu, decided to launch a major campaign against Chu. Wu Zixu, driven by both vengeance and the desire to display his undying loyalty to his new king, led the charge. Utilizing the ruthless and precise

Wu armies, Wu Zixu succeeded in crushing the enemy and storming their capital, Ying. Panicked, King Zhao of Chu abandoned his throne and made an escape.

However, Wu Zixu was not particularly interested in the fleeing king. He was now standing in the very palace where his family had been condemned. Without hesitation, he demanded that the tomb of King Ping of Chu, the one who was responsible for executing his father and brother, be opened. To Wu Zixu, revenge could be served even to the dead. And so, he had the corpse of King Ping exhumed and flogged. Some might see this action as desecration, but to Wu Zixu, this was retribution.

In the aftermath of Chu's defeat, Wu Zixu continued to play a decisive role in Wu's affairs. In 495 BCE, Wu emerged victorious over Yue at the Battle of Fujiao. This resulted in the submission of the king of Yue, Goujian, and seemed like the end of Yue. Wu Zixu, however, saw differently. He warned the court that Goujian's submission was nothing more than an act, a way for him to buy time. Unfortunately, none heeded his caution.

When Helü died from wounds he sustained in a battle against Yue, the throne was handed to his son, Fuchai. Again, Wu Zixu repeated his warning but with an even greater urgency. He pressured the new king of Wu to annihilate Yue completely instead of turning his ambitions elsewhere. Wu Zixu was certain that sparing Goujian would one day prove disastrous. But Fuchai was young and naive. Upon listening to the poisonous words of a courtier named Bo Pi—who was said to have been bribed by the Yue—Fuchai chose to spare Goujian. Believing that he had no intention to rebel against Wu, the king sent him back to his kingdom.

Wu Zixu's vision was beginning to turn into reality. While King Fuchai turned his gaze elsewhere, eager to realize his ambition of claiming hegemony among the Chinese states, Goujian was busy preparing for revenge. Wu Zixu pressed for Fuchai to consolidate and crush Yue while they still had the upper hand. But the king refused to listen. Irritated, Fuchai eventually saw Wu Zixu as an obstacle rather than an ally. Hence, in 484 BCE, the king ordered the loyal minister to take his own life.

As his final request, Wu Zixu asked that his eyes be gouged out and hung upon the eastern gate of the capital. This way, even in death, the minister could witness the destruction of the kingdom he had once so strongly protected.

Years later, his warnings came to pass. Goujian rose against Wu and exploited Fuchai's complacency. This shattered Wu's strength, and in 473 BCE, the kingdom fell. Fuchai, cornered and defeated, committed suicide.

From Friends to Enemies

This story begins with a friendship. Pan Juan and Sun Bin were students of the legendary strategist, Gui Guzi. Under his tutelage, the two studied the art of war in seclusion, taking in lessons that could shape the destinies of kingdoms. Although they were friends, they had different traits and personalities. While Pang Juan was the more ambitious one, always eager to apply what he had learned to achieve glory, Sun Bin was more reserved. He was brilliant but always remembered to temper it with humility. However, when it was made clear that Sun Bin's talent was superior to his, Pang Juan began to develop a hint of jealousy—which would grow as time passed.

Pang Juan wasted no time crafting a path of success for himself. He sought out military service in Wei and rose through the ranks rather quickly, becoming a general under King Hui. After achieving a list of victories, Pang Juan was elevated to the position of commander. Even though he had achieved so much, insecurity still lingered in his heart. Although Sun Bin had not yet achieved prominence, Pang Juan could not live with the thought that his old classmate would soon eclipse him. Perhaps it was better to silence the threat before it could even manifest. Therefore, he invited Pang Juan to the capital of Wei, pretending he was ecstatic for a reunion.

The unsuspecting Sun Bin accepted the invitation. He was welcomed warmly and showered with honor as a guest. This, of course, was only an act. Pang Juan then laid accusations against his old friend. He claimed that Sun Bin harbored intentions to destroy the kingdom of Wei. As a result, terrible punishments were ordered. Sun Bin was seized and subjected to *xing*, the removal of the kneecaps. But crippling him was not enough. His face was also tattooed with the mark of shame, branding him as a traitor.

Sun Bin was imprisoned and put under close watch at all times. He knew there was no way out unless he could prove that he was incapable of harming the state. So, he feigned madness. Sun Bin started scribbling nonsense on the walls, ranting incoherently, and waking the guards up at odd hours by laughing uncontrollably. Over time, his captors lowered their guard, believing that he was truly insane and harmless.

This was an opportunity for the envoys from Qi. Early on, they had heard of a crippled prisoner who was a brilliant strategist. After investigating the rumor, they eventually agreed that Sun Bin was indeed a man worth saving. The envoys secretly smuggled him out of Wei and brought him to Qi, where he later found a new purpose as the kingdom's respected military strategist.

It did not take long for Sun Bin to cross paths with his envious friend again. Led by his old classmate, the forces of Wei were besieging the capital of Zhou, Handan. When Zhou turned to Qi for help, Sun Bin knew this was the moment he had patiently been waiting for. Knowing it was unwise to go against a raging opponent head-on, Sun Bin feigned weakness. He intentionally launched an unsuccessful attack against Wei elsewhere, convincing the enemy that the Qi were not strong enough to defeat them.

Upon learning about the defeat of Qi, Pang Juan called for more troops from Daliang to continue besieging Handan. These troops left the Wei capital nearly unprotected. Seeing that his plans were going well, Sun Bin led an army to the capital city, prompting Pang Juan to make a mad dash to save Daliang. He was in such a rush that he left his infantry and supplies at Handan, taking only his cavalry with him. Since they were riding at full speed, Pang Juan's men fell into exhaustion just as they crossed the Yellow River. Little did they know, Sun Bin was already waiting for them with a large army. An ambush was launched, and Sun Bin emerged victorious. Pang Juan, his reputation now tarnished, managed to retreat.

The two former friends faced each other once more in 342 BCE at the Battle of Maling. Again, Sun Bin came up with a ruse to defeat the enemy. He ordered the Qi army to light fewer and fewer cooking fires each day so that the enemy would think his troops were deserting. Pang Juan fell for the tactic. Eager to crush Sun Bin and perhaps restore his image, the Wei general rushed his forces forward through a narrow valley at night. Unbeknownst to the Wei forces, they had entered a trap.

As Pang Juan and his men passed through, dozens of Qi archers fired at them, decimating as many men as possible. Later, Qi infantry poured in, fighting the enemy in close combat. Some said Pang Juan was among those who fell to the arrows, while others claimed he survived but then commit suicide.

Legend has it that, despite having claimed victory and exacted revenge on the man responsible for his unjust punishments years prior, Sun Bin was sad the moment he saw the body of his former friend. As for Wei, the kingdom was thrown into a deeper chasm, never to return to its glory ever again. Although the kingdom lingered for more than a century, Wei was left vulnerable to the pressures of not only Qi but also Qin on the west.

The Punished Historian

The name Sima Qian may be familiar, especially to those who have read the story of ancient China. However, long before his name rose to prominence, there was his father, known as Sima Tan. He served as the grand astrologer, an important position in the Han dynasty that demanded more than just watching the stars; his duties also included recording the annals of the empire to keep track of rituals, omens, and most importantly, the deeds of the mighty rulers and ministers. Of course, his work was not simply a matter of compiling names and dates. He was expected to ensure that the story of China endured through centuries, if not millennia.

Sima Tan was aware of the weight of this responsibility, but he embraced it wholeheartedly. History was his passion, and he had long dreamed of being given this very opportunity. He believed that such work should not only preserve the past but also teach the present and guide the future. However, fate had another story for him. Sima Tan contracted a life-endangering illness. Knowing that he would never realize his ambition, he called for his son, Sima Qian.

"The responsibility now rests upon your shoulders," he may have said as he entrusted his son with a final request. "Promise me that you will finish what I have begun."

Sima Tan died in 110 BCE, leaving all his scrolls and notes to his son. Wishing to honor his father, Sima Qian devoted himself to the history of China. He traveled widely across the land, searching for stories and events that shaped the empire. He visited ancient battlefields where soil was once soaked in blood, walked through palaces that witnessed coronations and assassinations, and sought the wisdom of elders who still remembered the events of past reigns.

A portrait of Sima Qian.[40]

At a glance, the life of a historian seemed far safer than that of a soldier who was expected to brave arrows from afar and blades at close quarters. But Sima Qian's story proves otherwise. It all began with Emperor Wu of Han, who was famously ruling with an iron hand. He had launched many violent expansion campaigns, which eventually drained the treasury and robbed his land of countless lives. It is not surprising to learn that his court was filled with suspicion, and those who dared to speak words out of step with imperial judgment could easily see the end of their lives.

The campaign that sealed Sima Qian's fate was the one involving the nomadic Xiongnu. Ever ambitious and eager to heighten his power, Emperor Wu launched a campaign led by his own brother-in-law, Li Guangli, who was supported by another general, Li Ling. With the support of one hundred thousand men, Li Guangli wasted no time marching north. However, the journey was perilous; the northern steppes were difficult to navigate, especially with the windswept plains. The Xiongnu, on the other hand, knew the land well. With this advantage, the nomads struck at their enemy swiftly and vanished quickly into the wilderness before the Han forces could react.

It did not take long for Li Guangli to realize that his usual strategy would not work on the Xiongnu. He began the campaign full of confidence, and his mistake was a simple one: he did not anticipate the speed and cunning of his enemy. His army withered faster than he could have imagined. In the end, of the hundred thousand men that marched into the north, only ten thousand limped back. His defeat was so humiliating that, at first, he was refused re-entry into Han territory. But the emperor was unwilling to admit failure on the part of his own kin. Hence, he needed a scapegoat.

That scapegoat was none other than General Li Ling. While Li Guangli commanded a large force, Li Ling had only five thousand infantry. Despite this small number, Li Ling went on against the Xiongnu, fighting them off for weeks. He and his men moved across the difficult terrain and never hesitated to stand against impossible odds. They fought the enemy bravely; his archers used up every last one of their arrows, and the rest fought until their blades were either blunted or fell from their hands. While they managed to cut down thousands of enemies, the Xiongnu outnumbered them. They could only win if somehow the gods descended from the heavens and intervened. And so, surrounded and exhausted, with his resources dwindling, Li Ling made the choice to surrender. It was an act of compassion rather than cowardice: the general did so to save what was left of his men from being slaughtered.

When news of this surrender reached the emperor, he was furious. But, at the same time, it gave him the scapegoat he needed. Thus, the emperor branded Li Ling a traitor. Although not everyone in court agreed with the condemnation, none of them dared to voice their opinion, for whoever questioned the Son of Heaven would certainly face dire consequences.

This was when Sima Qian entered the story. He rose in defense of Li Ling. He argued that the general had fought with unmatched valor. With only five thousand men, he had achieved what armies ten times that size could not. He exclaimed that the surrender was not an act of betrayal but a sacrifice for his soldiers.

His words, however, enraged Emperor Wu even more. The Son of Heaven reacted by arresting Sima Qian and throwing him into the palace prison. He subjected the historian to a death sentence by suicide. Sima Qian sat in his cell, staring at the cold stone walls, confronted with the end. Yet the promise he had made to his father, and the unfinished history he had dedicated his life to, gnawed at him. He was not ready to let it die with him.

Sima Qian's tomb and ancestral temple in Hancheng.[41]

He learned that there were two possible alternatives to escape the death penalty. The first option was to purchase a commutation into exile. Of course, such mercy came at a steep price, and unfortunately for Sima Qian, he did not have enough wealth. This left him with the second option, which was castration. This was considered the lowest degradation. To go through a castration meant that he would be plunged into a life of humiliation, derision, and contempt. He would certainly get cast out of respectable society. He would never get a chance to have a family and would be branded a scourge upon humanity. Many would rather end their lives than living with such disgrace.

But not Sima Qian. To die was to betray his father's dying wish. Thus, he chose to live. With this, Sima Qian was dragged, bound, and mutilated in 99 BCE. He was not the only one to go through this punishment. Alongside him was Li Ling, also cast into disgrace.

When he was released from prison, Sima Qian immediately experienced a change in his life. His friends no longer greeted him warmly. Instead, they avoided him altogether. His colleagues and even strangers looked at him in disgust. He was officially a living shame. Sima Qian wrote to his friend, Ren An, expressing how he felt. He talked about the unbearable shame he had to endure each time he stepped outside and the endless nights of contemplating suicide.

But his father's legacy demanded he live. This was possibly the sole reason he continued to wake up each morning. Despite the torment, he bent himself back to the brush. Eventually, out of this disgrace came the *Shiji*. Completed in 91 BCE, it consisted of a hundred and thirty chapters and spanned two thousand years, from the age of the Yellow Emperor to the reign of Emperor Wu. The author himself died in 86 BCE only a few years following the completion of his greatest work.

Chapter 7 – The Favorites

The practice of keeping concubines was not something new in the long history of ancient China. The practice traces its roots to many centuries ago, stretching back to the feudal courts of the Zhou and the Warring States period. During these turbulent times, rulers often accepted daughters of noble houses as concubines in the name of alliance. Then came the unification of China under the Qin in 221 BCE. From then on, concubinage changed. It moved from a regional custom to an imperial institution.

Since he was considered the supreme ruler of everything under heaven, the emperor was expected to preside over a harem that reflected both his power and the breadth of his empire. After all, this system of concubines ensured a constant supply of heirs should the dynasty need them. Hence, concubines were brought into the palace from across the realm. Some were given as tributes from noble houses. while others were chosen by officials after going through selection processes. Some were also taken as the spoils of war.

According to Sima Qian, Emperor Qin Shi Huang himself maintained a harem of about ten thousand women. Scholars, however, agree that this number was meant to be a rhetorical exaggeration; in ancient Chinese writing, "ten thousand" was often used to describe something beyond measure. Interestingly, despite having a harem and being married twice, Qin Shi Huang never elevated a consort to the rank of empress; he remains the only Chinese emperor in history never to have named an empress.

The reasons behind this remain a mystery, though some have pointed to his troubled past. His mother was said to have had a scandalous affair with a merchant-turned-politician named Lü Buwei and later a man referred to as Lao Ai. Perhaps these liaisons and the political conspiracies surrounding them scarred the young ruler, who in turn, associated women with betrayal, deception, and the dangers of divided loyalty. Another reason lay in his self-image. It is plausible that the emperor saw himself as not only a monarch but also a powerful figure who had surpassed all who came before. After all, he had a long list of achievements. To appoint an empress would have been to elevate one woman above thousands, granting her symbolic parity in the cosmic order. For a ruler who considered himself unmatched, perhaps no woman seemed worthy to stand at his side.

By the Han dynasty, concubinage had become one of the pillars of imperial life. The difference was that it was no longer a loose collection of women around the emperor but an institution as rigid and stratified as the bureaucracy itself. Concubinage in this period even had its own hierarchy. At the top was none other than the empress (*huanghou*). Below her were nine ranks of consorts, each given a title that symbolized her prestige. These different titles also dictated nearly every aspect of the concubine's life, from the number of attendants she was entitled to the silks she wore and even the dishes served at her table.

A concubine could be visited by the emperor and shared a bed with the Son of Heaven, yet this did not shield her from any danger that lurked behind the palace walls. To be in the lowest rank of the hierarchy meant she could end up being alone—many concubines never even had the honor of meeting the emperor—but being the ultimate favorite was equally dangerous. Jealousy and coups often took place among the concubines as these women vied for the emperor's affection. The story of Lady Qi, for instance, gives clear insight into the competition and jealousy that constantly existed in the emperor's harem.

A Peking opera actress portraying Wang Zhaojun, one of the Four Beauties of ancient China and the concubine of Emperor Yuan of Han.⁴⁸

With the emergence of the Tang dynasty, concubinage again expanded into something grander. The Tang court was famed for its cosmopolitan brilliance. Hence, it is not surprising that it ritualized the harem into an immense hierarchy of one hundred and twenty-two ranks.

For aristocratic families, offering a daughter to the emperor was both an honor and a political strategy. Since these women were highborn and offered in the name of alliance, they were given an entrance that was far from humble. They did not have to start from the bottom of the hierarchy but were granted a high rank from the beginning. The rest, however, could only secure a place in the palace through a more formal selection process.

When it was time to supply the emperor with new concubines, the court would issue an edict to "select beauties" (*xuanxiu*). Then, officials from Chang'an would be dispatched throughout the provinces to identify suitable candidates. However, not everyone fell under their radar; the officials would only look for candidates from what were called *liángjiā zǐ* (respectable households), usually in their mid-teens. Oftentimes, their eyes would be fixed on daughters of lower-ranking officials. Those born into families of merchants and artisans were excluded outright since these professions were located at the bottom of the hierarchy. The families of the chosen candidates—typically the fathers—were then given a summon for their daughters to appear at Chang'an for the next step.

Of course, to refuse an invitation by the court would certainly mean punishment. But the candidates were not expected to travel at their own expense. Typically, the provincial officials would send covered carriages or palanquins to the girls. They would depart to the capital accompanied by attendants and guards. As for their families, this scene was both an honor and a loss. Should their daughters pass all the inspections and tests, this would be the last time they would lay eyes on them. Concubines were not permitted to leave the palace grounds and could only meet their family under emergencies, though this was only permitted in extremely rare, supervised occasions. In return for their daughters, the families would be compensated with gifts—usually silk, money, or official promotions for the fathers and brothers.

Once they arrived at Chang'an, the candidates must go through an imperial audition. This was a series of trials that stripped away the last remnants of their old identity. First, the girls must go through the physical inspection. They were examined head to toe, typically by the eunuchs. These were the loyal servants of the emperor, most of whom had been castrated as boys. Some were sold by desperate families; others volunteered in the hope of rising to influence. (Eunuchs, too, had ranks and departments, and their roles could range from menial servants to some of the most powerful figures in court.)

Apart from teeth and hair, their posture was also measured and their skin checked. Even the smallest blemish could immediately result in dismissal, let alone a limp or a scar. Of course, their physical appearance was not the only thing that was important. The next stage involved a virginity examination. While later folklore spoke of mystical signs like the "gecko cinnabar" mark that supposedly revealed whether a woman had known a man, the palace relied on invasive examinations. Medical knowledge at the time associated virginity with certain physical signs, particularly the presence of an intact hymen. The task of determining virginity was placed onto senior maids or female physicians who would probe and prod the candidates.

A woman who failed the inspection would be dismissed and returned to her family. This might sound simple, yet for her family, it was a shame. No matter how trivial the reasons behind her dismissal were, being rejected by the palace could invite whispers that she was "tainted." However, sometimes rejected candidates were reassigned into lesser palace service such as that of a maid or attendant.

Those who passed moved on to the test of refinement and grace. Every bow, every glance, every word was observed by experienced eyes. The way she held her hands, the way she lowered her gaze, the rhythm of her steps, all were judged in the most critical way possible. A single awkward gesture could portray her as unworthy. The tension of this stage was undoubtedly almost unbearable, for it was not enough to be beautiful. To pass, a candidate had to appear naturally graceful, effortlessly poised, and innately suited to the rarefied air of the palace. Many girls faltered at this stage, undone not by lack of beauty but by nerves, if not clumsiness.

The remaining candidates were put to yet another challenge, which involved showcasing their talent. The Tang emperors were known to be patrons of culture, often surrounding themselves with sophisticated poets, musicians, and artists. Hence, it is not surprising that they demanded their companions reflect that refinement. One of the girls might be asked to compose a poem right there and then; her choice of words alone could either secure her a position in the Forbidden City or doom her future entirely. Some might be given a brush to paint a scene, their elegance in each stroke judged critically. Others might be told to play a melody, their tunes judged for both technical perfection and emotional resonance. This was the time for a girl of more modest looks than others to shine. Her gifts in poetry, painting, or music could enchant the judges far more than a flawless beauty who could only smile.

With the end of the trials, officials would come up with a list of finalists. Sometimes, the list was handed to the emperor, who would review the girls. But often the decisions were made by his senior consorts, the empress dowager, or his most trusted eunuchs. The lives of the girls who were accepted as concubines experienced a swift transformation. Officials would notify their families and reward them with lavish gifts. However, they could no longer see their daughters. From this moment on, their old ties were cut. It seemed as if the girls ceased to be daughters. Given the title *cǎinǚ* (selected lady), they were officially in the possession of the emperor.

Never again would they taste poverty; the concubines were showered with luxury. Yet, some viewed their lives differently: they were living in a prison. They could not leave. They could not marry because they were reserved strictly for the emperor. Yet, many would never even get a glimpse of the Son of Heaven, forced to spend their days waiting for a summons that never came. Loneliness was their only company. As for those who were fortunate enough to gain his attention, their nights would not be so lonely. They could even rise rapidly through the ranks. However, they also must always be cautious. Earning too much attention from the emperor could also be dangerous. Other concubines might be envious enough to plan sabotage. An envious concubine might bribe a eunuch or an attendant into her devious plans just so she could watch the other girl crumble.

The concubinage system endured for many centuries, even after the Tang. Later dynasties formalized the process still further, scheduling selections that swept in girls from every province and refining the ranks until the harem became a state within a state. Some concubines rose to rule empires as empresses, while others lived a far quieter life, their names lost even to history. The system lingered until the last days of the Qing and was only abolished in 1949 with the founding of the People's Republic.

The Emperor's Male Favorites

While the story of imperial concubinage in ancient China usually revolved around women, there were times when emperors had other favorites. Interestingly, the Sons of Heaven did not always confine their desires to women alone. Hints of same-sex affections at court appear as early as the Spring and Autumn period, though these stories were often overshadowed. To modern eyes, this may seem contradictory, especially to the patriarchal system of ancient China. But the reality was more nuanced.

This was a time when emperors were considered above all. They were expected to uphold Confucian ideals. Emperors must honor their ancestors, ensure the continuity of their lineage, and produce heirs to secure the dynasty. As long as these obligations were fulfilled, their private affections were their own business. Especially in the Han dynasty (a period when stories of male concubines are more apparent), there were no prohibitions against same-sex intimacy. Hence, there was no moral panic about it or any stigma of illegality. Criticism would only surface when a male favorite wielded undue influence. It would only cause an uproar if his presence distracted the emperor completely, taking him away from affairs of state and the mission of providing heirs.

In contrast to the female consorts, male concubines had no official structure or harem reserved for them. Instead, they were known only by an informal term, *nán chǒng*, which literally means "male favorite" or "male concubine." In short, a male favorite's entire existence and privileges depended strictly on the emperor's affection. If a certain young man managed to maintain favor with the Son of Heaven, he might enjoy influence and wealth beyond anything his birth could have provided. But his influence, status, and wealth were never guaranteed. Unlike female concubines who still belonged to the emperor even after his death (though their life was essentially gilded captivity), the position of a male favorite could vanish overnight if he lost favor or the emperor simply died.

This lack of an institutional framework is what made the role of a male concubine both dangerous and unique. Sometimes, the impact of a male favorite could extend far beyond the emperor's bedchamber. Emperor Hui of Han, for instance, was believed to be enamored by a young man named Hong Ru. One of the few ways to get on the emperor's good side was to mirror the tastes of the man he favored. Hence, Hong Ru's personal style turned into fashion, and court officials began imitating his looks. They added feathers in their hats and lightly powdered their faces. Some even wore ornaments dangling from their robes just like the young lover.

Since the path to becoming a male concubine was far less formalized compared to that of imperial women, how exactly could one stumble upon such a destiny? The answer lay in chances: a man could find himself elevated to the intimate circle of the emperor not by design but by chance. Before becoming a male concubine, one could be a low-ranking official or even an entertainer who once performed a song or recited a poem before the Son of Heaven. Eunuchs, too, sometimes found themselves crossing the line from servant to companion. What mattered was not lineage or a family's political ambition but the man's abilities to enchant the emperor with his looks or perhaps wit.

It is safe to conclude that these male concubines were not confined to a gilded cage. While their counterparts had to leave their families behind once selected by the emperor, a male favorite was allowed to maintain his own household outside the palace walls. He could even marry a woman, raise children, and build a family since he was not technically absorbed into a harem system. His relationship with the emperor, however, could leave an impact on his family in terms of fortune. Once a male concubine was favored, the emperor often showered his family with gifts, land, and even opportunities to hold court positions.

Of all the Han emperors, the one known to be closely associated with male concubines was Emperor Wu. He was known for his long reign—he sat on the Dragon Throne for over five decades—and martial prowess. It was under Emperor Wu that the Han dynasty achieved its greatest territorial expansion; the empire stretched from the Fergana Valley in the west to northern Korea in the east and northern Vietnam in the south. With all those years on the throne and his vast achievements, the emperor was constantly surrounded by courtiers and officials. Among all, one of the few who stood closest to him was known as Han Yan.

According to the *Shiji* and the *Book of Han*, the two had already known each other for years, back to when the emperor was referred to by his name, Liu Che. Both Han Yan and Liu Che shared calligraphy lessons when they were young. Details of their early days are scarce, but many historians agree that it was this early companionship that planted the seeds of a closeness that eventually endured into adulthood. By the time Liu Che sat on the throne, succeeding his father, Emperor Jing in 141 BCE, Han Yan was already a familiar presence.

Emperor Wu of Han, accompanied by his two attendants.[48]

Sources claim that Han Yan was a striking character, both in appearance and ability. Indeed, ancient records describe his beauty and charm, but they also emphasize his physical skills. Han Yan was a horse whisperer; he could ride, control, and guide a steed with elegance and mastery. He was also exceptional in archery, a skill that perfectly aligned with Emperor Wu's martial inclinations. Perhaps Emperor Wu found in Han Yan a mirror of his own spirit. Sima Qian claimed that it was common for the two to rise in the morning together, hinting at the deep comfort they found in one another's company.

Of course, the emperor's favor transformed Han Yan's entire life. He was honored with gifts. Emperor Wu showered him with fine silks, jewels, horses, and all other kinds of privileges typically reserved for ministers and royal bloods. His influence at court was undoubtedly immense. Knowing he had the ear and the heart of the most powerful man in the empire, Han Yan walked with confidence. This confidence eventually turned into arrogance. Over time, the emperor's favorite began to push boundaries. He disregarded the etiquette that had long kept the imperial household in balance. The story goes that he even hunted within grounds forbidden to all except the Son of Heaven himself. However, courtiers could only voice their disapproval in silence. They knew that Han Yan had a shield and dared not invoke the wrath of the emperor.

His privilege, however, had a limit. Han Yan's downfall came when his name was mentioned in a scandal. Rumor has it that Han Yan attempted to seduce a maid. Other sources claim he was bold enough to have taken Princess Longlü, the emperor's sister, as his lover. Whichever version was true, the aftermath was the same. His action was reported, and word eventually reached the ears of Empress Dowager Xiaojing. Enraged, she made her decision, bypassing even the emperor's hesitation.

This time around, Emperor Wu's affection could not save Han Yan. He was finally summoned and ordered to take his own life.

Unsurprisingly, Han Yan was not the emperor's only male favorite. Another of his favored companions was known as Li Yannian. Unlike Han Yan, who came from the aristocracy of palace life, Li Yannian had a rather humble beginning. He was said to have committed a crime resulting in his castration. He was then made a eunuch in the palace, where he was forced to work in the royal kennels. However, his exceptional talent in the realm of music made it possible for Li Yannian to escape lowly servitude.

Some claim that Li Yannian could captivate audiences with compositions so moving that they would halt the chatter of an entire court. His melodies also managed to attract the attention of Emperor Wu. Soon, he found himself sleeping and waking up in the Son of Heaven's bedchambers. This was only the beginning of his influence in court.

Li Yannian also once performed a song titled "Jiaren Qu." The song, which he wrote himself, was about a woman whose beauty was beyond this world. Legend has it that the moment the emperor heard the song, he had a question.

"Is there truly a woman of such beauty among us?" the emperor may have asked.

The question was answered by his sister, Princess Pinyang. She told the emperor that the musician had a younger sister whose beauty was ethereal, to say the least. When Li Yannian's sister, Li Furen, was brought before the Son of Heaven, he immediately agreed that she did, in fact, matched the description sung by Li Yannian. Enthralled by her beauty, he made her his concubine.

A painting of Li Furen, after being made the emperor's concubine."

This was a unique situation where a brother and sister were both loved by the emperor. Through this dual connection, Li Yannian's family rose to prominence. Apart from being one of the emperor's male lovers, Li Yannian was also given the honor of leading the re-established Imperial Music Bureau. Even Li Yannian's brother, Li Guangli, was made a general in the Han army.

Unfortunately, prosperity was not meant to linger in the Li family for long. Their influence waned when Li Furen died after giving birth to the emperor's son. Details are murky, but both Li Yannian and Li Guangli ended up being executed for treason. While some claim this was a direct result of the men having affairs with court women, others suggest their death was the work of Empress Wei Zifu, the emperor's second wife.

If Emperor Wu's favorites demonstrate how deeply personal relationships could entwine with power, the story of his grandfather, Emperor Wen, shows just how far such affection could go. In many books of history, Wen is described as a ruler of frugality and benevolence. He was remembered as a stabilizer of the Han dynasty after its turbulent founding. But even a man like Emperor Wen could be swept into devotion by chance and what he believed was divine fate.

It all began with a dream. In it, the emperor caught a glimpse of heaven high above. Yet, he struggled to ascend. He climbed up multiple times, but each time, he slipped back down. That was, however, until a mysterious man wearing a yellow hat entered the scene. He gave the Son of Heaven the push he needed to reach into the celestial realm. When Emperor Wen woke up, he was certain the dream was a sign sent by the gods.

One day, the emperor prepared for a trip. He boarded a boat and set sail along the river. A few moments later, he spotted a humble fisherman wearing the same yellow hat he had seen in his dream. He approached the man and asked for his name. Much to his surprise, the fisherman introduced himself as Deng Tong, a name that, to Chinese ears, sounded like "to ascend." This convinced the emperor that their encounter was not a mere coincidence. And so, he took the humble fisherman to his court.

Deng Tong did not step into the palace grounds as a servant but as the emperor's intimate companion. Soon, their relationship became one of devotion. When a fortune teller predicted that Deng Tong would face a grim end starving in poverty, Emperor Wen scoffed: "How can he starve, if I, the Son of Heaven, could bestow upon him all the riches this empire possesses?" He dismissed the prophecy entirely.

And with that, the emperor began granting Deng Tong vast fortunes. He even went to the extent of giving his lover the rights to control a bronze mine. Even more shocking, Deng Tong was given the privilege of minting his own coins, an authority reserved for the central government. Just a few years after their first encounter, Deng Tong's coins circulated widely, making him one of the wealthiest men in the world.

According to legend, when the emperor suffered from painful boils, it was Deng Tong who remained by his side day and night. In one of the most startling displays of devotion ever recorded, Deng Tong once placed his lips to the sores and sucked out the pus to relieve the pain. Many would consider this a grotesque act, but to Emperor Wen, this was an intimate move that proved ultimate loyalty.

"Answer me one question, Deng Tong," the emperor may have said. "Who loves me more than you?"

At first, there was silence. Bowing his head, Deng Tong answered: "No one, apart from the crown prince."

His reply was bold. It placed him alongside the heir in the emperor's affections. But Emperor Wen's love for Deng Tong grew deeply, much to the dismay of the crown prince, Liu Qi. Some accounts say that later the emperor demanded Liu Qi perform the same act of devotion, sucking at the boils as Deng Tong had. As expected, the prince gagged, recoiled, and vomited. This response not only infuriated Emperor Wen but revealed that none could ever be as loyal as Deng Tong. As for the crown prince, this was a humiliation he would never forget.

And so, when Emperor Wen died, Deng Tong's world collapsed. Liu Qi, now sitting on the throne as Emperor Jing, worked fast to curb Deng Tong's influence. He stripped his father's favorite of his wealth and accused him of illegal dealings. No longer protected by imperial affection, Deng Tong was a step closer to his demise. The fortune teller's prophecy came true after all. Deng Tong, once one of the richest men in China and the intimate favorite of an emperor, starved to death in poverty.

Chapter 8 – Love and Demise

There once lived a wealthy family in Shangyu. They had just welcomed a child. Named Zhu Yingtai, she was the only daughter among nine brothers. Her life was perfect. She was cherished by her parents and fortunate to have been born into an upper-class family. Yingtai, however, was unlike any other young girl. She was always intrigued by knowledge. She could memorize the classics recited by her brothers and would often ask questions beyond her years. Over time, Yingtai grew a desire to study properly. Yet, even if women lived in a privileged environment, they were often denied such opportunities. Girls were trained for weaving, music, and the duties of the household. To seek scholarly learning, to sit beside men in the lecture halls, was forbidden.

Even though she knew this was the norm for everyone who shared her gender, Yingtai never planned to abandon her hunger for knowledge. Every day, she would plead to her parents to allow her to study in Hangzhou, and each day, they firmly said no. One day, Yingtai dressed herself in her brothers' clothes. She tied her hair neatly into a scholar's knot and donned the robes of a young man. Once more, she confronted her parents. This time around, her parents relented to her wish, but with one condition: she was to keep her true gender a secret.

A monument of Zhu Yingtai and Liang Shanbo in Verona, Italy.⁴⁴

Yingtai was ecstatic. Almost immediately, she prepared herself for the journey to Hangzhou. On her way, she met a fellow scholar. He introduced himself as Liang Shanbo. Unlike Yingtai, who grew up in a wealthy family, Shanbo was born into a rather modest family. Although not swimming in wealth, he was often described as earnest and kind; some even summarized his character as a man of quiet virtue. Once the disguised Yingtai discovered that Shanbo was heading to the same destination, Yingtai invited him to travel together. Within minutes of their first meeting, the two clicked, falling into easy conversation. It was as if their bond was meant to be. By the time they reached Hangzhou, the two had grown so close that they swore to become study mates.

The two studied in Hangzhou for three years, and Shanbo never discovered Yingtai's true gender. Still, it was as if they were glued to each other. In the morning, they would study books, sitting side by side. When afternoon came, they recited passages. In the evening, the two could often be seen walking the fields, discussing topics like virtue and fate. It is safe to say that Yingtai matched Shanbo in wit and insight. While Shanbo saw Yingtai as the truest companion (or brother) he had ever known, Yingtai began to develop feelings for him. She would occasionally drop hints, speaking of mandarin ducks that never live apart, but Shanbo never understood. There were times when he poked fun at Yingtai for comparing herself to a woman.

One day, Yingtai received a letter from her parents, summoning her home. This was the moment when things changed. She did not want to leave the love of her life, but at the same time, she could not ignore her parents. She prepared to leave Hangzhou and said her goodbyes. Of course, the farewell weighed heavily upon her. Shanbo felt the same. Unwilling to part so soon, he decided to walk with her for eighteen miles beyond the city walls. Again, Yingtai tried to subtly reveal her secret, telling Shanbo that she was not what she seemed. And yet again, Shanbo failed to grasp her meaning, replying with only a warm smile. At last, Yingtai decided to tell him that she had another sister who was beautiful and unwed. She encouraged Shanbo to visit her family one day and promised that she herself would arrange a union between him and her sister. Shanbo was perplexed by the request but promised to visit regardless.

When Yingtai returned home, her secret life ended. She put away the robes she had worn in Hangzhou, unbound her hair, and continued her duty as a daughter. Then came her parents, who informed her of the reason behind the sudden callback. As it turned out, they had already promised her hand to a wealthy man named Ma Wencai. Yingtai's heart was crushed. She begged her parents to break the match.

"My heart belongs to another," she may have said. Yet, their answer was final. After all, to cancel a promised marriage was to bring embarrassment to the family. And so, a marriage ceremony was set in motion.

Shanbo, on the other hand, tried to live his life as a scholar as usual. However, it was different without Yingtai. This was when he remembered his promise. Shanbo then journeyed to Yingtai's house, hoping to see his study mate once more and perhaps meet the mysterious sister that Yingtai had spoken about.

When he arrived at the door, it was Yingtai (without her disguise) who greeted him. Just by looking into her eyes, Shanbo finally understood the hints that Yingtai occasionally threw at him. Joy struck him, knowing that the sister was Zhu Yingtai herself, his beloved companion from those years of study. Shanbo confessed his love right there and then, and Yingtai returned it. However, their fate was already bound by her parents' decision.

When Yingtai informed him that she was to be married to another man, Shanbo's world turned dark. He returned home in despair. Grief consumed him to the point he fell seriously ill. His strength failed, and within weeks, he died with Yingtai's name still carved in his heart.

When news of her true love's death reached her ears, Yingtai could feel sorrow overtaking her entire being. Yet, there was nothing she could do. Her wedding to Ma Wencai was still on schedule. She did, however, request that her bridal procession pass by Liang Shanbo's grave. Her parents, thinking the request harmless, agreed.

When the day finally came, Yingtai found her hands trembling within her sleeves. As promised, the procession wound its way through the countryside until it reached Liang's resting place. As they drew near, a fierce wind suddenly blew. The horses reared and refused to press on despite the attendants' pressuring. Yingtai, knowing that it was a sign by the heavenly gods, leapt from her carriage. She stripped off her fiery red wedding garments, revealing beneath them the white cloth of mourning. She made haste to Shanbo's grave, where she dropped to her knees. There, the bride-to-be wept continuously.

The winds howled louder, this time accompanied by lightning that appeared as if it was splitting the heavens. Suddenly, the grave split open, and without hesitation, Yingtai threw herself into the dark chasm. Before anyone could get close to the grave, the earth closed again, sealing the two lovers together, forever.

Later, when the sky calmed down and the thunder and lightning were no more, the sun began shining over the land. Several farmers soon noticed two small butterflies fluttering from the grave.

Meng Jiangnü's Grief

This story took place during the Qin dynasty. It involved a young woman who went by the name of Meng Jiangnü. Legend has it that she belonged to a family that was neither rich nor powerful. Her kindness, beauty, and gentle nature, however, were her most precious traits and often captivated the hearts of the people around her.

Meng Jiangnü lived in a quaint village where she spent her days tending to her family and garden. One evening, as Jiangnü was admiring the autumn leaves, she heard a faint rustling noise coming from a bush. Curious, the young woman went and checked to see what made the sound. Perhaps it was a cat or a squirrel, she may have thought to herself. The closer she got to the bush, the more Jiangnü's heart began to race. Turns out, the noise came from a man hiding in the bush. Panicked, Jiangnü called for her parents. The man, afraid that she would cause a commotion, jumped out and explained his circumstances.

His name was Fan Qiliang, and he was hiding from the government officials. This was a time when the emperor, Qin Shi Huang, demanded endless labor from his subjects to build his grand wall. It did not matter whether they were willing to contribute; many were seized from their homes and forced into the construction work. They had to work regardless of the weather or even their health. As a result, many ended up perishing from hunger, cold, and exhaustion. Hence, it made sense for Fan Qiliang to run away, hoping he could escape this daunting fate.

Having heard his reasoning, Meng Jiangnü grew sympathetic. Instead of turning him in, she offered the man refuge. She brought him food and water, treating him like a guest. In time, her kindness blossomed into love, and the two were married. For a short while, it seemed like their lives were filled with joy. However, happiness was fragile under Qin rule. In just a matter of days following their wedding, government officials came to the village, searching for more able-bodied men. Fan Qiliang was eventually discovered and dragged away, taken to labor on the Great Wall. Meng Jiangnü could only stand and watch, powerless to stop the soldiers.

Meng Jiangnü patiently waited for the return of her husband, praying each night for his safety. Weeks turned into long months, yet not a single letter arrived from Fan Qiliang. She asked around one day, hoping someone had heard news of her husband, but unfortunately, she returned home empty-handed. That night, Meng Jiangnü had a dream. In it, she saw Fan Qilian shaking and trembling as he worked without rest in the cold winter weather. Worried that her husband might be in trouble, Meng Jiangnü sewed warm clothes, packed food, and began the long journey northward, determined to find her husband.

The road was harsh, and the journey long. She crossed rivers, climbed hills, and braved cold winds. She tirelessly asked every passerby if they had seen Fan Qiliang among the laborers. Many shook their heads. At last, she reached the construction site. There, she was able to witness first-hand the place of misery and despair so many men were terrified of. Thousands of men toiled under the lash of overseers, their faces hollow with hunger and their hands bloodied from lifting stones. Indeed, the wall rose high and wide, but beneath its stones also lay countless bones of those who had died from exhaustion.

Meng Jiangnü searched desperately, asking each worker if they knew of her husband. When the sky had almost lost its light, Meng Jiangnü finally got her answer, though it was far from what she wanted to hear. One of the laborers told her that Fan Qiliang had perished a few weeks prior. His body was buried within the very wall he had been forced to build.

An illustration of Meng Jiagnü weeping before the Great Wall.[46]

Meng Jiangnü was left speechless. She could not feel her body. She fell to her knees before the towering wall, still clutching the winter clothes she had sewn for her beloved husband. She remained at the foot of the wall for days, crying continuously. Legend has it that her sorrow was so deep that it moved even the gods. Her cries grew more piercing as the days went by, until one day the earth responded with a tremble. A thunderous crack echoed through the land as a section of the Great Wall collapsed. From within this rubble, the remains of Fan Qilian were revealed.

The destruction angered the emperor, who came to the site so he could punish Meng Jiangnü. However, the moment he laid eyes on her, the emperor was starstruck; he had never seen a woman as beautiful as her. Hence, instead of punishing her, the emperor proposed marriage. Meng Jiangnü, her cheeks still wet with tears, reluctantly agreed, but only if the emperor allowed her to provide a proper burial for Fan Qiliang. To this, the emperor agreed.

She gathered his bones one by one with her trembling hands and buried her husband. But could she bring herself to marry the emperor? How could she when her heart belonged to Fan Qiliang and the emperor was the reason he died? When the burial ceremony was done, Meng Jiangnü requested the emperor to fulfil another one of her wishes: to visit the ocean. It was clear that her heart was broken beyond repair. The moment she got on a ship with the emperor, Meng Jiangnü threw herself into the sea, her body quickly devoured by the waves.

The Ups and Downs of Love

Sima Xiangru is said to have been born in 179 BCE at the dawn of Emperor Wen's reign. Since he was born into a family of some wealth in Chengdu, Xiangru enjoyed a fine education. He was indeed a lover of literature. Even from a young age, he often immersed himself in books, mastering the classics and sharpening his prose. He also received training in the realm of music, mastering the lute to the point that every melody he plucked could stir both the heart and mind of anyone nearby. Of course, poetry and music were not the only fields he was well versed in. Xiangru also studied the art of war, eventually growing up to be a respectable swordsman known for his discipline and agility.

This combination—moderate health, immense knowledge, and exceptional martial ability—undoubtedly made him popular. He later got the attention of Emperor Jing of Han, who sat on the throne between 157 and 141 BCE. Impressed by his complete set of skills, the emperor welcomed the young man into his service. In court, Sima Xiangru was made one of the emperor's personal guards. Although this position gave him stability and standing, it brought him little joy. He preferred art, philosophy, and music to guarding the Son of Heaven. After all, according to the historian Sima Qian, Emperor Jing had little taste for literature.

And so, Xiangru began to look elsewhere, hoping he could attain fulfillment in his life. His opportunity soon arrived when Prince Xiao of Liang came to the imperial capital. He was accompanied by an entourage of not only scholars but also a band of talented musicians and rhetoricians. Their brilliance immediately captivated Xiangru. In their company, the young man got a taste of a life full of refinement, discourse, and artistry—a life that he longed for. Therefore, he made up his mind: Xiangru chose to leave his post as a guard and follow the prince to Liang.

At Prince Xiao's court, Xiangru was surrounded by great minds, giving him a chance to hone his rhetoric, improvise his verse, and perfect his melodies. Liang was indeed a melting pot of men with talent, so it was not surprising that Xiangru was able to flourish in its halls. He remained here for years, and his reputation grew steadily across the land. Things only changed in 144 BCE, when Prince Xiao died. Without his patron, Xiangru was left with no choice but to return to Chengdu. Upon his return, more bad news came. In his absence, his family fortunes had greatly withered.

With wealth and comfort at home a thing of the past, Xiangru made his way to Linqiong. He was hoping to meet with a friend who served the city as a magistrate. Since Xiangru already had influence—due to his poetry and his life as a courtier of princes—it was not hard for him to settle in. In Linqiong, he was treated with respect. His name drew the attention of the local elite. Families of influence vied for his company, inviting him to banquets and seeking the honor of his presence at their tables.

One rather wealthy merchant, Zhuo Wangsun, once hosted a lavish feast and invited the poet as his honorable guest. It was one of the grandest events in Linqiong, attended by the most prominent members of the district. They indulged in endless food and flowing wine and spent the evening socializing with each other. Xiangru, however, had his attention elsewhere. He had caught sight of a certain Zhuo Wenjun, the daughter of the host.

Wenjun was well known in the district not only for being the daughter of Linqiong's well-respected merchant but also for her extraordinary beauty and refinement. She had once been married, but not for long; her husband died within a year of their union. Hence, she returned to her father, living within his household once more. Like father, like daughter, Wenjun too was a lover of music and arts. Unsurprisingly, when she heard the tunes coming from the lute played by Sima Xiangru that night—he was purposely plucking the finest melody to attract her attention—Wenjun immediately fell in love.

And so, she made her choice. She fled her father's house and eloped with the talented poet. Their union shocked the entire district. Indeed, Xiangru was popular, but he was not above or at least at the same social level as Zhuo Wangsun, whose vast fortune and influence far outweighed the poet's modest means. Wenju's decision to elope so enraged her father that he stripped her of his wealth. Hence, the couple lived their early days together full of hardship.

Still, their love prevailed. Wenjun worked alongside her husband to survive. They opened a small business selling wine in the market. Some whispered scorn, mocking the fallen daughter of Zhuo Wangsun. Yet, the two never took these cruel remarks to heart. Her father, on the other hand, grew restless with the gossip. He was embarrassed to see his daughter, once dressed in fine silks, now dressed like a commoner and working in a mere tavern. So, he relented. He restored part of Wenjun's dowry, sending servants, wealth, and resources to the couple. From then on, their lives grew easier, and with leisure restored, Sima Xiangru devoted himself once more to literature.

Again, Sima Xiangru's name reached the highest circles, and he eventually caught the attention of Emperor Wu, who succeeded Emperor Jing in 141 BCE. A man of literature and art himself, the emperor summoned Xiangru to his court. The poet dazzled with his compositions, such as the "Shanglin Fu," a long descriptive poem that captured the natural beauty of a royal hunting park, Shanglin Park.

True, Xiangru's reputation grew tremendously, but success also carried temptation with it. At court, he was surrounded by luxury and praise. He began to drift from the humble devotion that had bound him to Wenjun. Days stretched into weeks, then months. Wenjun waited in Linqiong, expecting news that her husband would bring her to the capital. Sadly, none came.

One day, a letter arrived. It contained only thirteen characters. In it, Sima Xiangru coldly confessed his intent to take a concubine, as was common among men of his current standing. The letter broke Wenjun.

However, she chose not to unleash wrath. Neither did she beg desperately for his compassion. Instead, she crafted a poem known as "Yuanlang Shi" (Blaming My Husband). In the verses, she poured out her grief, expressed beautifully the betrayal that she felt, and wrote the remembrance of all they had shared. She reminded him of the night she fled her father's house, the years of poverty endured at his side, the scorn she had borne willingly for love. She did not throw bitter insults but rather piercing honesty. Later, she followed with another poem named "Baitou Yin" (Song of White Hair), in which she talked about how love is fragile, just as beauty and youth.

When Sima Xiangru read her words, shame engulfed him. The woman who had risked everything for him, who had labored beside him when he was penniless, now humbled him with poetry that revealed his betrayal. He chose to abandon his intention to take a concubine and returned to Wenjun. In the end, the two lived together until death.

The Broken Emperor

Emperor Xuanzong of Tang first came to power in 712 CE. He reigned wisely, guided by trustworthy ministers, and presided over what scholars later called the Kaiyuan Golden Age. But as the years passed and his youth faded, so did his interest in the serious duties of governing. He had also lost his other half, the consort Lady Wu. The emperor longed for companionship, but it was not easy to find someone who could check all the lists.

That was, however, until he laid eyes on Yang Yuhuan. She was young, only nineteen, with radiant skin, delicate features, and eyes that seemed to sparkle with mischief and life. Her beauty was beyond the world; some claim she had a face that would shame even the prettiest flower on earth. History, too, would remember her as one of the Four Great Beauties of China. However, there was an obstacle to Xuanzong claiming her for his own: she had already been married to his son, Li Mao.

Still, the smitten emperor could not erase his feelings. Yet how could the ruler of the mighty Tang dynasty openly take his own daughter-in-law without scandal? If he did so, it would certainly be a blow to imperial prestige. But Xuanzong came up with a plan. He told his son to pressure Yang Yuhuan into walking the path of religion. As a result, Yang Yuhuan became a Taoist nun, severing her marriage. Outwardly, she became "Lady of the Dao," her hair bound and her days devoted to prayer. But, under the cover of night, she would slip into disguises and meet the emperor. This, however, was an open secret. But she lived this double life for seven years.

When Li Mao eventually remarried, Xuanzong wasted no time. He summoned Yang Yuhuan back into the palace and gave her the title *guifei*, or "noble consort," which was the emperor's favorite. From then on, Yang Guifei became the center of his world.

Yang Guifei enjoyed this new level of prestige. She used this opportunity to lift her family's fortune. She showered his brothers and sisters with wealth and lands. Her cousin, Yang Guozhong, was also elevated to the position of prime minister, one of the most powerful offices in the empire. But many viewed Tang Guozhong as unfit for the role. Not only was he clumsy, but he was also corrupt in politics. This incompetence slowly poisoned the government and sowed seeds of resentment. Although these seeds of nepotism would one day turn into a calamity, none dared to speak up.

Yang Guifei mounting a horse.[47]

Yang Guifei herself lived a life of extraordinary luxury. Her wardrobe was filled with nothing but the most exquisite silks dyed in the rarest colors. Each of them was typically embroidered with phoenixes and peonies, two of the most favorite motifs among the nobles. Hundreds of maids also attended to her every step, and the emperor would move heaven and earth to satisfy her cravings. According to one story, Guifei loved lychees. This fruit, however, could only grow in fields far from the capital. So, to please her, the emperor ordered his officials to travel far, just so they could source the fruit. For weeks, horses and couriers raced across provinces, carrying the precious fruit at full speed so that the emperor's dearest consort could enjoy it fresh. The scramble left ministers grumbling about the absurdity of palace priorities, but no one dared speak too loudly, especially against the emperor's favorite.

Emperor Xuanzong and his favorite, Yang Guifei.[48]

Beauty was not her only strong suit. Yang Guifei was also bestowed with a gift for music and dance. She often composed songs for Xuanzong. She played the pipa and flute and performed graceful dances in the palace halls. The emperor could watch her for hours, getting so entranced that he would forget the affairs of the empire.

Of course, like any other love story, theirs was not without quarrels. Yang Guifei was described as fiercely jealous. It was difficult for her to tolerate those who gained the emperor's affection. Once, after a bitter quarrel, Xuanzong banished her to her cousin's home in disgrace. But the emperor could not bear to live a life without his favorite consort and soon sent for her to return. Another episode of banishment came a few years later. This time, it was due to the consort's alleged theft of a flute. Again, the banishment did not last long.

Knowing that the emperor held a soft spot for Yang Guifei in his heart, many courtiers began to realize that their path to heightened influence lay through her. They knew that those who pleased Yang Guifei could win the emperor's ear. Thus, these nobles showered the consort with gifts and flattery. The one who excelled at this was a general who commanded the armies on the northern frontier. His name was An Lushan, and his charming personality sat so well with the consort that she was said to have jokingly referred to him as her adopted son. Little did she know that An Lushan was the key to her demise.

The general had ambition to sit on the throne, so in 755 CE, he led a rebellion. His armies marched with terrifying speed, seizing cities and threatening even Chang'an. Panic swept the court. Even Xuanzong and his entourage fled westward, seeking refuge in the mountains of Sichuan.

Things took a dark turn for the emperor and his consort along the road at Mawei. There, the imperial guards, who had grown extremely exhausted and furious, turned their anger toward the emperor's favorites. They slew Yang Guozhong, blaming him for corruption and misrule. Then, they pointed their fingers at Yang Guifei, demanding her execution.

The emperor was torn. He pleaded and wept, but his soldiers stood unmoved. They would go no further unless she was gone. At last, Xuanzong relented. Yang Guifei was led beneath the trees of a wayside Buddhist shrine. There, she was strangled with a silken cord. The emperor's beloved, the woman for whom he had bent the empire, now lay lifeless on the earth.

The emperor lived, but he was a broken man, beyond fixing. Though the Tang armies eventually crushed An Lushan's rebellion under the leadership of Xuanzong's son (who ruled as Emperor Suzong), the dynasty never fully recovered its former strength.

Conclusion

Looking at China today, it is easy to assume that its story has always been one of unstoppable power. The truth, however, is different. China's history is anything but steady. It is named the world's oldest continuous civilization not because it was unshakable but because it was constantly being shaken—and rebuilt over and over again.

Across these short pages, we have saw dynasties rise and fall, sometimes spectacularly. Famines and rebellions were recurring themes of Chinese history. Cities that once became a melting pot of merchants and scholars were never guaranteed endurance; Loulan, for one, eventually vanished into the desert despite being one of the most precious centers fought over by major powers. Entire cultures, such as Sanxingdui, left us with more questions than answers about their story and disappearance despite leaving behind dozens of impressive artifacts. Even the great Han dynasty faltered, paving the way for ancient China to eventually fracture yet again. Indeed, continuity was never promised. But China survived only because of the people—both named and unnamed— who never failed to pick up the pieces and carry them forward.

Of course, it was not only the Son of Heaven who held the line. There were many others who contributed to the civilization's survival. While emperors and dynasties gave their names to eras, it was often generals on the frontier, scholars in their studies, poets in exile, and even women in the palace who kept the thread of continuity from snapping. Shangguan Wan'er and Princess Pingyang, for instance, went against the norms of a patriarchal society; one used her expertise in words to see to matters of the state while the other raised an entire army as part of a rebellion. There were also those like Wu Qi and Tan Daoji, who led the empire to triumph yet were rewarded with tragedy and injustice. Love stories in ancient China likewise had themes of tragedy and misfortune woven into the plot.

It is clear that China's endurance came not from being unshakable but from being resilient. Continuity lived in forgotten cities, in overshadowed rebellions, and even in poems written by kidnapped victims. Vulnerability was always a part of the nation's long history, and so was the will to start again. True, the stories were not always glorious, but they were always human. That is why these forgotten voices and overlooked episodes matter. They fill in the spaces between the grand narratives and remind us that history is not only the story of emperors but of people.

Part 3: Ancient Japan

Discovering Lost Stories from Ancient Japan

Introduction

It is easy to fall in love with Japan at first glance. In fact, Japan is one of the most visited countries in the world today. Each year, over thirty million people flock to explore the archipelago, drawn by the country's unique blend of old and new traditions. People gaze at the delicate sakura petals when spring finally comes, wait impatiently for the skies to clear so they can get the perfect view of the iconic Mount Fuji, and peacefully walk through the thousands of vermillion torii gates standing in the forest. For visitors and admirers alike, Japan seems like a country that has mastered the art of timelessness. There is always elegance in its traditions, no matter how old they are.

When it comes to Japan's past, though, many immediately think of katana-wielding warriors, imperial palaces full of court nobles dressed in flowing silks, or a troop of samurai, all clad in heavy armor, riding into battle. These images are not incorrect, but they are only fragments of Japan's past. Like many other countries and civilizations, Japan's past is long and complex.

What we now think of as "Japan" was not always a unified concept. Long before the arrival of the samurai and the age of shoguns, the archipelago was a patchwork of competing clans, shifting belief systems, and regional identities struggling to define themselves. It was a time when the line between myth and reality blurred. It was a time when divine wrath was chosen as the cause of a natural disaster rather than science.

Although the Yamato period began as early as the 2nd century CE, it was not until many centuries later that the imperial court could truly assert its dominance over distant provinces. Wars and battles were a common scene in ancient Japan. They fought not only invaders and foreigners but also those who had long called the land their own, like the Emishi and the Hayato. Even when peace was established, there were times when the imperial court ruled more in theory rather than in practice. Multiple clans emerged from behind the scenes, always eager to maximize their influence and even manipulate the imperial succession.

Buddhism and Shinto peacefully coexist today, but back then, violent conflicts erupted when Japan received its first Buddha statue. Temples, though now appearing serene, were once training grounds for warrior monks wielding swords, bows, and arrows. They remained peaceful at times, but when their demands were not met by the court, these religious institutions would not hesitate to march into battle.

Of course, the history of ancient Japan was not only shaped by warriors, assassinations, and court intrigues. Women played prominent roles back then, though their names were rarely recorded in official chronicles commissioned by the imperial court. Some left a legacy by becoming priestesses, a few others chose the path of a warrior and took part in battles, fighting alongside popular figures, and some even succeeded in gaining the throne and ruled with real authority, not as mere puppets. There was also a handful of women who left their mark on literature.

Outside the palaces and temples, everyday life in ancient Japan was filled with customs and beliefs that may seem peculiar—or even unthinkable—by modern standards. These aspects are rarely highlighted in history books; they are often reduced to footnotes, if they appear at all.

Yes, the elegance we often associate with ancient Japan is real, but at the same time, it also existed alongside turmoil, contradiction, and change. This book does not seek to retell the most well-known accounts of ancient Japan but rather to look to the margins—to the lesser-known figures, the regional tensions, the spiritual disputes, and the forgotten voices that helped shape a civilization.

Chapter 1 – The Hayato People

Two figures could be seen quarreling. They were brothers, though they lived in a time when the land of Japan was still struggling to take shape. It was a time when boundaries between gods and men were blurred.

The younger of the two brothers was a hunter named Hoori (also known as Yamasachihiko), who was also the prince of the mountains. The other was a fisherman and the prince of the sea, who went by Hoderi (also called Umasachihiko). Together, they were thought to be the children of the celestial deities known as Ninigi (the great-grandfather of Japan's first emperor, Jimmu) and Konohana Sakuya (the goddess of Mount Fuji and other volcanoes in Japan).

An illustration of Hoori.[40]

According to the ancient Japanese chronicle known as *Kojiki,* their quarrel began with a simple exchange. The two brothers had previously been given two divine gifts by their father. Hoderi was given a magic fishing hook, and Hoori was gifted with a powerful bow. One day, Hoori asked his brother to exchange their gifts. Hoderi was reluctant at first since his fishing hook was personal and treasured, but his brother persuaded him. And so, with their magical tools exchanged, the brothers went on to test their skills. As predicted, both of them fared poorly. Hoderi could not hit a single target with his brother's bow. Hoori failed to catch a single fish. Worst of all, he lost the magic hook in the ocean.

Hoori immediately told Hoderi of the incident and apologized for his carelessness. He then crafted five hundred hooks from his sword and offered them to his brother. Hoderi refused to accept them or his brother's apology. The magic hook had been his most prized possession.

Desperate to seek forgiveness from his brother, Hoori made a journey to the bottom of the sea. However, as he was searching for the hook, Hoori found himself deviating from his goal. He arrived in the realm of the dragon god, Ryūjin. Hoori married the god's daughter, Toyotama-Hime, and chose to remain in the realm, where he was showered with luxuries beyond imagination. Three years later, he suddenly longed to go back home. He recalled his goal to find Hoderi's magic hook, and with the help of Ryūjin, he successfully retrieved it.

Hoori asked Ryūjin for permission to return home. Although he was disappointed at first, Ryūjin gave his blessing. Before Hoori departed, the dragon god bestowed upon him two tide-controlling jewels. One could be used to raise the tide, while the other was used to wash away the tide. He then warned Hoori that his brother would not be content with his return; instead, Hoderi would wage war with him.

Ryūjin was right. Hoderi was already angry when the magic hook had been lost, and he had grown jealous of his brother's newfound fortune. So, even when Hoori returned the hook, he was not content. Hoderi wished to wage war with his brother, which prompted Hoori to use the magical jewel. Raising it into the air, Hoori called upon a flood, which almost drowned Hoderi. Desperate to save his life, Hoderi apologized and promised that he and his descendants would serve Hoori and his descendants for all eternity. Agreeing to the peace offer, Hoori used the other magical jewel and washed away the tide.

This myth was glorified by the Yamato. They believed themselves to be the descendants of Hoori and that the Hayato people, who were thought to have descended from Hoderi, were meant to be subjugated. Through this myth, court scribes were able to frame their campaigns not as conquest but rather as the natural order of things.

The Hayato, however, did not see themselves this way.

People of the South: The Hayato Before Yamato

Map showing the region of Kyūshū, inhabited by the Hayato.[50]

The Hayato lived far from the imperial capital. They dwelled amidst the mountains and across the rivers that flowed through Kyūshū. They built their communities in the south, particularly in areas that we know today as Kagoshima and Miyazaki, long before anyone spoke of emperors or courts.

However, to describe the Hayato as just a single tribe is to simplify what was never simple. They were not one, united people but rather a network of autonomous groups. Each of them had its own leaders, customs, and dialects. Living on lands dotted with volcanoes and bamboo forests and surrounded by jagged cliffs and steaming springs, the Hayato lived a life that followed the local rhythms of nature. They farmed, hunted animals, and fished. Archaeological evidence from burial jars and pit dwellings suggests the Yamato preserved cultural practices that dated back to the Jōmon period (the prehistoric period of Japan).

They did not build big cities or grand palaces like the Yamato, who came much later, but the Hayato organized themselves through clan ties, oral traditions, and through kinship that undoubtedly flowed deeper than written law.

However, the Yamato, who were descendants of the Yayoi people who migrated to Japan from the continent, viewed them through a different lens. They thought of the Hayato as strange. Court scribes recorded them as wild and at times barbaric. These descriptions were commonly used in court records, especially when a certain group of people did not conform to the ideals of Yamato rule. The Hayato, for instance, did not rely as heavily on rice farming as the Yamato did. Not only did they share lands communally within their clans, but the Hayato also cultivated fields by agreement rather than edict. Their leaders were chosen based on prestige and lineage rather than state appointment. This kind of decentralized structure stood in direct contrast to what the Yamato court sought to impose.

But the Hayato were not completely isolated. They engaged in trade with their neighbors to the north and people across the sea, exchanging a variety of goods like deer hides, sea salt, and woven items. It is safe to assume that the entire Japanese peninsula was aware of their identity, legends, and warriors. Even the Yamato recognized them as a people—a people worth conquering.

The Yamato court had greatly expanded its wings by the late 7th century CE. Inspired by Chinese models of centralized rule, the court adopted a political and legal framework known as the Ritsuryō system. Through this system, land across the realm was to be nationalized and then redistributed equally to citizens. In return, the people had to pay taxes to the government in the form of goods, labor, and rice. To put it simply, everyone served the emperor, from humble farmers to state officials to even regional clans. To the Yamato, it was a system of fairness and order. To those far from the imperial capital, it was a tool of control.

The Hayato, in particular, could see little sense in the system. Their lands were not something to be measured and divided. Their soil belonged to their families and clans. For many centuries, they were passed down by memory and agreement. They also could not conform to rice farming even if they wanted to. The Hayato lived on volcanic soil. Southern Kyūshū's humid subtropical climate made wet-rice cultivation nearly impossible. They relied on millet, wild root vegetables, hunting, and fishing. Some would agree that imposing the Ritsuryō tax structure on these people was like fitting a square peg into a round hole.

Nevertheless, the court pushed on. The Yamato established new provinces like Ōsumi on the Hayato lands. Governors were placed in their territories. Census-takers arrived with their wooden tablets and ink brushes. They expected the Hayato to submit easily. They wanted them to pay tribute and serve the emperor.

And for a while, the Hayato relented. Since it was difficult for them to cultivate rice, they paid tribute with other goods like deer and cow pelts, handwoven cloth, and a certain delicacy known as ama-zura-sen. According to the Heian-era book called *Makura no Sōshi* (*The Pillow Book* by the court lady Sei Shōnagon), a sweetener was made from ivy sap. These tributes were delivered by young Hayato men to Daizafu (the western administrative capital in northern Kyūshū) first and then to the capital in Nara, Heijō-kyō.

Unfortunately, these young Hayato men had to fork out their own money to pay the travel expenses. The burden, however, did not stop after they delivered the tribute. They had to remain in the capital for six years, serving in menial or ceremonial roles. Meanwhile, back home, their families struggled in their absence. The Hayato were left without their strongest workers to till the land and hunt. They also had to suffer the cost of tribute, food, and travel.

In 720 CE, the volcanoes of southern Kyūshū were not the only things that simmered. The Hayato had had enough of the injustice. A rebellion erupted in the province of Ōsumi, located at the southern tip of the island. Of course, only a little survives from the Hayato side of the conflict. What we know today is mostly taken from the court chronicle known as *Shoku Nihongi*. Like all official records commissioned by the imperial court, *Shoku Nihongi* narrates the rebellion through the eyes of the victors.

It was said that the conflict took place right after the murder of the first governor of Ōsumi, a man named Yako no Fuhitomari. We do not know exactly how he died, but ancient sources point their fingers at the discontented Hayato. To the Yamato, this act of defiance meant war and punishment, so bloodshed was inevitable.

Turning their seven hilltop fortifications into strongholds, the Hayato prepared for war. Rather than having massive troops guard each entrance, they relied on the craggy ridges, bamboo forests, and narrow mountain passes to protect their flanks. Later, the court launched a full-scale military expedition. Spearheaded by a respected member of the imperial family and a seasoned commander named Prince Ōtomo no Tabito, the Yamato were confident that victory would be theirs in just a matter of weeks. After all, they had the technology needed to crush a mere rebellion; the Yamato were equipped with siege units, engineers, and warriors gathered from across the empire.

The fight, however, was more brutal and took longer than expected. The Hayato were versed in the lay of the land. They knew which mountain pass was faster and which forest could confuse their enemy. They relied heavily on guerrilla tactics, striking the Yamato with speed before fading into the terrain in the blink of an eye. They were adamant about keeping their land, even if it meant bloodshed. Some accounts suggest that entire families fought together and that women helped in the defense, ferrying supplies or reinforcing ramparts under the cover of night.

After eighteen months of defending their land, the Yamato proved they were the more powerful of the two. After days of siege warfare, one of the Hayato strongholds at Soonoiwaki fell when supplies were completely cut off. The Yamato also succeeded in toppling the fort at Himenoki. By the end of 721, the rebellion had been crushed. At least 1,400 Hayato were killed or captured.

Those who survived were left with no other choice but to accept incorporation. Many Hayato men, especially those hailing from influential clans, were sent to the capital, where they were organized into specialized guard units. These warriors were then stationed at the gates of the imperial palace, tasked with guarding the emperor himself. They were typically equipped with long spears and large wooden shields.

Interestingly, instead of using shields bearing imperial symbols, they used the ones featuring a reverse-S-shaped spiral motif. This particular motif was believed to have the ability to ward off evil spirits and misfortune.

A monument featuring a Hayato shield.[51]

Apart from these symbols, the Hayato were known for their ritual howls. This loud and chilling cry was thought to increase morale. Like the symbols on their wooden shields, the howls could also scare evil spirits. When the Hayato, typically dressed in red and white cotton garments and scarlet shawls, led processions for imperial visits, these ritualistic howls were thought to have cleared the emperor's path from unwanted misfortune.

Apart from military roles in the imperial palace, the Hayato were also acknowledged for their craftsmanship. Since their homeland in southern Kyūshū, especially areas around Kagoshima, was full of high-quality bamboo, the Hayato were talented in weaving, shaping, and bending bamboo into fine crafts. They made kasa hats, traditional Japanese hats worn by all classes for different types of occasions and ceremonies. They also crafted folding fans, which, again, were both practical and ceremonial. These Hayato-crafted items were ironically court favorites, especially in Nara.

A monk wearing a type of kasa hat.[53]

The Hayato also provided performances in the imperial court. On occasion, they were summoned to the palace to showcase their wrestling skills. These matches are referred to by some scholars as an early form of sumo. Of course, these early matches were far from being grand tournaments with dohyō rings and salt purification like we typically see today. Another ancient chronicle, the Nihon Shoki, recorded a sumo match between Ata and Ōsumi Hayato being held at court in 682 CE during the reign of Emperor Tenmu. The victory belonged to the Ōsumi wrestler. Another match mentioned in the record was held at Asukadera, a temple in Nara, in 695 CE.

The reputation of the Hayato as fierce warriors endured, even years after their subjugation. When the court was troubled with news of a rebellion in 740 CE, led by the governor of Dazaifu, Fujiwara no Hirotsugu, the Hayato were summoned yet again to lend a helping hand. It began when two figures named Genbō and Kibi no Makibi were promoted to higher positions in the court despite the two coming from a family that lacked prestige. Hirotsugu, no longer able to contain his dissatisfaction over the promotions, openly defied the imperial court.

Since Hirotsugu was a man of high importance and influence, the court did not dare to wait; if no actions were taken, the conflict would undoubtedly snowball into a full-scale insurrection. The court immediately mustered troops, calling on men from across the empire to quell the rebellion. Among them were, of course, units of Hayato warriors.

Their inclusion was not because of desperation. The Hayato hailed from Kyūshū, so they knew the lay of the land better than most. These warriors were agile and well accustomed to mountain paths and open field tactics. While some participated solely under the imperial court's order, others viewed Hirotsugu's rebellion with disdain. After all, his seat of power was in Daizufu, the very city that had long burdened the Hayato with tributes and injustice.

Fujiwara no Hirotsugu was eventually defeated. The rebellion ended just slightly over a month later. Hirotsugu attempted to flee to Silla (one of the three kingdoms of Korea) following his defeat, but the weather did not permit his escape. Relentless storms forced him to turn back. He eventually landed on the northernmost Goto Island and remained there for almost two months before finally being captured and beheaded.

Although the Hayato were mentioned only a few times in the Yamato chronicles, they played an important role. However, as the decades passed, their names began to fade from history altogether. This was possibly due to the nature of assimilation. Integration had long been one of the quiet strategies of the Yamato to erase the legacy of certain communities. The court encouraged regional peoples to adopt imperial names, languages, and roles. This resulted in many Hayato taking up Japanese surnames. Many also married into local clans and raised children who were taught imperial culture rather than their old beliefs, stories, and even dialects. Slowly, their distinctiveness softened until it became difficult to tell where the Hayato ended and the Yamato began.

Some Hayato continued to serve ceremonial roles. Glimpses of the Hayato acting as guards protecting the emperor or participating in ritual processions still existed into the 9th century, though it was not as common as in the years before. By the mid-Heian period, mentions of the Hayato had largely disappeared from court records.

Chapter 2 – Assassination Games That Took Over the Chrysanthemum Court

Far beyond the Mediterranean Sea, news arrived that shocked many. A man who had all the authority of the Roman Republic had fallen not on the battlefield or to famine or plague but to the knives of his own allies. On March 15ᵗʰ, 44 BCE (also known as the Ides of March), Julius Caesar, dressed in his purple toga and a golden wreath on his head, made his way to the Curia of Pompey. He was to meet the rest of the Senate for a meeting. Little did he know that what should have been a session of discussion and debate would turn into an ambush.

As he began giving his speech in the meeting hall, one of the Senate members approached him. Sensing that Caesar had his guard down, he took the opportunity and stabbed the dictator. This was a signal for the rest of the conspirators to close in and plunge their daggers into the once-mighty dictator's torso. These conspirators were the very same men Caesar once called friends. After getting stabbed twenty-three times, Caesar was left to die in a pool of his own blood.

Of course, Caesar's death was only one of the many episodes of assassinations that have been immortalized in history books and other media. Another prominent episode took place on a completely different continent. Two centuries prior to Caesar's death, the world saw an assassination attempt made on King Zheng of Qin. This happened during the Warring States period. Prince Dan of Yan orchestrated the plot. He sent a man named Jing Ke to carry on the mission.

Jing Ke arrived at King Zheng's court under the guise of diplomacy. When the opportunity arose, he attacked the king with his blade, which he had hidden in a roll of cloth. However, the attempt failed. His attack was swiftly deflected, giving time for King Zheng to unsheathe his sword and kill Jing Ke. Unlike Julius Caesar, King Zheng survived the attempt. He eventually succeeded in uniting China, becoming its first emperor and taking the name Qin Shi Huang.

Of course, these assassinations were not always personal. In many places across the ancient world, survival required more than just lineage. It demanded silence, awareness, and a kind of political intuition that could sniff betrayal before it took form. But still, even the most cautious fell. Some were murdered in their own chambers, while others were handed a blade and told to die with dignity. There were also those who were too cautious that they turned paranoid. They acted recklessly, eventually resulting in their closest companion strategizing their murder.

Suffice it to say that not only kings and emperors were exposed to the possibility of being assassinated. A prince, a reputable general, a philosopher, and even a poet could find themselves in danger if they drew too much attention or stood in someone else's path. Yes, ambition was admired, but only up to a point.

The ancient Japanese knew this dangerous world all too well. Its early courts were refined, governed by ceremony and lineage. However, beneath the surface lay the same struggles seen elsewhere: rivalry, fear, and quiet violence.

The Isshi Incident: An Assassination That Took Place Before the Empress's Presence

When the Japanese entered the Asuka period (538–710 CE), they began to witness an era of major transformation. Buddhism had recently been introduced to the populace, bringing in new beliefs that contradicted Shintoism and caused conflicts among the courts, though the religion eventually coexisted peacefully with the ancient Shinto religion. The Japanese court also saw a tremendous increase in the arrival of foreign envoys. In short, this was a period when Japan was beginning to shape itself into something more than just a collection of powerful clans. However, for all the signs of cultural and political development, one thing remained the same: power belonged to those who could hold it, even if that meant removing those who stood in the way.

By the mid-7ᵗʰ century, one particular clan had risen to great heights. Under the leadership of Soga no Emishi and his son, Soga no Iruka, the Soga clan was the real power behind the throne. It not only controlled court appointments, but the Soga also played a hand in manipulating royal marriages. The emperor was still the face of the state. He wore the crown and sat on the Chrysanthemum Throne, but it was the Soga who whispered in his ear, influencing every decision he made. This went on for many years. Unsurprisingly, not everyone was content with the power that the Soga had.

However, challenging or even complaining about the Soga could result in punishment. Only a few were bold enough to voice their opinion. One of them was Prince Naka no Ōe. The son of Emperor Jomei and Empress Kōgyoku, the prince had spent enough time watching the Soga clan's power grow unchecked. Plus, Naka no Ōe had a dream of his own. He wished to sit on the throne one day and rule the land. In his eyes, there was only one way to ensure his ambition would come true; he had to remove the Soga from the court. Always clever and calculating, the prince was well aware that a direct confrontation would be suicide. He knew that he needed a plan that required both timing and a partner.

That partner came in the form of Nakatomi no Kamatari. Although he was from a lesser noble house, Kamatari was popular for his sharp insight and deep loyalty. The story goes that the two met in secret under the guise of casual friendship. Instead of meeting quietly in a hall or a chamber within the palace, the two typically met under the open sky. Located west of the Asuka-dera (also known as Hōkō-ji, one of the oldest temples in Japan, built in 596) was a public ground where nobles would gather to play kemari. This was a game of kickball imported from China. Ancient sources suggested that this was where Naka no Ōe and Kamatari conspired to end Iruka's control.

The day of the coup came in 645 CE when a court ceremony was to be held. It was the reading of memorials sent from the Three Kingdoms of Korea—Baekje, Silla, and Goguryeo. Since it was a formal and diplomatically significant day, both Naka no Ōe and Kamatari expected the event to be filled with major figures of the court. It was indeed a perfect setting for their plan to materialize.

Every detail had been carefully prepared by the two conspirators. Nakatomi no Kamatari was not present during the event of the assassination itself, but he made sure to actively play a role behind the scenes. He bribed the palace guards, ensuring they remained silent. The palace gates were also ordered to shut immediately after everyone had entered the ceremonial hall. That way, no additional reinforcements could interrupt. Interestingly, the assassination was not to be carried out by Naka no Ōe's own hands. The prince had arranged for four armed men to be present during the ceremony. They were the ones ordered to strike Soga no Iruka. However, Naka no Ōe had a backup plan in case the attack went south. He concealed a blade inside the ceremonial hall, close to where he would be sitting when the ceremony began so he could defend himself should the need arise.

The prince was right to doubt the smoothness of the plan. When the time came, the four men he had bribed to attack Iruka froze. Perhaps they got cold feet now that they were in the presence of Empress Kōgyoku, or perhaps they were suddenly terrified by the thought of them failing to execute the plan and the punishment that would follow. Regardless of the reason, the four men remained still, as if they were paralyzed.

Realizing that the plot might be foiled, Prince Naka no Ōe chose to take matters into his own hands. He stood up and drew the blade he had hidden close to him before rushing to Iruka. Without hesitation, the prince slashed Iruka across the shoulder. The wound was deep, blood staining Iruka's ceremonial attire. Yet, it did not kill him. Iruka stumbled backward and turned toward the imperial throne in disbelief. Clutching his wound, he threw himself at the feet of the stunned Empress Kōgyoku. He desperately cried out for the empress to take action against her son, Naka no Ōe.

It was a stunning scene. The most powerful man in the palace, who had long orchestrated plots and influenced the decisions in the court, was now covered in blood, begging for the empress to help prevent his demise. The empress, however, was left shaken. Caught in between the two sides, Empress Kōgyoku chose to withdraw from the scene to consider the matter.

An illustration depicting the assassination of Soga no Iruka after Empress Kōgyoku left the hall.[58]

Now that the empress was gone, the four men bribed by the prince suddenly rushed forward and attacked the wounded Iruka. He was struck multiple times until he breathed his last. Other sources claimed he was decapitated.

Chaos ensued following his death. With news of his son's assassination, Soga no Emishi was engulfed in despair. He lit his house on fire and committed suicide, leaving behind only ashes and memories. The Soga clan's dominance in the Yamato court effectively came to an end.

As for the empress, what she experienced was not easily forgotten. Although the court had been successfully reclaimed by the imperial house, the bloodshed that had occurred in her presence was not without consequence. In Asuka Japan, death was not viewed as merely a loss but also as a source of spiritual pollution. The idea of *kegare*, or defilement, held deep cultural meaning. To be in the presence of a violent death, especially within sacred or imperial space, was seen as a spiritual stain on the soul. In Kōgyoku's case, the empress had witnessed the murder of her most powerful minister, so she believed she had been touched, physically and ritually, by death. She made the decision to abdicate the throne to her brother, Emperor Kōtoku.

However, this was not the last we see of Kōgyoku in the record. After Kōtoku's death, she reascended to the throne under the name Saimei. She reigned over Japan until her death in 661 CE. Only then would Naka no Ōe rise, ruling from the Chrysanthemum Throne as Emperor Tenji. Of course, he did not forget the deed of his partner in eradicating Soga no Iruka a few years prior. Nakatomi no Kamatari was granted the *kabane* (hereditary title) of Ason, which was the second-highest noble rank at the time. He was also given a new clan name, Fujiwara. This marked the foundation of the Fujiwara clan, which, ironically, would later dominate court politics for centuries.

Emperor Sushun: The Emperor Who Got Tired of Being a Puppet

It is not surprising when we learn that the Soga clan was not always the victim of a blade. Long before Soga no Iruka fell lifeless before the imperial throne, the Soga themselves had drawn the blade. It is safe to say that their rise to power had not been passive. They had grown their influence through various methods, from strategic marriage ties to religious patronage and, of course, through force when necessary. As for this particular story, the central character was Soga no Umako, the ōomi or chief of the Soga clan at the time and the grandfather of Soga no Iruka. Similar to Emishi and Iruka, Umako was the hand that controlled the court from behind the curtain. When the imperial line refused to move in the direction he chose, he did not hesitate to make adjustments.

The story begins in 587 CE. After a period of violent succession disputes, Umako succeeded in installing a new emperor on the throne. Known as Emperor Sushun, he was the twelfth son of Emperor Kinmei (r. 539–571 CE) and Empress Hirohime, who was the daughter of Soga no Iname (the father of Umako). The Soga expected Sushun to remember that the emperor had to govern in line with their interests. Sushun did for a time until it was clear that Umako's influence had grown more visible. The emperor began to feel restless. He disliked how decisions were made before they reached his ears. He also hated the sight of the court bowing to Umako before bowing to him. His temper was growing unpredictable, especially when it came to matters involving Umako and the Soga clan.

One time, the emperor was out hunting. He managed to kill a wild boar. Holding the boar's head in his hands, Sushun was said to have muttered, "I wish to slay the one I despise, just as I have slain this beast,"

A portrait of Emperor Sushun.[54]

No one asked who the emperor was referring to, but everyone knew. Some sources claimed that Umako learned of this incident. Whether he heard those words directly or received them through his informants, it was clear that Sushun had grown dangerous.

Unlike the story of Soga no Iruka, the emperor was not killed during an official ceremony or before the court. Instead, Soga no Umako hired a person named Yamatoaya no Ataikama to get his hands dirty. Details about him are scarce, but he was likely a retainer loyal to the Soga clan. We have no evidence of how exactly the emperor was assassinated, but it is safe to assume everything happened quietly. Emperor Sushun died in 592 CE at the age of seventy-two. He had reigned for only five years.

Umako grew more powerful following Sushun's death. He never faced any consequences for the assassination. No one dared to mention Sushun's name again; even his burial was done hastily without any of the usual imperial rituals. Ancient sources also state that Umako eventually fell out with the assassin he hired. Umako had him hung from a tree.

Fujiwara no Tanetsugu

The imperial court in Nara was growing restless in the final decades of the 8th century. This was a time when temples had grown extremely wealthy, allowing them to participate in the political sphere more actively. Eventually, their religious influence, once seen as a source of protection for the court, threatened to pull them into factional disputes and spiritual rivalries. Emperor Kanmu, who rose to the throne in 781 CE, knew that his subjects needed a new beginning, away from Nara's monastic power. With an aim to reestablish the true power of the imperial house, Kanmu's first step was to relocate his capital.

This was where Fujiwara no Tanetsugu made his entrance into the story. As one of Kanmu's most trusted advisors, he proposed the quiet and fertile area along the Yodo River as the new site of the capital. This area was known as Nagaoka.

It is safe to assume that Tanetsugu earned his rank. He had to climb the political ladder before finally being awarded the rank of *chūnagon* (a counselor of the second rank in the imperial house). Competition was high, especially since he was of a lesser branch of the mighty Fujiwara clan. Yet, Tanetsugu was able to soar high in his career, eventually getting the promotion he deserved through his own merit and loyalty to the emperor. Therefore, it is not surprising that Kanmu listened when he recommended Nagaoka as the new seat of imperial power.

However, before he could make a decision, Kanmu had to launch an official inspection of the new site. A team was assembled, comprising Tanetsugu himself and other noblemen who held important positions in the court, such as Fujiwara no Oguromaro, Saeko no Imaemishi, Ki no Funamori, Ōnakatomi no Kōyu, and Sakanoue no Karitamaro.

The team brought back good news. The area was ideal. It had open space perfect for palace grounds and flowing water for both transport and irrigation. More importantly, it was far from the watchful gaze of Nara's powerful Buddhist institutions. After reading through the report, Emperor Kanmu approved of the site, kickstarting the construction of the new capital, Nagaoka-kyō, in 784 CE. Tanetsugu was trusted to oversee the construction. Things, however, would turn south even before the palace walls were fully raised.

A model of Nagaoka-kyō.[55]

A year later, Tanetsugu was suddenly attacked. While he was carrying out his duties at the site of the new capital, he was shot by an arrow. Tanetsugu survived the night, but the wound claimed his life the following day. The emperor was away when the attack happened. He was visiting Yamato Province when the bad news arrived. It is safe to assume that the sudden death of his trusted advisor might have struck him with both grief and unease. The situation in the imperial court turned chaotic. Not only had they lost a reliable figure in the court, but Nagaoka-kyō was also stained before it could stand.

An investigation was launched to catch the individual who shot the arrow and those with whom he conspired. First, the authorities arrested Ōtomo no Takeyoshi. He was interrogated, but more questions arose rather than answers. Within days, ten more men were arrested and executed, including Ōtomo no Tsuguhito and Saeki no Takanari. Even Ōtomo no Yakamochi, who had died a month prior to Tanetsugu's assassination, was not spared from punishment. He was posthumously named as the ringleader of the plot. Whether or not the accusation was true, we will never be certain. Yakamochi was an influential statesman and one of the five great poets at that time, but his legacy was formally erased by the court. His name was removed from the official register of honored officials, as if his poetry and service never existed. His son was also affected. Not only was he stripped of his rank, but he was also forced into exile, though he regained his rank years later.

Although the one who first recommended the site was no longer around, work at Nagaoka continued. However, misfortune followed. Nagaoka was struck by floods and epidemics, leading the Japanese to believe that the land was cursed. Each day, the court grew more wary. Emperor Kanmu made the decision to abandon the city after a decade. The court relocated once more in 794, this time to Heian-kyō, which would later become known as Kyoto. This city remained as the imperial capital for over a millennium.

Ankō, the Emperor Whose Reign Ended as It Began

The nineteenth emperor of Japan, Ingyō, finally breathed his last in 453 CE. He reigned over the land for slightly more than four decades. However, a problem arose over who should take the mantle and ascend to the throne. In keeping with imperial custom, it was understood that the firstborn would succeed his father. In this case, the candidate was Ingyō's eldest son, Prince Kinashi no Karu. However, things began to change when Karu found himself in a scandal. He had fallen in love with his own half-sister, Princess Karu no Ōiratsume. He was said to have seduced the princess. When the incestuous relationship between the two was made known to the court, the majority of the officials shunned him. This particular information was not only limited to those in the palace; as time passed, the public also became aware of the relationship. Karu's reputation collapsed as a result.

This gave way for Karu's younger brother, Prince Anaho, to step forward and claim the throne. Since Karu was losing all the support he had from his retainers, Anaho thought he was the best fit to succeed their father. A struggle between the two brothers ensued. Details of their conflict are scarce, but Karu was said to have been overwhelmed by his brother. He eventually fled and took refuge at a noble family's residence. Here, he took his final stand, but his fate was already written. In the aftermath of the conflict, Karu committed honorary suicide.

The *Kojiki* offers a different version of Karu's fate. According to this version of events, Karu chose to surrender to Prince Anaho. As a result, he was banished to Iyo. His lover and half-sister was also said to have remained loyal to the end. Karu no Ōiratsume reunited with Karu afterward and later committed suicide together.

Regardless of the different versions, the aftermath of the event remained the same. Prince Anaho ascended to the throne in 453 CE, ruling under the name Emperor Ankō. Little did he know that he would not remain on the Chrysanthemum Throne for very long.

As part of his effort to secure power and manage alliances, Emperor Ankō decided to unite his younger brother, Prince Ōhatuse no Wakatakeru, with a woman from a noble branch of the imperial line. This woman was the sister of his uncle, Prince Ookusaka, who went by the name Hatahihime. Ankō dispatched his servant to negotiate the arrangement.

Prince Ookusaka received his guest and almost immediately expressed his consent to the marriage. Delighted, he entrusted the servant with a jeweled coronet. This token of approval was supposed to be presented to the emperor. Perhaps greed suddenly consumed him, as the servant chose to keep the coronet for himself. Upon returning to the palace, he lied to Emperor Ankō. He claimed that Prince Ookusaka refused to consider the marriage proposal. This enraged the emperor, leading him to act hastily. Without investigating the situation, Ankō sent his soldiers to Ookusaka's residence. They killed him and seized his wife, Nakashi, the daughter of Emperor Richū (the seventeenth emperor of Japan). Hatahihime was also taken and married to Ōhatuse, just as the emperor had planned.

Nakashi was brought to the palace and stripped of her mourning. Without having a choice, she was married to Ankō in 455 CE. The emperor, who claimed to have loved her deeply, made her empress. Ankō even adopted her six-year-old son named Mayuwa.

Mayuwa became part of court life, but Ankō never trusted the boy. After all, Mayuwa was the son of the very person he had killed. The emperor eventually confided his worry to Nakashi sometime in the autumn of 456 CE. He expressed his worry that one day Mayuwa would learn the truth and seek to avenge his father's murder. The story goes that Mayuwa overheard this conversation. After finding out the truth, he was said to have quietly crept to the side of the emperor as he lay asleep in Nakashi's lap. Armed with a sword, the boy beheaded the emperor. Just like that, Ankō, who was fifty-six years old at that time, left the throne vacant. He left no children of his own.

Chapter 3 – Natural Disasters of Ancient Japan: The Works of Mother Nature or Divine Retribution?

Earthquakes, plagues, famines, and eruptions were recurring episodes in the history of Japan. However, these events were rarely viewed as misfortunes that occurred due to science or nature. Instead, they were thought to be messages, signs, or warnings sent from the spirits, gods, or the restless dead. To their eyes, mountains smoking because of an eruption might signal divine fury, while a sudden outbreak of an illness meant they had angered a spirit. In their ancient beliefs, harmony, or *wa*, was the ideal that bound heaven, earth, and mankind together. When that balance broke, something had to answer for it.

This understanding was governed by two spiritual systems. The first one was Shinto, the indigenous belief system of Japan. Those who embraced Shintoism were taught that all things in the world had a *kami* or a spirit dwelling within them, be it the many mountains in Japan, the flowing rivers, trees, or even pebbles at the side of the road. These kami could be gentle or wrathful. Respecting them would ensure rewards like good harvests and protection from evil. However, when dishonored, these spirits would not shy away from showing their wrath.

The *onryō*, for example, were spirits that were believed to be the cause of many natural misfortunes that struck Japan. These vengeful ghosts were typically born from injustice, betrayal, or unresolved resentment. They were thought to have the ability to summon a variety of natural occurrences, like storms, plagues, and earthquakes, to punish those who wronged them and, at times, everyone around them.

One of the most popular onryō in Japanese history was none other than Emperor Sutoku. Once respected and held in high esteem, his story ended terribly. Even after death, many pointed their fingers toward him as the cause of disasters.

Sutoku reigned over the land during the early 12th century CE. He eventually became entangled in a brutal succession crisis following his abdication. The conflict escalated into the Hōgen Rebellion of 1156. In the end, Sutoku and his forces were defeated. The former emperor was exiled to the remote province of Sunuki.

Here, Sutoku was said to have gained a new interest. He devoted himself to copying Buddhist scriptures. Hoping to win back his honor, he sent these sacred texts as offerings to the imperial court. However, the court rejected them, worried that Sutoku had ill intentions and cursed the papers. When the scriptures returned unopened, the former emperor felt both humiliated and angry. He then declared his wish to abandon his humanity and return one day as a demonic spirit.

Sutoku eventually passed away in 1164. Legend has it that by the time of his death, the former emperor had a rather daunting appearance. His hair had grown wild, and his nails were extremely long. It was as if he had already begun his transformation into a demon.

A painting depicting Emperor Sutoku's transformation as an onryō.[56]

Soon after news of his death, Kyoto faced multiple calamities. Great fires threatened the capital, and lightning destroyed palaces. Plague also spread across the land, and those who once sided with Sutoku's rivals began to die mysteriously. Eventually, the people concluded that it was Sutoku's spirit that wreaked all this havoc. Desperate to rid their land of the evil spirit of the former emperor, the imperial court held rituals and memorial services to appease him. Hoping they could turn his rage into protection, the Japanese chose to enshrine Sutoku as a kami at Shiramine-jingū.

The worship hall of Shiramine-jingū.[57]

Of course, the belief that these natural disasters were the result of human wrongdoing was not only restricted to Shinto. Buddhism, which arrived in Japan during the 6th century CE, also added its own explanations to these unfortunate events. The religion introduced the Japanese to the law of karma. This is the idea that the suffering of today is the result of moral failures in the past done by either an individual or a community. However, it is worth noting that Buddhism in Japan did not erase ancient beliefs. Instead, it layered them together. A vengeful spirit might be seen as both an onryō and a soul trapped by karmic anger. To appease or repel these spirits, Shinto called for ritual purification, while Buddhism typically prescribed sutras, offerings, and merit-making.

Indeed, to modern eyes, these may seem like superstitions. However, they were also tools of interpretation. They gave meaning to tragedy, allowed people to act in the face of the uncontrollable, and shaped some of Japan's most important religious, architectural, and political decisions.

Mount Asama

Mount Asama may have the appearance of a normal mountain. Sitting in central Honshū, in between the provinces of Shinano and Kōzuke (known today as Nagano and Gunma), the mountain's last eruption occurred in 2019. Yet it still puffs white smoke, as if it is continuously reminding people that it is very much alive.

Mount Asama viewed from the south.[58]

While to the rest of the world Mount Asama is just another active volcano, the Japanese consider it sacred. To them, the mountain is the seat of a powerful kami. Since Mount Asama is also the home of Kongoshoji Temple (believed to be the shield of Ise Jingu, the most important shrine in Japan dedicated to the sun goddess Amaterasu), it was a must for pilgrims to visit the mountain first before ending their journey at Ise Jingu. Despite being a sacred location, the people also feared it. They believed that if they were to disrespect the kami residing in the mountain, a catastrophe would befall them.

The 12th-century nobleman Fujiwara no Munetada, for instance, once witnessed the wrath of the kami of Asama. He recorded the event, which took place in 1108, in his diary. According to the nobleman, the episode began when he suddenly saw strange things in the sky. He witnessed sunsets that appeared redder than usual and ashfall reaching distant provinces. When reports of crop failure and odd signs arrived at the court, he knew that something sinister was about to happen.

He was right. The eruption of Mount Asama began on August 29th, 1108, and possibly lasted through the first few weeks of October. The mountain stood far from the capital in Kyoto, yet the effects could be felt throughout the entire Japanese peninsula.

For days, the volcano spewed ash and gas, eventually covering the land like a blanket. In the nearby provinces, villagers woke to skies the color of rust. Their routines had changed too. With the fields of rice wilting, they were unable to till the land. Not only were food supplies dwindling, but the water was also turning bitter. Over time, many fell ill, especially the children and the elderly. Despite the distance between Mount Asama and the capital, it was impossible for the imperial court to ignore the state of the people affected by the eruption.

However, an eruption of such a scale was not seen as merely a natural event by those in the Heian period. They thought of it as a divine rebuke. For years, the mountain had been sitting quietly. Surely, the kami of Asama was pleased with them at that time. Now that the terrible eruption had happened, the Japanese were sure that it was the result of the kami feeling displeased by their actions. Whispers went around, questioning what had gone wrong. Had a certain ritual gone unfinished? Perhaps the emperor himself was at fault? Had he failed in his spiritual duties, or was corruption growing in the court?

To find out what was going on, the court put the priests to work. Some were sent to nearby shrines, and others were dispatched directly to the mountain's slopes. These priests were tasked with seeking answers from the heavens. Rites of purification took place. Prayers were chanted day and night in the hopes they could tame the anger of the mountain's spirit. Even court rituals in Kyoto were adjusted in response to the event.

Fast forward to about two months later, and the Japanese were finally able to breathe easy. The misfortune had passed, and the fierce mountain had calmed down, as if returning to its slumber once more. Perhaps the rituals had worked after all. Unfortunately, this was not the last time the mountain ever wreaked havoc across Japan.

It would wake from its deep slumber many centuries later, in 1783. This eruption caused catastrophic famine and the deaths of tens of thousands. Just as before, the Japanese thought of the event as a punishment. Many pointed their fingers at the Tokugawa shogunate's neglect of the poor and their harsh policies. It is safe to say that the idea that disaster reflected injustice endured long after the Heian era.

But while the ancients sought meaning in spirits and curses, modern science sought patterns. Modern researchers analyzed the 1108 eruption of Mount Asama, and they found evidence that its impact was not limited only to Japan. Ice core samples in Europe, particularly in Greenland and the Alps, show a spike in volcanic sulfate that matches the Asama eruption's estimated timing. It was also around this same period that European sources recorded a sharp decline in the temperature. The region was said to have experienced unseasonal frosts. Because of this major temperature change, their crops saw widespread failures. In certain parts of northern Europe, famine began to take place in the years following 1108. Starvation and civil unrest soon became common. This study led both historians and climatologists to arrive at the conclusion that the ash and sulfur from Mount Asama might have entered the stratosphere and triggered a hemispheric cooling effect—a distant consequence of a volcanic plume from a mountain most Europeans had never heard of.

The Wronged Prince Who Was Posthumously Named Emperor

Prince Sawara was the son of Emperor Kōnin, the forty-ninth emperor of Japan. He was bestowed with the title of crown prince in the year 781 when his elder brother, Prince Yamabe, sat on the Chrysanthemum Throne as Emperor Kanmu. At first glance, it all seemed to go well; the imperial line would continue in harmony. Things, however, went south when the court received the news of an unfortunate death. Fujiwara no Tanetsugu had died after an arrow struck him as he was overseeing the construction of the new capital at Nagaoka.

Since Tanetsugu was a person of high influence and respect—he was Kanmu's most trusted official—the court was adamant in finding those who were involved in his murder. They took even the slightest suspicions seriously. Many were arrested and interrogated. Even Prince Sawara himself was not free from the suspicious gaze of the court.

The prince was said to have voiced his concern and opposition to the emperor's decision to move the capital. He was then arrested, as the court claimed that he had played a hand in orchestrating the assassination of Fujiwara Tanetsugu. The court did not wait for conclusive evidence and instead stripped the prince of his title. He was then exiled to Awaji Island, which was a common punishment for disgraced nobles.

Fate, however, had another path for the wronged prince. It is believed that he never reached Awaji. As a sign of protest, the prince chose to fast. Knowing that he had been treated unjustly, Sawara refused food and drink, which ultimately cost him his life.

For many, this was the end of Sawara's story. The Japanese, however, were soon forced to face the consequences of his death. In the years that followed, an invisible retaliation took form. The mother of Emperor Kanmu, Takano no Niigasa, and his own wife, Fujiwara no Otomuro, suddenly died in succession. Even the newly appointed crown prince fell ill. Misfortunes did not only strike the imperial court and the nobles. Famine soon swept the land, followed by floods and disease that disrupted the construction at Nagaoka. This series of unfortunate events led the people to believe that it had been done by none other than the dead Prince Sawara, who had become a *goryō*—a wrathful spirit, usually nobles and high-ranking individuals, who died unjustly (often the result of political intrigue).

The ancient Japanese believed that death, especially one that happened violently or unjustly, would result in *kegare*, or spiritual pollution. For a court that held strong Shinto beliefs, they saw the disasters as more than just coincidences. They thought of it as messages from the dead. Emperor Kanmu grew anxious when this chaos happened during his reign without rest. So, he decided to begin various acts of appeasement. Hoping he could calm the spirit of his brother, Kanmu posthumously elevated Prince Sawara to emperor. He bestowed upon him the name Emperor Sudō.

The Shinto shrine for Emperor Sudō.[59]

Knowing that it was important for a spirit to have a resting place, Emperor Kanmu ordered the construction of a shrine in 794 CE. Known as the Kamigoryō Shrine, it was built on the former site of a Buddhist temple north of Heian-kyō (present-day Kyoto).

The Kamigoryō Shrine in Kyoto.[60]

This was where the spirit of the wronged prince was enshrined. Since a goryō could only be calmed through ritual and worship, the Japanese made offerings to the spirit and held festivals. Through these efforts, they transformed Sawara's wrath into protection for the city.

Today, the shrine is home to eight figures, who either died unluckily or as a result of being entangled in political strife during the Nara and Heian periods. Also known collectively as the Eight Goryō Deities, those enshrined alongside Prince Sawara are Empress Dowager Inoue, Prince Iyo, Fujiwara no Yoshiko, Tachibana no Hayanari, Funya no Miyatamaro, Kibi no Makibi, and Yakusanoikazuchi (the collective name for the eight kami of thunder).

The Smallpox Epidemic of 735

Japan was forced to face another episode of catastrophe in the mid-8th century when a wave of smallpox tore through the population. Beginning in Daizafu, which was also the administrative center of Kyūshū, the disease moved rapidly northward, obliterating the lives of many for about two years. It is safe to imagine that Nara (known back then as Heijo-kyō, which was also the capital at that time) trembled as reports arrived before the gates non-stop, carrying news of how villages had been emptied by the disease overnight and how corpses were left unburied, either because none were left alive to do so or because the people were scared to go near the bodies.

The Japanese had never seen such a disease taking over the empire before; this was the first time smallpox ever made an appearance across the Japanese peninsula. The people saw the catastrophe as a spiritual punishment rather than a natural outbreak. They believed that the spirits had been angered by their acts of negligence, injustice, or sin. They believed that the disease had been brought onto them by a certain demon known as Hosogami.

The smallpox demon was said to have carried the disease with him as he traveled from one town to another. Along the way, he would infect the people with smallpox. The demon was also thought to have a fearsome temper, which was reflected in the ferocity of the disease itself. Interestingly, Hosogami was terrified of dogs, and he hated the color red. Scholars suggest that this hatred was due to the color being the symbol of good health. When the body of those with the disease was covered in a red rash, this was thought to be a sign of recovery.

The ancient Japanese made sure to make use of the demon's weakness. Since the color could repel the demon, many houses had red woodblock prints known as *akae* hanging around. They also wore red clothing more than usual and had other protective talismans close by, which included dolls and toys in the shape of dogs and the red-haired sea spirits named shōjō. The people also used images of Daruma (the popular traditional Japanese doll modeled after Bodhidharma, the founder of Zen Buddhism), the large and bearded demon queller Shōki, and the folk hero named Kintarō.

There are also records of the ancient Japanese hosting community rituals as part of an effort to save themselves from the terrible disease. Known as Hōsōgami Okuri, this ritual was said to have been done to send off the demon from their villages and towns. The people would play drums, flutes, and bells as they paraded through the streets. They played songs and performed dances, sometimes in front of those infected, as acts to ward off the sickness.

These repellants, however, were not the only way for the people to protect themselves from the disease. Although Hōsōgami was a demon, he could also be appeased by rituals and offerings. There were some cases, especially in houses already affected by smallpox, where shrines for the demon were erected. These people saw Hōsōgami not as an evil spirit but as the savior of the people from the deadly disease. And so, they prayed to Hōsōgami so that he could spare the lives of their loved ones. Those who survived the disease also continued to offer their gratitude to Hōsōgami.

Those who viewed the demon as the cause of smallpox chose to leave their fate to other powerful deities and figures. The kami of hot springs, Sukunabikona, for instance, was increasingly worshiped during this period of time, given the deity's attributes in healing abilities. Another figure highly revered at that time of turmoil was the warrior Minamoto no Tametomo.

Minamoto no Tametomo defeating the smallpox demon.[61]

The belief that he had the ability to keep Hōsōgami away originated from a certain episode involving Tametomo fleeing during the Hōgen Rebellion. Following his exile to Izu Ōshima, the warrior made his escape to Hachijōjima. This was a time when smallpox was ravaging the empire. Interestingly, every region felt the wrath of Hōsōgami, except for Hachijōjima. This led the locals to believe that it had something to do with Tametomo's presence.

All the rituals and rites were not enough to drive Hōsōgami out of their empire in time. It is estimated that one-third of Japan's population perished from the disease by the time the epidemic had passed. Not even the richest and most influential nobles were spared during this time of turmoil, including the four high-ranking brothers of the Fujiwara clan. Their deaths undoubtedly disrupted the balance of power at the imperial court. This dark time greatly affected Emperor Shōmu, which resulted in him launching a few temple-building projects. One of the most famous that came from this project was none other than the Tōdai-ji in Nara, which housed one of the largest bronze statues of Buddha (Daibutsu) in Japan.

A Plague Quelled by the Appointment of a Certain Priest and Sake

Smallpox was not the first disease-related catastrophe that ever ravaged the empire. Before temples dotted Nara and many years before the emperors ruled from Kyoto, the Japanese witnessed a plague that turned their empire into chaos. It happened during the reign of Emperor Sujin, the tenth emperor of Japan, who ruled from 97 BCE according to the traditional order of succession. Although he is widely accepted to be a real figure, some still doubt his existence and consider his rule to be legendary due to the lack of information.

According to ancient sources, the land was buckling beneath the weight of death as an unknown plague raged across the land. The *Nihon Shoki* highlighted the extent of the plague; it was said to have killed at least half of the population. In addition to the plague, crops struggled to grow, eventually withering. Livestock also perished, leaving the people in both hunger and despair. It was high time for them to seek answers from the divine. Emperor Sujin turned to rituals and prayers to heal his empire. Yet, none of the existing rites seemed to ease the suffering.

Things began to change when the emperor experienced a dream. In it, he saw the guardian spirit of the sacred Mount Miwa named Ōmanonushi. The guardian spirit spoke to him and demanded that rituals be conjured not by any priest but by a man named Ōtataneko. Only then would the plague subside, and the Japanese would be spared from further suffering. Emperor Sujin woke up with a racing heart, but he knew his dream was real. He wasted no time in sending emissaries throughout the land, hoping they could locate the man mentioned by Ōmanonushi.

Mount Miwa and the torii gate leading to Ōmiwa Shrine.[62]

When he was finally found, Sujin asked why the guardian spirit had asked specifically for him. Turns out, Ōtataneko was a descendant of Ōmanonushi. Without wasting any more precious time, the man was appointed head priest of Mount Miwa, where he was in charge of leading the many rituals and rites. This was believed to be the establishment of the worship of Ōmanonushi in the Shinto tradition. Just as the emperor had hoped, the plague began to subside. Perhaps now that Ōmanonushi was pleased, Japan was allowed to heal and thrive once more.

It is said that the appointment of Ōtataneko was not the only effort made by Emperor Sujin to appease the mountain spirit. He also called upon a renowned brewer named Takahashi and commissioned him to create a special batch of sake. They were then presented as a gift to Ōmanonushi at Mount Miwa. To this day, Lake Biwa, which was located near the mountain, is considered a sacred site, as its water is important for sake production. As a token of gratitude, Takahashi was later enshrined as the god of toji or brew master at the subsidiary shrine of Omiwa-jinja, known as Ikuhi-jinja.

Chapter 4 – Buddhism, Monks, and Scrolls

Emperor Kinmei had just received guests. It was the mid-6th century (possibly 552 CE), and an envoy all the way from the Korean kingdom of Baekje (also spelled as Paekche) had arrived in the capital, bearing gifts. They presented a small golden statue of Buddha Shakyamuni to the emperor, along with several volumes of Buddhist scriptures. They sought to introduce the religion to Japan.

The chronicle *Nihon Shoki*, for one, described that the emperor and his court were awestruck by the gifts, particularly the bronze statue of Buddha. This was not the first time Buddhism had entered Japan; the land already had immigrants from China and Korea who practiced Buddhism. However, this was the first time that the religion arrived in the palace. Emperor Kinmei, despite being said to have marveled at the Buddha's image, hesitated. He wondered if it was a good idea to adopt this foreign religion and introduce it to his people. He was afraid that embracing the religion with open arms might offend Japan's spirits and gods.

Therefore, the emperor turned to his top advisors. Almost immediately, the court split into factions. The powerful Soga clan was headed by Soga Iname at that time. He championed the new faith, explaining that every great civilization on the Asian continent had embraced Buddhism. "It makes no sense for Yamato alone to refuse it," he might have voiced.

On the other side of the ring were none other than the Mononobe and the Nakatomi clans. The Mononobe was spearheaded by Mononobe no Okoshi. While the Mononobe were the ones who handled the weapons and armor of the imperial palace, the Nakatomi were responsible for overseeing rituals of kami worship. These two clans were close allies, as they viewed themselves as the guardians of Shinto traditions. They were strongly against the adoption of Buddhism. They argued that abandoning their kami, the ones who had always protected their lands, would certainly invite their wrath and bring forth destruction and chaos.

Of course, underneath this religious debate was a struggle for political supremacy. The Soga clan was considered a relative newcomer during the period. Some believed their roots traced back to the Korean Peninsula. Because of their continental connections, they saw Buddhism as an opportunity to greatly enhance their influence at court. In comparison, the Mononobe clan had been around for a long time. Although the year of their establishment remains a mystery, they rose to prominence in the Kofun period, sometime in the 4th century CE. The Mononobe claimed to have descended from a kami named Nigihayahi no Mikoto (a legendary figure who ruled the land before Emperor Jimmu, the founder of the imperial dynasty). It makes sense that the Mononobe were rather conservative and wanted no change in the realm of religion and politics.

Seeing that the debate was getting heated, Emperor Kinmei came up with a temporary solution. Instead of adopting the religion right away, he entrusted the Buddha statue to Soga no Iname, allowing the clan to privately venerate it. Some viewed the emperor's decision as an experiment. If the foreign faith brought blessings, then perhaps Japan should consider embracing it; if misfortune followed, then it was clear that the Mononobe clan was right.

Soga no Iname brought the statue into his residence. He then built a shrine to house the image. From here on, the Soga clan began practicing Buddhist rituals. They began bowing before the gleaming statue sent from Baekje. However, things turned south for the Soga when disaster struck. Not long after they enshrined the Buddha statue, a plague occurred, sweeping through the capital. This mysterious pestilence claimed the lives of many, and it also threw the court into panic. Many nobles thought of the plague as no mere coincidence. They saw it as divine punishment for doubting the kami and embracing a new, foreign faith.

Kōgen-ji, the first Buddhist temple built by Soga no Iname.[68]

Mononobe no Okoshi was quick to seize the moment. Together with Nakatomi no Kamako (the leader of the Nakatomi clan), they went to persuade Emperor Kinmei. They claimed that the kami was extremely angered by the Soga clan's worship of the foreign god. The two anti-Buddhists also warned the emperor that things would only get worse if he allowed Buddhism to take root.

Witnessing that the plague was spreading as days went by, the emperor issued an order to halt the Buddhist rites and call for his subjects to immediately appease the Shinto kami. Following pressure from both the Mononobe and the Nakatomi clans, the emperor eventually ordered the destruction of the golden statue, along with the Buddhist shrines and temples. Without wasting any time, Mononobe no Okoshi gathered his men and stormed Soga Iname's residence. They made their way to the newly built temple and tore down the altar without remorse. They also seized the small Buddha statue. Determined to rid the land of the pollution brought by the new faith, the Mononobe burned the Buddhist temple to the ground.

Legend has it that Mononobe no Okoshi attempted to destroy the Buddha icon using a hammer, but interestingly, the statue proved unbreakable. So, he took the idol to a canal in Naniwa (near what is now Osaka) and cast it into the depths of the river. With his task done, Mononobe no Okoshi rushed to the palace to report his deeds to the emperor. Buddhist records, however, narrate that Okoshi's actions did not put a stop to the chaos. All of a sudden, a thunderstorm arrived, despite the clear sky. Perhaps as a result of dishonoring a sacred relic, a bolt of lightning was said to have struck the imperial palace, giving way to a merciless fire.

The debate of whether or not Japan should embrace Buddhism was not settled within a few days. The clans continued to argue, each side viewing the natural disaster as divine vindication. The Mononobe used the same excuse of the new faith enraging the ancient kami. They pointed their fingers and cited every misfortune, such as crop failures, illnesses, and ill omens, as evidence that accepting a foreign deity would only deepen the land's misery. The Soga also refused to back down. They claimed that the misfortunes were the Buddha's way of punishing those who obstructed the path to enlightenment. At the same time, they rebuilt Buddhist shrines, preserved remaining scriptures, and quietly trained monks.

The conflict went on for years. It was clear that the imperial court stood divided like never before. Back and forth the struggle went. Instead of facing each other on battlefields, the clans expressed their disagreements via temples and shrines. The Soga would rebuild temples just for the Mononobe and the Nakatomi to burn them again. Matters got even worse when the land received news of Emperor Yōmei's death sometime in the late 580s. With a vacancy on the throne, the rival clans raced to place their own candidate as the next emperor. Soga no Umako, now the head of the Soga clan, supported Prince Hatsusebe, who favored Buddhism. The Mononobe, now under Mononobe no Moriya, had another name in mind; they planned to put Prince Anahobe, the son of Emperor Bidatsu, on the throne.

A portrait of Prince Shōtoku on Japan's banknote (first issued in 1958 and suspended in 1986).[64]

A full-scale civil war soon took place, culminating with the armies of both the Mononobe and Soga gathering near Mount Shigi for one last fight. The Soga clan also had the support of the sixteen-year-old Prince Shōtoku. Believed to be a devout Buddhist, Prince Shōtoku was said to have made a vow before marching into battle. Legend has it that the prince cut down a sacred tree and carved it into an image of the Four Heavenly Kings of Buddhism (known in Japanese as Shitennō). Along with Soga no Umako, Prince Shōtoku prayed to the Four Heavenly Kings, vowing that they would build a temple dedicated to the Shitennō if the heavens blessed their journey and gave them a victory. The sight of the two influential figures praying boosted the morale of the Soga troops.

The battle was fought sometime in July 587 CE, three decades following the start of the rivalry between the Mononobe and the Soga. Suffice it to say that the battle was brutal. Blades clashed, and volleys of arrows filled the sky. However, as if the heavens were siding with the Soga, Mononobe no Moriya faced his demise. Near the end of the battle, an archer successfully shot his arrow directly toward the Mononobe leader. With the death of Moriya, the rest of the Mononobe forces were forced to retreat.

Finally, the last great obstacle to Buddhism's rise was swept aside. When Empress Suiko rose to the throne following the death of Emperor Sushun, Buddhism could be seen in nearly every inch of the capital. Court ceremonies began to incorporate Buddhist elements, and monasteries received imperial backing. Scriptures were copied, and more monks were sent to study in China and Korea.

As for the Mononobe, the clan became a subject of the past. Many died in battle, while those who survived were dispersed. Some moved on under a different name. As for the Soga, this was only the beginning of their story. While Soga no Umako's influence soared, giving his clan's name a higher reputation in the court, Prince Shōtoku worked on fulfilling his promise to the Buddhist god. He built the Shitennō-ji temple in 593 CE in honor of the Four Heavenly Kings of Buddhism. The temple still stands in Osaka today and is known as one of Japan's earliest Buddhist temples.

Shitennō-ji temple, Osaka.[65]

Kūkai and the Forbidden Scrolls of the Tang

Although Shintoism was never erased from ancient Japan, Buddhism continued to flourish. Then, in the early 9th century CE, the people saw the birth of two new schools of Buddhism: Tendai and Shingon. Before the arrival of these two schools, Buddhism in Japan, especially during the Nara period (710–794 CE), was heavily scholastic. Buddhists typically entered six main schools, which included Hossō, Sanron, and Kegon. These schools contributed to a strong academic foundation, but they were also deeply rooted in the intellectual traditions of the Chinese mainland. They focused on doctrinal study and monastic discipline. These traditional doctrines made enlightenment feel rather distant and abstract since it seemed like a pursuit reserved only for scholars and monks buried in scrolls day and night.

More often than not, these sects emphasized that enlightenment could not be attained within a single lifetime. Believers had to go through countless cycles of rebirth before they could glimpse enlightenment. That is, if they succeeded in accumulating enough wisdom and virtue. For most common people, reaching salvation seemed almost unreachable. Without an elite education, access to sutras, or the capacity to engage in intensive study and meditation, most laypeople could only hope to accumulate merit for a better rebirth, not transcend the cycle altogether.

The newly introduced schools, however, deviated from the traditional doctrines. Tendai was established first by the monk Saichō upon his return from China in 805 CE. The school was based on the Lotus Sutra. It emphasized the idea that all beings possess a Buddha nature, which meant it was possible for everyone to attain enlightenment. Tendai also advocated a flexible, inclusive approach, blending meditation, precepts, doctrinal study, and even esoteric practices. The center of this school was on Mount Hiei, just northeast of Kyoto. Tendai would also give birth to some of Japan's most influential monks many years later, including the founders of later sects like Pure Land and Zen.

Meanwhile, Shingon offered a more mystical path. It was the brainchild of a monk named Kūkai (who was also known as Kōbō Daishi). Similar to Saichō, Kūkai began to lay the foundations for his school upon his return from China. Being Japan's first ever fully fledged Esoteric Buddhist school (known in their tongue as *mikkyō*), Shingon emphasized that enlightenment could be attained in this life through secret rituals, symbolic gestures (mudras), visualizations, and sacred chants (mantras). While Tendai focused on accommodating many teachings, Shingon honed in on the cosmic truth embodied in the Mahāvairocana Buddha, the Buddha of the Great Sun.

Similar to Tendai, the school of Shingon received imperial support despite the differences in their teachings. Shingon would thrive as one of the most popular sects of Buddhism in Japan, but few are actually aware of how its founder, Kūkai, secretly smuggled esoteric scrolls and ritual texts from Tang China into Japan.

In contrast to Saichō, who already had a reputation for his knowledge and wisdom in the imperial court, Kūkai had no major political patronage when he set sail for China. In fact, Kūkai's family background had a darker history. Born in Sanuki Province on the island of Shikoku, he was a part of the Saeki family. This cadet branch of the aristocracy was once connected to the capital, but for reasons lost to time, the Saeki fell out of favor and was eventually exiled from Heiankyō. This was not a major problem for Kūkai, as he was destined to flourish in the realm of religion.

Ancient sources claimed that he was gifted. One episode recalled the seven-year-old Kūkai climbing atop a mountain near his home. Here, he declared that if he were to serve Buddhist law, then he would be saved no matter what. He then leaped off the mountain and was miraculously caught midair by heavenly beings. Another tale spoke of Kūkai receiving a sign of his talent as he was in deep ritual meditation. The morning star was believed to have descended from the sky and entered his mouth. This scene was interpreted as a celestial sign that he was to become a saint later on.

A depiction of Kūkai as a boy, flying on a lotus to heaven.[66]

Although the stories are considered more myth than fact, it is impossible to dismiss that Kūkai's actual life was remarkable. He entered monastic life while he was still young, and by the age of seventeen, he had moved to the capital, where he spent most of his time studying Confucian philosophy at the state-sponsored college. His mentor was his uncle. A scholar himself, he taught Kūkai classical Chinese and poetry. However, after a few years of burying himself in knowledge, Kūkai soon found Confucian teachings insufficient for the questions that stirred his soul.

So, he turned to the Buddhist texts that were circulating around the capital. This was when he became increasingly fascinated with the esoteric phrases and mantras embedded in untranslated sutras. Day and night, he sought the deeper and hidden teachings behind them. Through his exceptional command of the Chinese language, which developed after years of never-ending study, Kūkai became part of the Japanese diplomatic embassy to Tang China. However, he barely had a reputation at that time. He participated in the embassy not as an important figure but as a low-ranking monk whose name was barely remembered by those in court.

In Tang China, Kūkai followed the guidance of Huiguo, the master of Esoteric Buddhism and the abbot of the Ching Lung (Green Dragon) Temple. Kūkai was initiated into the most profound teachings of the two main esoteric texts: the *Mahāvairocana Sūtra* and the *Vajraśekhara Sūtra* (*Kongōchō-kyō*). For nearly two years, Kūkai showed his ultimate dedication to the teachings and wisdom of Huiguo. Perhaps impressed by the young monk, Huiguo named Kūkai his successor. He granted the young monk full transmission and urged him to return to Japan so that he could spread the teachings.

It is safe to assume that Kūkai was eager to continue his journey and spread these teachings. Unfortunately, there was a complication. The Tang government had strict limitations on the export of their religious texts and images. Many of the core scriptures of Esoteric Buddhism—texts like the *Mahāvairocana Sūtra* and *Vajraśekhara Sūtra*, along with ritual manuals and complex mandala diagrams—were considered restricted. Some versions of these scrolls were not yet officially catalogued or translated. Therefore, it made sense for the authorities to put restrictions on them.

Taking them back to Japan could easily be seen as theft of cultural and religious secrets. Harsh punishment would surely follow if he were caught. But Kūkai was headstrong enough to return to Japan with them. How exactly he managed to do so remains a question.

Many suggested that Kūkai was given full permission and even assistance. Based on certain records, monks in Tang China were said to have worked tirelessly to copy the sacred scriptures in time and help him prepare for his return. After all, Huiguo had named Kūkai his successor, so it made sense for them to prepare everything before his departure back to Japan.

However, there is another theory. Kūkai was said to have broken the rules and brought back certain scrolls and ritual items without formal approval from the Tang authorities. Modern scholars believe this was what happened, especially since Kūkai was described as a low-ranking monk when the embassy took place. He was almost unknown at court and certainly had no political influence to demand state-sanctioned exports of sensitive religious materials.

The number and value of items he returned with also raised suspicions. Kūkai arrived in Japan with complete sets of mandala diagrams, commentaries, Sanskrit treatises, ritual manuals, and bronze ritual implements, all of which seemed excessive for someone of his reputation. The scholar Ryuichi Abe, in his work called *The Weaving of Mantra*, notes that while Kūkai's mission to bring Esoteric Buddhism to Japan was clearly transformative, it might have involved sidestepping bureaucratic and diplomatic protocols.

However, whether sanctioned or secretly obtained, Kūkai played a hand in reshaping the Buddhist landscape in Japan. The scrolls, manuscripts, and relics that he brought back formed the basis of Japan's first complete Esoteric curriculum.

The Stolen Relics From Silla

Japan not only welcomed knowledge from Tang China but also embraced it from its closer neighbor, Silla (Korea). By the 7th century, Silla was already known to be deeply Buddhist. The kingdom was also believed to have been the home to many important relics, including bone fragments and ashes of the Buddha. They were kept safely in grand temples, such as the one famously known as Hwangnyongsa.

A model of the Hwangnyongsa pagoda. The real structure was destroyed in 1238.[67]

Then, by the mid-8th century, a controversial event happened that involved a group of Japanese monks or emissaries. Possibly acting under the orders of the emperor, they were sent to Silla to pay homage and bring back sacred relics of the Buddha himself. This was possibly due to the belief that the relics could protect the state and sanctify the temples.

Some sources suggest that the Japanese negotiated with Silla. In exchange for these sacred treasures, the Japanese promised trade, tribute, and alliance to Silla. It is plausible that the negotiation never bore fruit. Silla either refused the exchange outright or gave only partial access to the treasures. The scholar Jonathan Best wrote in his book *A History of the Early Korean Kingdom of Paekche* that Silla was extremely protective of its relics. It was common for Silla to decline export requests from its neighbors, including China and Japan.

Interestingly, the *Nihon Shoki* consisted of several entries that noted the arrival of relics from Silla. Details of how exactly they were obtained were written rather vaguely. This raised suspicions among scholars and historians. Some scholars suggest there is a possibility that the relics were taken from Silla without official approval. Perhaps the Japanese were able to reach an agreement with lower-level Silla monks, but the request was never approved by the royal court.

Of course, there is no concrete evidence to conclude that the relics were illegally taken from the Korean kingdom. The historical record on this is too thin, and the details provided in the *Nihon Shoki* are too ambiguous. But still, the possibility is not to be dismissed entirely, especially when there are records of rising tensions between Silla and Japan in the late 8th century CE. Although they never fought direct wars with each other during this period, a few accounts claimed Silla once lodged complaints about the Japanese acting unilaterally and disrespecting the royal family in certain exchanges. While these grievances were not explicitly tied to the theft of relics, they point to a broader pattern of friction, possibly reflecting episodes where Japan bypassed formal diplomatic channels and perhaps even secured sacred objects through unofficial or unsanctioned dealings with individual monks or factions within Silla.

Chapter 5 – The Emishi People: The Antagonists in the Eyes of the Yamato

Prisoners had arrived in the imperial capital of Kyoto. They were escorted under full guard. Each of the soldiers bore an insignia of the imperial army, and they were all armed to the teeth. Their arrival did not go unnoticed. The people of the city lined along the edges of the street, hoping they could glimpse the prisoners. Not only did their arrival attract the attention of the market vendors, but courtiers running morning errands and even monks returning from prayers at the nearby temple stood along the street to watch. They knew that these people were not just some rebels caught from minor skirmishes but high-profile enemies that the Yamato had been fighting for decades.

Although their hands were bound, the prisoners walked upright. Their eyes were steady, as if they did not regret their actions. When they finally reached the entrance of the imperial compound, the two prisoners were made to kneel. Just a few steps from them was a figure who was well respected by the court. His name was Sakanoue no Tamuramaro. Dressed in his court attire rather than his polished armor, he observed the prisoners with a mix of feelings. He was the one who had led the victorious campaign against them, and it was because of him that these men had been captured and brought into the city. They had been causing trouble for the Yamato for many years, yet Tamuramaro felt like it was his duty to speak on their behalf. After all, these prisoners had surrendered willingly. They did so not because they were defeated but to prevent more bloodshed. Tamuramaro believed that counted for something.

A drawing depicting Sakanoue no Tamuramaro.[68]

With a stern voice, he submitted a petition to the imperial court, requesting clemency. He laid out his reasoning. He saw value in the survival of these prisoners. They were leaders of their people, so they had influence. Surely they could help the Yamato stabilize the north.

However, despite his confident voice, Tamuramaro knew reason alone was not enough in Kyoto. Even though the decision had not yet been announced, deep down, he already knew what would happen to the prisoners.

The Story of the Emishi

Tōhoku, a region of Japan's Honshu island, was the home of the Emishi first, before the imperial forces raised their banners above the pine forests. Yet, to court scribes, they were nothing more than strangers and, later, monsters in their eyes.

The Japanese chronicles were never kind to the Emishi. They painted them as wild outsiders. Although they only met them on the battlefield, they wrote as if they had lived in their communities for ages. Some records claim that the Emishi were uncivilized people whose men and women lived together promiscuously. These records tell us of how the Emishi lived in holes rather than the typical thatched cottage (known as *minka*). When summer came, they lived in nests. Not only did they dress in nothing except fur, but the Emishi also drank blood. The Yamato had a few terms for these outsiders; they called them "Eastern savages" or "barbarians." Another popular term used in their records was *mōjin*, which simply means "hairy people." These terms were used by the Yamato to separate the "civilized" from the "uncivilized."

Now, why were the Emishi described in ancient records in such a degrading way? The answer is quite simple. The Yamato court was eager to legitimize its influence across the Japanese peninsula. When the Emishi refused to bow down to them, they cast the Emishi as barbarians to be subdued, much like the neighboring Chinese dynasties that spoke in the same way of civilizing their frontiers. However, beyond this propaganda lies a more complex reality.

The Emishi were far from a primitive society. In fact, they had a rich culture and society adapted to the northern wilderness. They were skilled hunters, gatherers, and fishers who lived in mountain forests and river valleys. Like the Yamato, they also cultivated the land. They planted and harvested crops like millet and barley. Paddy fields could also be found, especially in communities located in the northern lowlands, where the temperature was warmer. The records claiming that they lived in holes were nothing more than a simplification. In the eyes of the Yamato, any way of life that differed from their own was seen as primitive.

In contrast to their descriptions, the Emishi were not cave-dwellers. Like many other people who lived in colder climates, they adapted their homes to the changing of the seasons. When winter came, they hunkered down in warm pit-houses, which they dug into the earth. These structures were reinforced with timber and thatch to trap heat and block the cold wind. These semi-subterranean dwellings were practical, especially since they offered insulation against the long northern winter. During the summer, the Emishi would typically move into above-ground huts, which were built with raised floors to avoid moisture and pests.

Perhaps one of the few things that the Yamato got right in their chronicles was how the Emishi dressed themselves. They typically wore clothing made from fur and deerskin. Interestingly, they had tattoos adorning their bodies, a practice also observed among the indigenous people of Hokkaidō, the Ainu. Emishi men had full beards, and more often than not, their hair was tied in either topknots or buns. Interestingly, this style was depicted on ancient Jōmon clay figurines. At times, the men also tucked arrows into their hair. They also spoke a different language, which was incomprehensible to the Yamato to the point where officials needed interpreters whenever they ventured north.

Early encounters between the Yamato and the Emishi were not always violent. They engaged in a mix of trade and alliance. The year 658 CE, for instance, saw the Yamato join hands with the Emishi. It began with the frontier general named Abe no Hirafu, who, under the order of Emperor Tenji, led a naval expedition up the northwest coast. He later forged an alliance with local Emishi chiefs. Together, they attacked a rival people known as the Mishihase. While this alliance was rare, it does not erase the fact that the Emishi were diplomatically savvy. It was only during the late 7th and early 8th centuries that relations began to turn sour. As imperial ambitions grew larger, the Yamato began pushing their grip northward. New roads were established. Fortresses sprang up on land that was completely unfamiliar to them.

The Yamato finished building a fort at Ideha (located in Dewa, along the Japan Sea coast) sometime in 709 CE. The Emishi struck the Yamato almost immediately. They raided this new outpost and scattered settlements as a warning that these lands were not empty for the taking. Of course, these attacks did not deter the Yamato. Another great fortress was constructed in 724 CE. Known as Taga Castle, this *jōsaku*-style fortress was located near modern Sendai, which was the boundary between the Emishi people of the northeast and the lands ruled by the imperial court in Kyoto. This was undoubtedly the largest symbol of imperial presence in the north.

From here on, the Yamato forces pressed on. Under commanders like Ōno no Azumahito, they constructed more and more fortresses and administrative posts. These moves were answered with guerrilla raids launched by the Emishi. They attacked the invaders using the cover of forests and misty mountains. No matter how wide the moats were and how tall they built their watchtowers, the Emishi always had a way to overcome them. To the imperial court, the Emishi people's attacks were seen as rebellion. The Emishi saw their moves as acts of survival.

The rivalry between the Yamato and the Emishi exploded into open warfare by the late 8th century CE. The imperial court in Nara, eager to expand its power, dispatched large Chinese-style armies to "tame" the rebels in the north. Fully equipped with heavy armor and well trained in continental tactics, these forces were confident that they would return to the capital with good news. In their eyes, the Emishi tribes were poorly equipped. They had inferior technology as well.

Much to their surprise, the Emishi had already strategized. They were well versed in the lay of the land compared to the Yamato. Always exceptional on horseback, the Emishi mounted archers made use of elusive hit-and-run tactics. They rapidly descended upon their enemies from the lush forests and unleashed volleys of arrows on them. When the Yamato infantry could finally regroup, the Emishi had already vanished into the wilderness.

Another episode that clearly displayed the Emishi people's military prowess came in 789 CE. The Yamato forces, numbering over two thousand strong, were advancing under the command of General Ki no Kosami. They eventually reached the Kitakami River, where a battle would soon ensue. Having seen the Emishi fight before, they improvised their strategy. The Yamato forces were convinced that this time would be different. It would indeed be different, but not in the way they hoped.

At that time, the Emishi were under the leadership of a man named Aterui. None could confidently confirm where he came from. Many suggested that he was of the Isawa clan, while others believed he had grown up along the Kitakami River. What we can conclude for sure is that Aterui understood the land and his people better than anyone else. The Emishi saw him as a protector.

Cunning as ever, Aterui deployed a smaller force to fight Kosami's men head-on. After they got the enemy's full attention, the small force suddenly fell back. The imperial troops, thinking that their enemy was panicking, quickly gave chase along the riverbank. Little did they know that the smaller Emishi force was feigning retreat and was actually leading them into an ambush. When the Yamato finally arrived at a place called Subuse, they found themselves completely surrounded. Mounted Emishi archers rode down from the flanks and rear, encircling the army. They showered them with endless arrows from all sides. Almost immediately, panic plagued the imperial soldiers. There was no way for them to retreat since they were trapped against the river. Desperate to save themselves, they cast off their heavy armor and weapons and jumped into the river. They attempted to swim for their lives to no avail.

The defeat at Subuse was massive. Even the imperial chroniclers found it impossible to omit the episode; one chronicler bitterly admitted that the Yamato lost more men to water than to Emishi blades. The ambitious Emperor Kanmu halted campaigns for a time following this disaster. For much of the 8th century, the Yamato could achieve nothing except a stalemate. Indeed, more forts and roads were constructed, yet the Emishi were still far from their grasp.

Desperate to turn the tide, the Yamato state finally began to adapt. The imperial army was used to fighting on foot but was adamant on subduing the "barbarians." So, they began donning lighter armor and adopted horseback archery into their tactics, which was ironically modeled on the Emishi style. The turning point of this conflict came in the 790s. Emperor Kanmu appointed a new Sei-i Taishōgun (Japanese for barbarian-subduing general) to lead the conquest of Emishi. The man was none other than Sakanoue no Tamuramaro. Described as a young yet brilliant general, Tamuramaro introduced a fresh strategy. At this point, not every Emishi tribe was hostile toward the Yamato. Some had made peace and agreed to form alliances. Tamuramaro chose to leverage these alliances. In addition to combining Yamato troops with Emishi allies, he also dispatched friendly Emishi as scouts. With this new strategy, the imperial army was finally able to storm its way into the northern strongholds.

Records suggest that Tamuramaro's strategies worked wonders. He managed to achieve in a few years what decades of costly fighting had not. By the early 9th century CE, the two powerful Emishi leaders, Aterui and his comrade More, chose to surrender to Tamuramaro. Through their submission, the two Emishi generals hoped the Yamato would stop the bloodshed. They wanted to end the suffering of their people.

Tamuramaro accepted their surrender with respect. He even viewed them not as defeated rebels but as worthy adversaries. "These people are far from being criminals," he might have argued. "Execution is not the answer. You can turn them into martyrs or spare them and gain allies."

Unfortunately, even before he made the case, the imperial court had already made its decision. When the decree was read, some expected it, but there were those who were shocked. Despite already sensing that their fate had been sealed, Tamuramaro was disappointed to hear of this. Nevertheless, orders were orders.

Aterui and More were taken to the banks of the Katsura River in 802. Here, they were beheaded for the crime of defending their own land. Although they were the antagonists in ancient records, today, a monument honoring them can be found in Kyoto's Kiyomizu-dera temple. It was erected in 1994, and although it was not as big as the famous ancient wonders of the world, this monument inverted the old narrative by commemorating the Emishi side of the conflict.

A monument commemorating Aterui and the Emishi.[69]

With the end of organized Emishi resistance, the imperial government wasted no time in establishing new provinces in the former Emishi lands. Named Mutsu and Dewa, these provinces were fully equipped with officials and garrisons tasked with maintaining order. However, the region was located far from the imperial center, so it was difficult for the Yamato to keep a close eye on it at all times. This paved the way for local warlords to emerge as semi-autonomous rulers. Some of them were direct descendants of Emishi chiefs; the only difference was that they wore Japanese armor and had Japanese names. Others were noble families from the south that had moved north and married into Emishi families. In the 10ᵗʰ and 11ᵗʰ centuries, Japan saw the rise of powerful clans like the Abe, Kiyohara, and, later, the Northern Fujiwara. These clans held major influence in Tōhoku. They were loyal to the emperor, but at the same time, they ruled the north as if they were independent lords. They also meshed Emishi customs and Yamato culture.

The Emishi who chose not to remain under imperial rule moved northward, making their way beyond the new border. During the 9ᵗʰ and 10ᵗʰ centuries, it appears that some migrated into Hokkaidō, the great northern island that remained free of Yamato control at that time. Scholars believed they eventually blended with or contributed to the development of Ainu culture.

Although some Emishi chose to submit to the imperial order and assimilate with the Yamato, their legacy was never erased completely. It persisted in subtle ways. The military culture of Japan, for instance, witnessed some changes after the Yamato engaged with the Emishi. Perhaps after observing their enemies, the Yamato adopted mounted archery and light cavalry tactics. Believe it or not, this skill that they learned from the Emishi out of necessity was the precursor of the samurai class. Even more interesting, some of the earliest *bushi* (Japanese warriors) of the Heian era were of Emishi descent. These skilled mounted warriors were loyal vassals of the court. Emishi warriors who had once fought against the Yamato were also integrated into the imperial forces, bringing their skill to the empire's service.

This integration was not always peaceful. Rebellions and wars occurred in later centuries, often sparked by the powerful semi-autonomous northern clans. One such case could be seen in the mid-11ᵗʰ century. Known as the Zenkunen War (also called the Former Nine Years' War), it involved the Abe clan in Mutsu. Believed to have Emishi blood running in their veins, the Abe defied the central government. Led by the samurai Abe no Sadato, the war raged on for slightly over a decade. The imperial forces emerged as the victors. Abe no Sadato surrendered in 1062 CE, ending the conflict.

Two decades later, another conflict erupted, leading to the Gosannen War (also known as the Later Three Years' War). This time around, the war involved the Kiyohara clan and led to the half-Emishi warlord known as Fujiwara no Kiyohira establishing independent rule over Tōhoku. His dynasty, the Northern Fujiwara, built a prosperous mini-state that lasted nearly a century. The court in Kyoto tolerated this as long as formal allegiance was maintained. The Northern Fujiwara's Hiraizumi domain represented a resurgence of Emishi identity blended with Japanese high culture. It was not until 1189, when Japan was well into the feudal era, that the last Fujiwara ruler was toppled by the rising Kamakura samurai government. With his fall, the political autonomy of the old Emishi lands finally came to an end. But by then, Emishi blood and heritage had long since spread through the veins of the Japanese nation.

Chapter 6 – The Women of Ancient Japan

If one were to describe the ancient world with only a single word, they would certainly come up with words like warfare, empires, dynasties, myths, or even religion. But almost no one would think of the word equality. This is because the ancient world was not a place of equals, at least not often. Across great river valleys and fortified cities, men were the ones who typically wrote the laws, sat on the throne, and had their names in the historical records. Women were acknowledged for contributing to the shaping of these early civilizations, but their names were seldom recorded.

Athens, for instance, restricted the role of their women. Their place was behind the walls, where they remained hidden from not only politics but also education and even public discourse. More often than not, a woman's worth was measured by three main aspects: her obedience, her dowry, and her womb. Women in Athens neither had the right to vote nor to own land. They also could not appear in court unless they were accompanied by a male guardian. It is safe to conclude that Athenian women lived an extremely private life and were both silent and confined.

The same could not be said of ancient Egypt. Here, women were allowed to own property and operate businesses by themselves. They could even initiate legal actions and attend court without the company of a male guardian. Egypt also had powerful female pharaohs like Hatshepsut, Sobekneferu, and Cleopatra. True, some historical records describe them in a negative light. Cleopatra, in particular, is often referred to as a seductive vixen in Roman records despite her achievements in bringing Ptolemaic Egypt to greater heights. Hatshepsut's name was erased from ancient documents and her statues defaced after her death. Still, it is safe to conclude that women in ancient Egypt enjoyed more rights and legal autonomy than their counterparts in most other ancient civilizations.

The status of women in the Egyptian kingdom also extended to the realm of mythology and religion. The goddesses Isis and Hathor played major roles in Egyptian myths. They were thought to be mother-deities who nurtured and ruled. However, their influence did not surpass that of their male counterparts.

Then there was Japan. Their supreme deity was neither a lightning king nor a sun god who had the head of a falcon. Instead, they worshiped a woman known by the name of Amaterasu. The emperors claimed descent through this sun goddess. She was held in high regard in both the heavens and on earth. She was the goddess who withdrew into a cave as a sign of protest against her brother, plunging the world into total darkness. When she eventually reemerged, her brilliance shone so brightly that the world resumed its activities at once. Her relic is a mirror, which to this day is part of Japan's imperial regalia.

It is ironic that the divine in Japan was female. Yet, over time, power in the human world would slip further and further into male hands. Of course, this was not always the case. The earliest chronicles of the Yamato court—compiled in the *Kojiki* and *Nihon Shoki*—hint at a more ambiguous past. Before men took complete control of the court narrative and many years before Kyoto rose to prominence as the flourishing capital, women played important roles in the history of Japan. This was a time when the Japanese archipelago was made up of loosely connected clans. Although they did not always see eye to eye, these early communities, referred to as *uji*, shared rituals and myths. Especially during the Yayoi and early Kofun eras, it was common for women to take up the mantle as female shamans, or *miko*. As intermediaries between human beings and the spiritual world, the miko were the ones whom clan leaders often sought to interpret omens and lead seasonal rites.

However, when the Yamato state came to prominence in the 4th to 6th centuries, the political landscape witnessed a change. Chinese influence—through writing, Confucian values, and bureaucracy—brought about a more rigid, patriarchal worldview. Over time, women were given more restrictions, even in the world of education. But still, contradictions remained. The imperial line continued to claim descent from Amaterasu, the sun goddess. Ironically, the emperor's legitimacy was tied not to conquest but to a divine female source. This made the image of women both sacred and politically potent—yet also dangerous. A woman could serve as regent or high priestess, but her rise to lasting power always came with obstacles.

Then came the Heian period, which saw Japan increasingly absorbing and localizing many Buddhist monastic codes (Vinaya), merging them with native Shinto taboos. In Shinto, the concept of *kegare* (pollution) dictated that death and blood (especially from menstruation and childbirth) were impure. When concepts of the two religions merged, restrictions became even more formalized. Women were eventually barred from entering certain areas of temples and shrines. Most of the time, they were not allowed to enter the main halls (*honden*), temple kitchens, and altars. A few sacred mountains like Mount Ōmine and Mount Kōya were off-limits for women. Some sects even had designated halls for women known as *nyonin-dō*, while others only allowed women to worship from the outside. It was only during the Meiji Restoration (1868) that temples slowly began relaxing these restrictions.

Of course, these restrictions did not put a stop to women carving their names into history. Even as religious institutions imposed boundaries and the imperial court favored men, some women managed to defy these constraints. They seized the mantle of leadership, stepped into the roles of warriors and rulers, and wrote their names—real or legendary—into the scrolls of Japan's past. Among them was Empress Jingū.

She was born as Jingū Kōgō. Although records of her early life are scarce, the *Nihon Shoki* tells us that Jingū was the wife of Emperor Chūai (the fourteenth emperor of Japan according to traditional succession). Her story began when Emperor Chūai died suddenly. He was thought to have paid the price after disrespecting a kami. Following his passing, the throne was passed to his wife, Jingū. However, instead of filling her days with mourning, the empress chose to make a move that shocked many.

Jingū, who was heavily pregnant at the time, launched a campaign to invade a mysterious kingdom across the sea, which many have interpreted to be the ancient Korean kingdom of Silla. Equipped with both divine guidance and the loyalty of her generals, the mission began with little inconvenience. Ancient records also claim that the empress allegedly delayed the birth of her son, the future Emperor Ōjin, by tying a magical stone to her belly. As a reward for her discipline and devotion to her kingdom, the gods bestowed protection upon her. Not only did the empress return to Japan safely, but the invasion was also done without spilling a single drop of blood.

A woodblock print of Empress Jingū.[70]

Apart from being named an empress, Jingū is sometimes remembered as one of Japan's earliest examples of *onna-bugeisha*. This is a term used to describe female warriors from the noble class who were trained in weapons and battlefield tactics. Unlike the more commonly known samurai, which became a male-dominated role by the medieval period, onna-bugeisha were believed to have played active military roles in earlier times.

However, it is important to note that Jingū's story must be read with caution. Modern historians claim that Jingū was nothing more than a legendary figure. This is largely due to the lack of contemporary records of her campaign. Apart from the *Nihon Shoki*, which was compiled many centuries after her supposed reign and typically blended oral traditions with state ideology, there seems to be no mention of Jingū. Korean sources made no mention of the Japanese invasion during this era. Therefore, many concluded that Jingū's narrative was crafted to solely legitimize the Yamato's expanding power and the regency of women in times of political transition.

Regardless of whether or not the empress was a real figure, Jingū was venerated for centuries. She was eventually deified as a kami and had shrines built in her honor. Even her image was featured on Meiji-era banknotes as a symbol of divine authority and female virtue.

Empress Suiko, on the other hand, was a real figure. She ascended to the throne in 593 CE, sealing her name as Japan's first historically verified female monarch. The daughter of Emperor Kinmei and his wife, Soga no Kitashihime, she claimed the crown after Japan witnessed the assassination of Emperor Sushun. Prince Shōtoku was made regent the following year she ascended to the throne, but the empress was far from being just a puppet. This could be seen in a certain episode that took place in 624 CE. At that time, the court was controlled by the Soga clan. Its leader, Soga no Umako, once requested that he be granted the imperial territory known as Kazuraki no Agata. Suiko was against the idea. She refused Umako's request, showing that the empress had the ultimate power in deciding important matters in the imperial court.

An 18th-century painting of Empress Suiko.[71]

Suiko remained on the throne for thirty-five years, which further suggests that the empress possessed political prowess. She also presided over a court undergoing radical transformation. At that time, Buddhism was beginning to gain prominence. Continental systems of governance were being studied and adopted. It was an era when Japan was slowly beginning to define itself as a centralized state.

During her reign, Prince Shōtoku's reforms were successfully implemented. This moral code was based on influences from Confucian and Buddhist principles. It was considered one of Japan's earliest formal articulations of statecraft. It is safe to say that Japan reached greater heights under Suiko's reign, especially in the realm of foreign diplomacy. This era saw more envoys being sent to China.

Suiko's gender was never publicly contested. In fact, the very nature of her rule challenged later assumptions about women's limitations in early Japan. She was both empress and high priestess, holding political and spiritual authority all at once. Unlike Jingū, whose story was viewed with skepticism, Suiko's reign has not been doubted by historians and scholars. Her actions were logged in official documents, and her legacy has been carried forward in court rituals.

Tomoe Gozen: The Female Warrior Who Was Afraid of Nothing

Japan was again thrown into a period of turmoil in the final decades of the 12th century with the arrival of the Genpei War. This civil conflict was fought between two samurai clans. One of them was the Taira clan, which had long held sway in the capital of Kyoto. The other clan was the Minamoto. This war was not the first time that the clans had clashed with each other. Previously, the Taira and the Minamoto fought each other during the Hōgen and Heiji Disturbances, both of which took place in the mid-12th century. The Minamoto were defeated terribly, but the Taira chose to spare the lives of a few Minamoto children, though they were exiled to lands far from the capital. This was a mistake for the Taira. The Minamoto, under the leadership of Minamoto no Yoritomo and his cousin, Minamoto no Yoshinaka (also known as Lord Kiso), would soon rebuild their strength and come back stronger, although the two would then clash with each other soon after defeating the Taira.

In the midst of this conflict, a female warrior named Tomoe Gozen rose to prominence. Described as a fearsome warrior with terrifying precision, Tomoe was said to be a retainer serving under Lord Kiso. Some whispered that she was more than just a warrior in Lord Kiso's eyes; she was his lover. Tomoe was often depicted in Japanese art charging into battle on horseback, wearing full armor. Her weapons of choice were a great bow and a long sword. According to *The Tale of the*

Heike, an epic that chronicled the events of the Genpei War, Tomoe was "worth a thousand warriors."

She displayed her military prowess in multiple battles during the Genpei War. One of them took place in the year 1181, the Battle of Yokotagawara. According to the epic, Tomoe led Lord Kiso's forces against the Taira, where she succeeded in slaying seven enemy horsemen herself. She then presented the severed heads of the enemies to her lord. Another victory came in 1183 when she commanded over a thousand cavalry at the Battle of Tonamiyama. She also played a major role at the Battle of Uchide no Hama in 1184. Here, Tomoe led a Minamoto force of only three hundred strong against six thousand mounted Taira troops. Although victory sided with the Taira this time, Tomoe was among the five people who survived the battle.

Her most dramatic moment came at the Battle of Awazu. This was also her final act on the battlefield. By this time, Lord Kuso's influence had waned. His ambition in taking Kyoto for himself had made him a threat to his more popular cousin, Yoritomo. Yoritomo sent forces led by his half-brothers, Yoshitsune and Noriyori, to stop Lord Kiso.

When Kiso's forces were reduced to only five people, he knew there was no way out. So, he turned to his most loyal warrior—and possibly lover—and told her to run. He claimed that it would be shameful for him to die alongside a woman. Tomoe had no intention of disappearing. She told Lord Kiso that she would obey his command, but only after she made one final move. Without wasting a single second, she turned her horse and charged straight into a pack of thirty enemy cavalry. She cut her way through them and eventually managed to decapitate the famed strongman named Onda no Hachirō. Using her katana, she was said to have killed another prominent samurai warrior named Uchida Ieyoshi. Then, upon the command of her lord, Tomoe vanished from the battlefield. As for Lord Kiso, he died when an arrow struck him.

Tomoe Gozen riding through battle with the severed head of Uchida Ieyoshi.[73]

What happened to Tomoe following the Battle of Awazu remains a debate. Some suggested that she was captured during the Battle of Kyoto. Instead of being executed, she was taken as Yoritomo's concubine and, later on, gave birth to a legendary strongman named Asahina Saburō Yoshihide. Others claimed she finally hung up her weapons and became a Buddhist nun. She dedicated her life to chanting sutras for Lord Kiso's soul. According to this particular narrative, Tomoe eventually died peacefully at the age of ninety-one. There were also those who spoke of her continued fight. Instead of becoming a nun, Tomoe chose to go down the path of vengeance. She allegedly hunted down Kiso's killers and retrieved the lord's severed head to prevent its desecration. In the end, she was said to have walked solemnly into the sea, head in hand.

No one can confirm which version of the story is true. In fact, even her entire existence and role in the Genpei War have been questioned. This is because her name does not appear in any official military records of the Genpei War. Tomoe Gozen was mentioned only in the pages of *The Tale of the Heike*. While some scholars argue that she was nothing more than a literary creation, others propose that she was a real warrior whose contributions have been erased. After all, history, especially when recorded by male-dominated courts, has a long habit of omitting the inconvenient. Perhaps her victories drew attention away from the noble male lineage of Lord Kiso himself; the authorities might have viewed it as necessary to omit her from the narrative.

The Creation of Kana and the Rise of Women in Literature

In ancient Japan, education was a privilege that belonged almost exclusively to men. Men born into the aristocracy were expected to master Han writing (*kanbun)*, which was made the official language of governance, diplomacy, and classical scholarship. Included in the syllabus were Confucian texts and poetry. Suffice it to say that proficiency in kanbun was a must if a man wished to advance through the ranks in court.

Women were excluded from receiving this form of education. They were not taught Chinese and were almost never granted access to the bureaucratic or scholarly world. A woman's education depended heavily on her family's standing and values. Some, especially those born to court scholars, might have learned kanbun through private tutors or familial exposure.

Things began to change, especially for women, when the empire finally stepped into the Heian period. For centuries, Japan had viewed Tang China in high regard; it was seen as the pinnacle of civilization. Japan adopted its writing system and models of governance, embraced its religious doctrines, and mirrored its architecture and city planning. However, by the 9th and 10th centuries, Japan began to take the first steps toward turning inward. The aristocracy in Kyoto sought to cultivate a distinctly Japanese sensibility. Although Chinese influence lingered, this was a time when the Heian court grew more interested in subtlety, seasonal beauty, and emotional refinement. Poetry was not only an art form, but it also became a political tool. Calligraphy was another area where refinement mattered. Each brushstroke was important, as it was judged for its grace, balance, and personal flair. The way a character was written could reveal one's character and upbringing. Even fashion became a language of its own.

Then came the birth of a new writing system known as *kana*. Kana could express sound directly. This way, writers could record the rhythms and emotional tones of their native language. However, kana was considered less scholarly and unfit for official documents. This new writing system became the domain of those who were already excluded from classical education: women.

Kana written in katakana (left) and hiragana (right).[78]

The development of kana allowed Heian women to write and record. However, rather than documenting politics and crafting policies, women of the Heian period wrote about the world they knew intimately. They kept diaries, composed poetry, and wrote fictional tales full of impressive details of court life beyond conflicts of emperors and clans. They spoke of longing, jealousy, pleasure, boredom, and loneliness—themes that often described their courtly lives. As time passed, what men dismissed as private or frivolous became the foundation of Japan's literary heritage.

Among the many writers who emerged from this era of culture, two rose above the rest. One was known as Murasaki Shikibu, and the other was named Sei Shonagōn. They wrote in a strikingly different tone, yet many would agree they were both equal in brilliance.

Both women lived within the same palace walls. Sei Shonagōn served Empress Teishi, the consort of Emperor Ichijō, and was the daughter of a provincial governor and poet. Best known for her quick wit and biting insight, she flourished in the early part of the emperor's reign, when her mistress still held influence. Sei's most famous work was known as *Makura no Sōshi* (*The Pillow Book*).

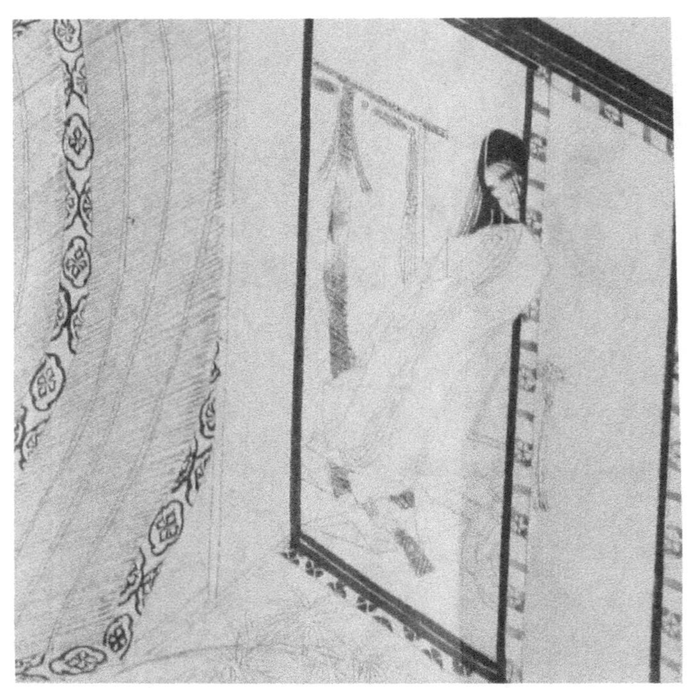

A 13th-century drawing of Sei Shonagōn.[74]

Her writings were not meant for the public, at least at first. Court women, especially those with lower standing in the court like Sei Shonagōn, were restricted from expressing themselves in public. *The Pillow Book* was merely a place for her to pour her inner thoughts and feelings. She turned the whims of her daily life into expressive poems, essays, and anecdotes. The pages were filled with her observations of the Heian world. She wrote about how seeing a gentleman playing the koto so elegantly could make her heart beat faster. She expressed how she found joy watching tiny children learn how to speak and kittens chasing butterflies. Sometimes, she also wrote about things that annoyed her. She claimed to have little patience for sloppiness, rudeness, and mediocrity. Most of the time, her tone was humorous, but it could also be biting. Apart from her personal thoughts and feelings, she also recorded gossip and events that took place in the Heian court, which shed light on the real lives of the aristocrats.

One day, Sei Shonagōn accidentally left her writings unattended as she was preparing to receive a guest. This guest read her musings and was said to have taken the book despite her pleas. What happened afterward remains unclear, but over time, her writings were copied, edited, and compiled into multiple versions before being circulated among the aristocracy. *The Pillow Book* was mostly a personal work, but Shonagōn's talents in writing turned it from just a simple diary into a work of literature.

Murasaki Shikibu was a lady-in-waiting under Empress Shōshi, who rose in prominence after Teishi's fall. She was said to have secretly learned kanbun by eavesdropping on her brother's lessons. To some, this was unsurprising since Murasaki was born into a scholarly family, as her father served as a court official.

A painting depicting Murasaki Shikibu.[75]

Her great work, *Genji Monogatari* (*The Tale of Genji*), is often regarded as the world's first novel. While Shonagōn's work comprised a collection of personal reflections and witty observations, Shikibu's *The Tale of Genji* offered glimpses into the court life through a tale. The protagonist was named Prince Genji. He was described as a handsome nobleman, but he was far from perfect. Not considered a hero in the classical sense, Prince Genji was created as a flawed character, yet deeply human.

The first forty-one chapters dive into Prince Genji's birth, rise, romantic relationships, and eventual fall from political power. Through his affairs and reflections, Murasaki creatively explores the themes of impermanence, desire, and regret. This book also narrates the silent roles women were forced to play in love and politics. The next set of chapters introduces new characters; one is named Kaoru, believed to be Genji's son but is actually the son of Genji's wife and another man, and another is Niou, the grandson of Genji. These chapters, written in a more somber and philosophical tone, explore the characters' romantic entanglements, identity struggles, and spiritual restlessness.

Copies of the manuscript began circulating among noble households soon after it was written. It was also said that Murasaki herself read the chapters aloud to Empress Shōshi and the other ladies-in-waiting. While her work was received exceptionally well by women, men reacted rather differently. While some male in the court expressed their appreciation, others were critical and dismissive. This was possibly due to the work being written in kana rather than kanbun. Murasaki lamented about this in her diary. She spoke of men who praised her writing but at the same time mocked her intellect behind her back.

Murasaki Shikibu and Sei Shonagōn likely never met face to face. Yet, Murasaki considered Shonagōn her rival. She said that Shonagōn was a woman of intellect but that her writings lacked real depth. She also claimed that her rival was full of herself. There is, however, no record of Shonagōn ever responding to her comments.

Chapter 7 – Secrets and Scandals in the Heian Period

A messenger arrived, handing a letter to a woman dressed in fine silk. The letter was folded with precision; three parts creased and bound with a crimson thread. The paper was thick, embossed with a subtle chrysanthemum motif, and she could smell the soothing scent of perfume as she unfolded it. With the letter still in her delicate hands, the woman moved closer to the light to read it. The message was brief. It was a single *tanka*, a thirty-one-syllable poem. Each line was elegant and romantic.

The woman had never met the sender before. However, she knew exactly who he was. Her parents had spoken of him. Not only was he a court

A poetry card featuring tanka and a portrait of Emperor Tenji.[76]

noble of promising rank, but the man also had a way with words. Her sisters would giggle whenever her parents talked about him. She knew that the man was a candidate whom her father had quietly approved of, so she was overjoyed when the messenger came.

In the Heian court, this was almost always the beginning of a union between two people. Typically, this began not with love but with arrangements and poetry. Families, often the parents, would choose potential matches based on lineage and social reputation. Personal meetings between the two came later.

As for the woman in our story, she was impressed by the poetry. She began crafting her reply. Whether she authored the response herself or asked for the assistance of her cousin, who was a skilled poet, mattered little. What was important was that the tanka be perfect. In this particular era, a woman's reply in her letters was, more or less, her mirror. Her suitor would analyze every little detail in it. And not only the poem itself, but also the calligraphy style, the thickness of the paper, and even the finishing of the ink. A paper of poor grade could imply either a lack of status or taste, while a smudged character could hint at carelessness.

The woman's response had none of those flaws. When the man finally received her reply, he was both relieved and overjoyed. He knew that he must take the next step if he were to continue the relationship.

The first visit happened at night. As tradition dictated, the visit had to be discreet. Although her household was aware that the man would soon visit, they said nothing. Even servants looked away, as if nothing was happening. Preparations, however, had already been done—corridors were swept clean, and the woman had spent hours looking her best. When the clear sky was lit only by the moonlight, the nobleman made his move. Ensuring complete silence, he walked straight to the noblewoman's room. Here, the two would spend the night together. However, no matter how intimate the night had been, the noblemen must leave before the first ray of the sun pierced the sky.

The waiting game began after the first visit. The noblewoman and her family waited in quiet tension, unsure if they would hear from the man ever again. If another messenger arrived at the door with a letter, that meant he enjoyed her company. If not, then everything would end unspoken. As for our character, tension was replaced with relief when they heard a soft knock. Within seconds, a messenger entered. In his hands was a scroll tied neatly with silk. The second poem had finally arrived. Just like last time, the noblewoman penned a response, triggering a second night. Again, the nobleman quietly entered her room, shared her bed, and left before dawn broke.

Then came the third visit. This was when everything would change. When the nobleman stepped into her chamber, he noticed a lacquered tray placed beside her mat. On it were two rice cakes prepared by the woman's family. These were not merely snacks for the couple to enjoy during their night together but a sacred offering. In the Heian period, marriage required neither extensive paperwork nor grand weddings. If a man visited a woman's home and shared her bed for three nights and both families had acknowledged their bond, then they were one step away from being considered married. All that was left for them to do was to partake in two small rituals.

First, the lovebirds had to share the rice cakes, which were made to symbolize Izanagi and Izanami, the divine couple of the Shinto creation myth. Then, the man had to join the woman's family for a modest meal. It is worth noting that the meal was only joined by the man, not his parents. This first sharing of a meal meant that the man had been accepted into the household. Later, another public feast would be held where both families would finally meet and formally recognize the marriage. After this, the two could meet in the open without anyone stopping them.

Interestingly, this ritual of night visits was not only reserved for the Heian aristocrats. Far from the capital, the commoners had their very own peculiar ways of courting women. However, this did not involve any exchange of romantic poems.

Known as *yobai* (night crawling), this courtship practice was typically woven into the daily lives of those who lived in villages dotted in the southwestern regions of Japan. It involved young men sneaking into the homes of women where they would attempt to share their bed without disturbing the rest of the household. Of course, in modern eyes, this practice is unacceptable, but to the ancient Japanese, these were not always seen as unwelcome intrusions.

Most of the time, young women, especially those interested in receiving a suitor, would leave their door open as they slept. This was an unspoken signal for her suitor to approach her that night. Some did so not for one particular man but for several, welcoming visits from multiple suitors throughout the night.

Since these visits were common, the women's household understood what was happening, though they usually kept quiet. Still, it was a must for the visiting man to enter the woman's room silently. Sometimes, this was a challenge since most houses in villages were far from soundproof. Screens rustled, and even the tatami mats creaked when stepped on. It was said that to remain stealthy, these men would remove the sash tied around their waist and lay it across the tatami mats. They tiptoed on it so that the sounds of their steps would be muffled.

Of course, women involved in yobai had the right to accept or reject a man's advances. If she refused and the suitor persisted, one shrill scream would awaken the house. Their brothers, fathers, or even neighbors would chase the man out, sometimes with sticks and shovels in hand. Similar to the courting practice by the nobles, men who were given permission to share the bed must leave the house before daybreak. More often than not, couples who participated in yobai eventually married, either after the woman conceived or perhaps after a few consistent visits.

Yobai was typically practiced by southwestern villages; it was very rarely practiced in northeastern Japan. This was largely because the region's hierarchical structures were more rigid. Clans tended to place greater emphasis on their bloodlines and status. Marriages were often arranged to avoid their family members from getting entangled with someone of a lower status.

More often than not, only men from the same village were allowed to participate in yobai. A stranger caught sneaking into a woman's house—especially from a neighboring or rival village—risked being beaten or forcibly driven out. While many communities stressed that yobai be practiced only by unmarried youth, some villages allowed otherwise. Widowed women or, in rare cases, married women left their door ajar, inviting their suitors to sneak in. There were also villages where the roles were reversed; women were the ones creeping into a man's home, searching for companionship.

It is not a surprise that the practice did not survive the era of modernization. When Japan entered the Meiji period (1868-1912), an era where the government worked to "civilize" rural customs and replace them with Western-style laws and moral codes, many old practices that went against the concept of modern morality were discouraged and erased. Yobai was included in this. Viewing it as backward and immoral, the controversial practice was officially banned. Still, in some remote villages, the practice lingered until as late as the 1950s.

The Heian period, which kicked off in 794 CE, is known as the golden age of classical Japan. This was the time when the imperial court at Heian-kyō (modern-day Kyoto) reached a new height in the areas of culture, art, and language. It was a time when the kimono was first worn by the nobles, when poetry became both a language of love and social maneuvering, and when Japan began to carve its own aristocratic identity, one that greatly differed from its Chinese influences.

Noblewomen were expected to wrap themselves in at least twelve layers of expensively dyed silk. Each color was not to be chosen lightly; it had to reflect the season, mood, and status. Long, flowing black hair was also an important part of their beauty standards. Both men and women of the aristocracy practiced *ohaguro*, or teeth blackening.

A woodblock print of a noblewoman practicing ohaguro.[77]

Pale, white skin was part of their beauty standard as well. Dark or tan skin was associated with laborers or lower-class people. The aristocracy preferred to remain indoors, and if they had to go outdoors, they would use parasols. Men also wore wide-brimmed hats to protect themselves from the sun.

Suffice it to say that it was an age where everything was highly choreographed, from the scent of one's layered sleeves to the way one opened a hand fan, from the thickness of papers used in letters to the style of calligraphy and the ink's quality. Even recuperation had its own rituals. The nobles loved visiting the springs. As *tojiba*, or places of healing and treatment, hot springs were visited by those who wished to escape from both physical ailments and emotional fatigue.

Prince Arima (the son of Emperor Kotoku) was a frequent visitor to hot springs, specifically the one known as Ki no Yu. Records in *Nihon Shoki* suggest that the prince was in the midst of a struggle with Naka no Oe (later Emperor Tenji). In order to excuse himself from the trouble, Prince Arima faked an illness, claiming that he could only get better if he went to the hot springs. Unfortunately, things did not go well for Prince Arima. He returned to the capital later on, feeling rejuvenated—his story about the hot spring intrigued Empress Saimei (Empress Kōgyoku) so much that she went to visit it later—but when the prince agreed to participate in a plot to overthrow the empress, his fate was sealed. The very person who had dragged the prince into the plot betrayed him by exposing the plan. Prince Arima was captured, and after a period of interrogation, he was hanged to death.

Although the nearly forgotten story of Prince Arima occurred long before the Heian period started (he died in 658 CE during the Asuka period), the hot springs continued to be seen as a place of recuperation. When Japan was embroiled in civil wars, some warlords established hot spring stations in their territories to treat wounded soldiers. After all, these hot springs, or *onsen*, do have healing properties due to their mineral content. Over time, toji was practiced by aristocrats, warlords, priests, and even commoners.

Unsurprisingly, beneath the surface of elegance and ritual, the Heian court was also an era full of secrets and emotional yearning. Marriage affairs were common. Jealousy, seductions, and silent heartbreaks were also recurring themes in this part of Japanese history. These stories are not so well known, especially since formal chronicles from this era were curated to maintain the public face of the Heian court. The quiet struggles, scandals, and desires of those in the court were usually omitted from the records authored by officials, but interestingly, some glimpses of them were preserved by women.

On the surface, women of the Heian court lived a life that seemed to be surrounded by wealth, peace, and all things beautiful. But beneath that image, many Heian women actually carried burdens they could never voice too loudly. So, they turned to writing. These women not only recorded their lives but also used ink to voice their concerns and disappointments. Some wrote about the bitterness of neglect, while others expressed their thrill at a lover's letter or the ache of loneliness. They lamented about their lives in their personal diaries, writing down episodes that captured their emotions; these were the kinds of episodes that were typically ignored by their other half.

Although their writings were not meant to be history, these diaries become a window for future generations to take a journey back to this particular age and get a view of what life in the Heian court was really like.

The Gossamer Years: A Story of a Marriage Slowly Withering

The woman who wrote *The Gossamer Years* (*Kagerō Nikki* in Japanese) was never named—at least not in a way a person wants to be named. She was simply referred to as Michitsuna's Mother. Details of her background are scarce; we only know her as the wife (or more accurately consort) of Fujiwara no Kaneie, a powerful figure who served as minister in the Heian imperial court.

Through pages of her diary, it is safe to assume she was not an aggressive person. Overwhelmed with heartbreak and sadness, her words were more like a sigh. Her main issue revolved around the relationship between herself and her husband, Kaneie. By 971 CE, she was caught in a marriage crisis. Kaneie was said to have become increasingly absent. Even when he was around, Kaneie brought only a form of intimacy that lacked meaning. Over time, it became rare for her to even hear his footsteps, let alone read his letters. But she still remained loyal. She stayed home and poured her love into caring for their son, Michitsuna, even though her husband was pursuing other women. She was almost hopeful, holding on to the idea that this nightmare would soon pass and that her husband would change one day.

Kagerō Nikki is, as some scholars have suggested, not just a record of a life but a record of a marriage dying by degrees. Over time, it was clear that what little thread holding their relationship together was wearing extremely thin. It pained her to accept the fact that her husband was straying further away from her. Yet, she refrained from raging. Again, she picked up her brush, dipped it in ink, and expressed her pain onto paper, turning it into poems. Her tone was gentle but also laced with anguish.

Other relationships also color her pages. She recorded her close bond with her son and her eventual adoption of a daughter (she was the daughter of Kaneie and another woman). There were pages that included moments of joy, although they never seemed to last; she always drifted back into sadness. In between these days of joy with her children, she slipped in episodes that confused her resolve. She spoke of the times when Kaneie visited after waiting for him for seasons. She spoke of how overjoyed she was by his rare return, although she knew her day would end in tears. She also narrated her sleepless nights when sorrow engulfed her entirely.

Then, her diary entered a new chapter. In search of peace, she decided to go on a pilgrimage. Her empty days were filled with visits to temples, mountains, and other places believed to bring peace and healing. After this pilgrimage, she was suddenly overcome by the thought of becoming a nun. She wanted to cut her last ties to court life and its cruel games and disappear into the mountain temples. Yet, it was not that easy for her to take Buddhist vows, as she dared not risk her son's future. She had to remain where she was, beside the absent Kaneie, and take up the weight of motherhood.

Near the diary's end, the tone changes. She was neither lamenting nor pleading. In fact, she spoke less often about Kaneie. After sixteen years, their marriage had finally come to an end. From here on, it appears as if she had accepted the reality of her life; perhaps the end of the marriage acted as closure for her. Instead of writing about longing and waiting for someone to come home, she wrote about caring for those who remained: Michitsuna and her adopted daughter.

Her last entry was during a festival, possibly the Tama Matsuri. She wrote that she heard a knock on her door late at night, but she never revealed who it was.

Sarashina Nikki: A Memoir About Dreams

While the story of Michitsuna's Mother feels like dusk, entries in the *Sarashina Nikki* feel more like dawn. The stories recorded in the early pages were full of wonder and the promises of youth. Like the *Kagerō Nikki*, the author of this particular diary is not known by her real name; instead, she is recognized only as the daughter of Sugawara no Takasue.

It is not a coincidence that both authors of these diaries did not use their real names. In the Heian period, it was customary for nobles, especially women, not to be addressed by their real names in public records or literature. This was not a matter of modesty but rather because of their cultural beliefs. Through the concept of *kotodama*, they believed that names carried power. If one learned the true name of another individual, there was a possibility for them to invoke the power of kotodama. This could allow them to control the person's fate or spirit.

Even though Takasue's daughter began writing her memoir in her later years, *Sarashina Nikki*'s first few pages are dedicated to her life when she was twelve years old. While other children played, Takasue's daughter longed for something else; she wished to read *The Tale of Genji* from beginning to end. When she finally got the complete copy in her hands, time seemed to pause. She spent day and night reading through the novel as if it were her religion. *The Tale of Genji* became more than just her favorite piece to read. She wished to step into that world. Every day, she dreamed of experiencing the romance narrated in the writing. Hopeful as a young girl could get, she believed that life would unfold just as it did in the bright tales that she read.

Life, however, rarely turns out to be the same as fiction. As she grew older, she realized that her life was far from the ones she read and dreamed of. She was protected in her father's home, and many suitors came expressing their interest in her. Yet none arrived with the same passion as Genji. Her prayers for literary romance were answered with mundane courtship, delayed proposals, and occasional disappointment.

Apart from these disappointments, she also recorded her travels. She played with words beautifully, describing many places and the beauty of Mother Nature. As she reached her thirties, Takasue's daughter eventually settled down with a middle-ranking government official named Tachibana Toshimichi. Although this was not the love story she had imagined when she was a child, the marriage was real. In time, she came to love this real-life romance. When her husband died later on, she mourned to the fullest. Her poems not only describe her sorrow and grief but also speak of the hollow quiet that followed.

She wrote her diary well until she was in her fifties. This was when she reflected on her life and all the fantasies of her youth. She blamed her own devotion to tales. Chasing those illusions caused her to neglect religious practice. In the end, she confessed that she was spiritually weak. Her writing faded a year after her husband's death. No one knows what happened to her or even how and when she died.

Chapter 8 – Marginalized Voices of Ancient Japan

Ancient Japan has some of the most interesting stories in history. However, most books prefer to only narrate those involving emperors, court ladies, and noble warriors. Indeed, their stories were well preserved and passed down through official records, poems, and painted scrolls. But what about the common people, the ones who actually built and sustained the lands across the archipelago?

This particular chapter is reserved for those who cultivated the lands, fired the pottery, and swept the compounds of the temples.

We do not know their names; ancient documents and chronicles only preserved the names of those in the palace. These people left no family crests, statues, or even poetry anthologies. However, what remains of their tools and crafts has been discovered. These artifacts, along with the land they once worked on, reveal their stories and the traditions they once practiced—some of which are practiced even to this day.

What follows is not exactly a list of facts or dates of wars and conflicts. Instead, it is five different days of people who lived in the ancient periods of Japan. They are reimagined and crafted closely based on what historians and archaeologists know. Each short story introduces a different person from a different time and a different walk of life.

A Day in the Life of a Yayoi Village Girl

The sun had just risen over the hills. There were no clocks to know what the time was, but there was the scent of damp soil and the tunes whistled by birds perched in the trees outside. Here, in a small and humble riverside village, a ten-year-old girl woke up. Her name was Yuka, and it was just another ordinary day for her.

A reconstructed Yayoi-style dwelling.[78]

Like every other day, Yuka did not need to be told it was time for her to wake up; she would arise at the same time every single day, as if she was programmed that way. She greeted her mother, who was already crouched by the hearth, stirring leftover grains into porridge. Yuka yawned—she went to bed late last night—but she ignored the feeling since she had things to do. Today, Yuka's task was to help her aunt. They were supposed to gather yams before the sun reached the highest point in the sky. Yuka quickly put on her hemp tunic. On her feet, she wore a pair of *waraji*, simple sandals made of woven straw. Although she knew she would return home tired, Yuka loved going out at this hour.

Their fields were not as huge as those of other villages closer to the cities, but they were big enough. Yuka passed by a group of villagers toiling on the flooded paddies. Curious, she asked her aunt where rice originally came from.

"Well, it was first introduced many generations ago," her aunt answered. "It was carried across the sea by travelers from the Korean Peninsula or perhaps even China,"

Seeing that Yuka was interested in learning more, her aunt explained how these newcomers introduced new tools; they brought sharper iron blades and wooden plows to make working the fields easier. They taught the locals a new way of living. These people, known by the Japanese as

Toraijin (meaning people who came by boat), showed them how to flood the fields for planting, how to store grain, and how to shape the bronze bells that rang during harvest rituals.

Yuka and her aunt finished their task by midday, just as the sun was about to shine directly on the top of their heads. With her hands still sticky with yam sap, the girl helped her aunt tie bundles with bark string. She then hurried to the village square. Coming from a family heavily dependent on agriculture, she did not dare to miss the planting ritual that was just about to begin. The ritual was led by an elderly woman who stood before a small altar of straw and stone. She chanted words that Yuka did not understand. Still, the girl hummed along, knowing that the ritual was held to ask the spirits of earth and rain for a good harvest.

She finally returned home when the sky turned orange. Every day, she would sit near the fire pit lit up by her father. Here, she took the time to relax after a day of working. She chewed on roasted millet cakes while listening to her brother telling an ancient story. This time, it was a story of a goddess whose retreat to a cave plunged the world into total darkness. It was a time of turmoil, and Yuka could not imagine living in a village where fields were filled with withering crops.

Before going to bed, Yuka made sure to make a stop at the tree growing behind their hut. She had heard hushed whispers of a fox spirit living there, guarding the village. As a sign of appreciation for the spirit's protection, she quietly pressed a tiny bead into the dirt near its roots. No one ever asked her to do it, and it was not part of any official ritual. Yet, she felt like it was the right thing to do. It was her way of saying thank you to the kami. Only then would she rush home, ending her day.

A Day in the Life of a Toraijin Potter

The kiln had been burning through the night. When Sun-Wu woke up from his deep sleep, he could already see smoke trailing above the roof of his workshop. This was nothing unusual for him. He was used to the smell of ash and soot on his fingers, as well as the sight of dark clouds of smoke in the air.

Sun-Wu lived during the Kofun era in the province of Kawachi (located today in Osaka). This was a major center for immigrant settlements, especially artisans who hailed from Baekje and Gaya (on the Korean Peninsula). Sun-Wu could trace his lineage back to the neighboring kingdom. He was born in Kawachi, but his grandfather was a migrant from Gaya. He had migrated to Japan sometime in 440 CE, when Japan was experiencing massive waves of migration. His grandfather did not come empty-handed; he also brought exceptional knowledge in the realm of pottery and iron-smelting. Sun-Wu inherited his grandfather's status as a Toraijin and his talent in crafting pottery and iron goods.

It was just another day of work for Sun-Wu. He began his day by unpacking yesterday's batch from the climbing kiln (a type of multi-chambered kiln called *noborigama* by the Japanese). However, he did not work alone; Sun-Wu had a few other craftsmen working on the hot jars, bowls, and roof tiles. Interestingly, most of their crafts were shaped in a style known as *sueki*. Brought over from Korea, this grayish-blue pottery could resist water better than anything the locals ever made before. They were typically used as funerary and ritual objects.

Sun-Wu was expecting the arrival of a chief steward from the nearby Yamato clan house. He was to visit at noon to collect his order: storage jars for grain and a ceremonial basin. However, it was still early, and Sun-Wu had at least a few hours before the chief steward would come knocking on the door. So, he made all the necessary preparations. He made sure that the wares were pristine and appeared perfect. Any form of cracks, warping, or visible fingerprints would not be tolerated. Last time, one of the potters missed a slight crack on a *yokobe* (a type of barrel-shaped vessel), and the steward refused to pay for the rest of their handiwork.

A sueki yokobe.[79]

When midday finally came, the steward arrived as expected. He said little, and upon inspecting his orders, he gave Sun-Wu a simple nod. No praise or insult for their fine work—only silence as a sign of his approval. This brief and cold interaction was not an uncommon exchange. Although the Yamato appreciated the work, they rarely valued the hands that crafted it. In their eyes, the Toraijin were useful but never equal to them. Payment was then made. Since Japan had no formal coin-based economy at that time, Sun-Wu was paid with a bundle of rice and millet.

Sun-Wu let out a sigh of relief and returned to his work. He reshaped a new bowl and then etched a simple geometric design on another vessel. He shut the kiln when evening finally came and walked to the nearby stream. Here, he washed his hands until the water ran clear. Only then would he return home to his small family of three.

While he spoke the Yamato tongue with ease as he dealt with business matters at the workshop and the market, Sun-Wu used the old Gaya dialect to speak to his family members at home. There were times when he wondered if his children would one day forget the old dialect that had been passed down by his grandfather. But as long as they shaped clay, he told himself, then they would at least carry something with them that could remind them of their roots.

A Day in the Life of a Young Slave at the Temple

A young girl named Kinu jolted up when the bell rang right before dawn. After taking a few deep breaths, she rose to her feet, ready for another day full of chores. She was twelve or thirteen that year—she was not even sure herself. The only thing she remembered vividly was the day her mother handed her over to the temple. Kinu's father had passed away a few years back, leaving her family in deep debt. In exchange for debt settlement and a few bundles of rice, her mother gave her away. Kinu was put to work. Some would call her a temple servant or a helper, but everyone knew what she was. She belonged to the temple like any other item found there.

Of course, Kinu was not alone at the temple. Others, both girls and boys, also shared her fate. Some were born into bondage, while others had been handed over by their families when they failed to settle a debt or pay taxes. There were also a few of them who were subjected to work at the temple as punishment for crimes committed by their parents.

Following the introduction of the Chinese-style Ritsuryō legal system in the late Asuka period, people like Kinu were classed as *nuhi*. This was a term used for slaves. They had no rights to land, marriage, or movement. While some nuhi were sent to serve in the houses of the aristocrats and in government offices, others, like Kinu, were tied to the Buddhist temples. Some were left with no choice but to till the lands, grind ink, and haul supplies for their masters. Those with rare talents—usually born into hereditary guilds—could be trained to serve in more refined roles. Some played music at the imperial palace or copied sutras in temple scriptoria. But for most nuhi like Kinu, their work was typically menial and uncelebrated.

After dressing up in her worn robe, Kinu moved to the kitchen, where older women were already working on their tasks. Some were chopping roots, while others stirred pots of millet. Kinu's task did not involve the stove. She had to wash the monks' bowls and fetch water from the well. Kinu had been at the temple for many months now, and she knew that it was always better to avoid eye contact. Some monks were kind, but others were not.

The temple that Kinu served at was a big one. It was funded by the imperial court and decorated with full grandeur. Nobles regularly paid visits to honor the heavenly beings. Kinu had heard stories of a time when the empress herself came to pray. Although the empress never interacted with nuhi at the temple—some only saw her crimson palanquin gliding past the compound—news of her visit gave them something to talk about for weeks.

As for the monks, they usually spent their days copying scrolls brought back from Tang China. When they were not copying these manuscripts, they would chant the Lotus Sutra, debate karma, and discuss Sanskrit. Kinu sometimes eavesdropped on their discussions, but she barely understood any of it. She did, however, like the sound of the chants. Sometimes, she would find herself unconsciously chanting the words as she swept the temple steps.

Then came an episode where she was sent to the side garden to deliver a pail of water. As she stood amidst the gingko trees with their gold-colored leaves, Kinu saw a pair of court officials passing by, followed by their loyal attendants. One of the officials made eye contact with her, though his expression was tight and dismissive. Kinu lowered her eyes as usual; she knew it was safer to do so.

Yes, it was an insignificant incident, but not to Kinu. The look on the official's face made her wonder if the concept of karma was true. She questioned if her current fate was a punishment for something she had done in a previous life. If so, she wondered if she had been cruel or perhaps too proud. Or maybe karma was nothing more than just a myth. Was this just how the world was?

Kinu was then assigned to clean the statue hall after lunch. This was her favorite place in the temple complex. She liked the warm smell of the burning incense and the way the great bronze Buddha sat silently on his pedestal. For some reason, the hall comforted her. Then, as she was about to leave, Kinu was approached by an old nun. No words were spoken, but the nun quietly handed her a piece of a bun. Again, Kinu lowered her eyes, worried that simple eye contact would be seen as a threat. Deep in her heart, though, she was thankful. However, Kinu did not eat the bun right away. She saved it for later so that she could enjoy it when the others were asleep.

Although the day went on smoothly, this was not always the case. She had seen many scenes that made her terrified of even sweeping the floors the wrong way. She had seen famished boys beaten severely for stealing a bun and girls banished after being caught near the monks' quarters. She had also heard of a time when a girl escaped the grounds. Days later, they found her down the river, curled up in the reeds. No one ever spoke about what exactly happened to her.

That night, Kinu lay awake in the dark, the bun hidden beneath her blanket. The bell would ring again soon enough. But for now, she listened to the rain tapping against the roof tiles. She recalled something her mother once said about how the Buddha saw everything, even the smallest ant in the biggest forest. Kinu was not sure there was any truth in it. But if the Buddha did see her, she hoped he knew she was trying to stay kind, even when the world rarely showed kindness to her.

A Day in the Life of a Lacquerware Apprentice and a Gagaku Instrument Maker

Akira was only fourteen years old when he started working at a workshop in Kyoto. He was the youngest apprentice there, serving under an artisan who specialized in creating lacquerware for the aristocrats. Akira's father, who had once been a merchant, had passed away several years earlier. The responsibility of taking care of the family fell upon his shoulders. His mother had sent him to the workshop to become an apprentice. This was indeed a golden opportunity for a commoner like him, especially in the Heian capital.

As an apprentice, it was expected that Akira would start the day by sweeping sawdust from under the workbenches. He dressed in a robe that smelled of pine soot and fermented rice glue—the signature scent of lacquer work. He then walked to the drying room, where wooden trays and boxes were stored, all coated in layers of black and red lacquer. One of the older craftsmen gave him a nod and moved away so that Akira could continue sweeping the floor. After all, dust was their greatest enemy. One speck touching a fresh coat could ruin weeks of work.

Lacquerware, or *urushi-nuri*, was highly valued, especially by the nobles. Apart from being just a decoration, it was also used in court banquets, tea rituals, and religious offerings. Crafting one, however, required patience and could even be dangerous. The raw *urushi* sap, tapped from lacquer trees, is toxic when wet. Coming into direct contact with skin invites blistering rashes. However, when an object is applied with the sap layer after layer and polished with charcoal and cloth, it forms a finish as smooth and deep as still water.

A lacquered cosmetic box (tebako) from the Heian period.[80]

As for Akira, his most important task that day was to prepare a new tray for a nobleman in the capital. He began his work by mixing the sap with pigments and fine clay. Then, using a bamboo spatula, he carefully applied the first base coat. His master never left his side, his eyes watching every stroke that Akira applied to the tray. However, since he was an apprentice, he was not yet allowed to complete and mark his own work. This would change if he managed to prove his skill and loyalty. Only then would he be granted the honor of completing a piece from start to finish. This was the promotion that Akira aimed to achieve one day. His ultimate dream was to have his own craft in the hall of the emperor himself.

Next to Akira's workshop was the workshop of an older man who went by the name of Choji. Perhaps because of his growing age, his hands were slightly trembling as he worked on his craft. Yet, precision was still his strongest suit. Choji ran a workshop where he produced musical instruments for the imperial orchestra. This business had been started by his father many decades ago. He had been an expert in carving the *hichiriki*, a Japanese flute commonly used in *gagaku* (a type of Japanese classical music). Choji, however, preferred working on the *shō*, which was a free reed musical instrument. Originating from Tang China, the instrument was first introduced to the Japanese during the Nara period.

A woman playing the shō.[81]

That day, Choji resumed his repair work on a shō that had been used in last month's performance at the palace. The process required both precision and gentleness. Choji began the work by heating the bamboo over charcoal. This was done to loosen the resin, allowing him to replace the cracked slat with one he had perfectly carved a few days ago. Once done, he tested the sound by blowing into the base. Almost immediately, a soft, ghastly chord could be heard echoing in the workshop.

It was indeed a job well done, but he received little thanks for the repair. Like many other artisans in the capital, payment was modest. He received dried persimmons, rice, and pouches of tea leaves. However, Choji never complained. He knew that the nobles would return to him again and again.

A Day in the Life of a Heian-Era Widow

Lady Tomoe was very familiar with the capital city. She knew which noble families lived in the grand homes that lined the winding streets. She knew them by name and often mingled with them whenever they had events at court. However, that life was in the past. Lady Tomoe no longer lived in that wealthy part of the city. She no longer donned fine silks, and her poetry reading sessions had ended over a decade ago.

In the Heian era, women's status depended almost entirely on their ties to a man—be it her father, her husband, or her son. Without a related male figure by her side, even women from the most well-bred households could slip into obscurity and poverty. In Tomoe's case, she had no one after her husband's death. Her family was distant and politically irrelevant. They offered her no support. She was forced to downgrade her lifestyle; she now lived in a humble wooden house near a temple that she rented from a retired guard.

She had not been among the highest ranks of court ladies. She was only married to a mid-level court official. But still, she held more status when her husband was alive. She used to have a servant bring her food, but now, she had to prepare her own rice. She did not have to worry about her income, but after her husband's death, even the smallest coin mattered. If she had extra, she would buy pickled plums to enjoy. If she had nothing, then she ate only plain rice with boiled greens gathered from the temple slope. It was not much, especially compared to her life a decade ago, but it was enough to fill her stomach.

Of course, Tomoe was not the only one who had experienced this spiraling moment. Others faced the same fate. While some women eventually remarried into low-ranking households, others chose to become nuns. Some, like Tomoe, eventually found modest work to sustain themselves. From palaces and grand houses, these women turned to the temples that dotted the capital. These became their informal sanctuaries. Tomoe filled most of her days here, where she prayed and did cleaning work.

Her day usually began rather early. She would join a group of other working women at the stream behind the temple, where they washed clothes for the monks. The water was cold in the morning, but Tomoe was used to it. Her hands had already shown signs of years of labor. She did not even mind how she looked. After all, her days of white powder and carefully drawn eyebrows had long passed.

When the sun rose high in the sky, Tomoe took the time to regain her energy. More often than not, she would head to the shrine beside the temple. Here, she listened to the priest chanting sutras. However, this time, she chose to sit on the shaded steps, gazing at the crowded market nearby. She caught sight of a few noblewomen passing by in their ox-drawn carriages. Each of them was dressed in twelve-layered silk robes. She used to get sad when she watched them, as they reminded her of the past. From the outside, they appeared as if they had everything in the world. However, Tomoe knew that behind that elegance was a cruel reality. A woman's worth at court could easily fade the moment she lost her husband. It took Tomoe years to get accustomed to her new life, but what was important was that she was no longer bitter, just clear-eyed.

Every now and then, Tomoe would make ink sticks by grinding soot with glue before pressing the mixture into carved molds. She sold these in the market. Although they never brought her a massive income, they were enough for her to get food on her table.

When the day turned to dusk, Tomoe would return to her humble home. That day, she received a visitor. It was the young son of her neighbor who brought her a bundle of kindling. In return, Tomoe shared her pickled plums with him. Even though it was just a simple exchange, Tomoe found it more comforting than all the flattery she once received back in her noble years.

Later that evening, she wrapped herself in a worn blanket and wrote in her diary. She found joy filling the pages with things from long ago—the cool breeze in the garden and the way her husband used to softly hum when reading scrolls—and things that happened in the present, like the sound of the bells at the temple, the sour taste of the pickled plums, and the cold water that rushed in the stream behind the temple. Of course, these details would never enter the official record, but they were her story.

Chapter 9 – From Sutras to Bloodbaths

After reigning for twenty-five years, Emperor Shōmu made a shocking decision. Known to be a devout Buddhist, he chose to follow the path of enlightenment; the emperor abdicated the Chrysanthemum Throne to become a Buddhist monk. He passed the crown to his daughter, Princess Abe, who reigned as Empress Kōken. From then on, Japan was thrown into another episode full of political conflicts.

Empress Kōken did not oversee her domain alone. Behind the scenes, there was Empress Consort Kōmyō. She never ruled in her own name, but her influence was very powerful. She was the wife of the retired Emperor Shōmu, the daughter of the powerful statesman Fujiwara no Fuhito, and the mother of the reigning empress. Her Fujiwara lineage played a role in her reputation, but her strategic alliances made her indispensable. By her side was the loyal Fujiwara no Nakamaro, who was said to have quickly risen through the ranks through the empress consort's favor.

Nakamaro, who was also Kōken's most trusted advisor, was known to be both ambitious and relentless. He wished to be the very best in court and would not tolerate anyone surpassing his influence. When the court frequently mentioned and praised another name, Tachibana no Moroe, Nakamaro refused to remain silent.

Moroe was not a newcomer. He was a respected official from the powerful Tachibana clan. His influence had grown tremendously, especially after he introduced policies aimed at easing the burdens of commoners. To some, he was a true official of the imperial court: just, competent, and moderate. Nakamaro, however, saw his rising popularity as a threat.

The opportunity to silence Moroe came when he allegedly made inappropriate remarks about Empress Kōken. Sources suggest that he was drunk at the time. Intoxicated or not, this was the very excuse that Nakamaro needed. Without wasting any time, he publicly demanded Moroe's resignation. Nakamaro also later accused him of plotting a rebellion. Although there was no record of Moroe ever planning such moves, he stepped down quietly, perhaps knowing that Nakamaro would stop at nothing.

Nakamaro thought he could now dominate the court unopposed. However, another obstacle lay in his path. Moroe's son, Tachibana no Naramaro, was not planning to let Nakamaro shine so easily. Naramaro, along with a group of conspirators, planned a coup to overthrow Nakamaro and remove Kōken from power. Unfortunately, the conspiracy ended before it could even begin, as their plot was leaked. It was said that Naramaro refused to back down. He confessed to planning the coup. Perhaps he expected execution, but to his surprise, Empress Kōken displayed mercy. She exiled Naramaro and the rest of the conspirators. However, this decision did not sit well with Nakamaro, who took matters into his own hands. The conspirators were beaten to death with a cane. While Naramaro's death was never mentioned, historians suggest he was included among those who died. It is plausible that the record of his death was erased later on by his granddaughter, who eventually became empress consort of Emperor Saga.

With all obstacles removed, Nakamaro stood as the most powerful man in the imperial court, second only to the reigning empress. With Kōmyō's continuous support, he began to behave like a regent in all but name. As ambitious as he was, Nakamaro had many plans in mind. He initiated military projects aimed at subduing northern Japan. Outposts were built, and garrisons were installed on the borders of modern-day Hokkaido, a region not yet fully under imperial control at that time. Nakamaro even expressed his plans to invade Silla, though the campaign never materialized.

His influence continued to grow tremendously. In 758 CE, Nakamaro and Kōmyō successfully pressured Empress Kōken to abdicate the throne to their puppet, Emperor Junnin. Things went smoothly for Nakamaro for two years. His power hinged on Kōmyō, so when she died in 760, Nakamaro saw a shift of power in the imperial court. Instead of witnessing a new figure rise to power, Kōken began to reassert her power.

Although she had abdicated the throne, the former empress was still very much involved in state matters. This was far from uncommon. Japan's political system had a tradition of cloistered power, where retired emperors or empresses continued to wield influence despite stepping down from the throne. After her abdication, Kōken retreated to the temple, where she became a Buddhist nun. Sources claimed that she even shaved her head. However, after Kōmyō's death, she seemed to have embarked on a journey away from the path of enlightenment so she could reclaim her authority. She courted other branches of the Fujiwara clan, formed new alliances, and strengthened the ones she already had.

Nakamaro sensed that this was the beginning of the end, especially since his power base was beginning to shrink. He was losing favor even with the Fujiwara clan itself. In a desperate effort to bounce back, Nakamaro began bolstering his military might. However, he made one fatal error. Nakamaro was said to have consulted a fortune teller to determine the best date for him to launch a rebellion. The fortune teller, however, chose to betray him. Either out of fear or loyalty to the empress, the fortune teller leaked his plans. What happened afterward was rather straightforward. Kōken stripped Nakamaro of his rank and his Fujiwara name. Nakamaro fled, but he was eventually cornered and killed. His head was brought to the capital.

Kōken went on to depose Emperor Junnin. He accused him of conspiring with Nakamaro and exiled the poor emperor to Awaji Island. Sources claim that Junnin tried to escape but failed terribly; he was captured and murdered. As for Kōken, she officially returned to the throne, ruling under the name Empress Shōtoku. However, the empress soon got herself embroiled in yet another conflict when she planned to pass the throne to someone unfamiliar. His name was Dōkyō.

A depiction of Empress Shōtoku.[82]

He was neither a royal nor an aristocrat. His background was rather modest, though no details of his early life survived. What is known is that Dōkyō was a Buddhist monk. His involvement in the imperial court began when he visited the empress (before her re-ascension), offering prayers. At that time, Kōken had fallen mysteriously ill. No one could cure her except for Dōkyō, who arrived and reportedly nursed her back to health. After this incident, Dōkyō became her most trusted confidant.

Some may question how exactly the empress grew close to an individual with no impressive background. It is worth noting that Kōken was not actually the first choice to succeed to the throne. Emperor Shōmu's initial heir was his son, Prince Motoi. Unfortunately, he died less than a year after his birth. So, Shōmu made his daughter the next empress. However, to avoid creating a new bloodline that could compete with other imperial branches, she was not allowed to marry or bear children. Alone and politically sidelined after her abdication, she found comfort in Dōkyō, especially as her former advisor, Nakamaro, grew more invested in Junnin.

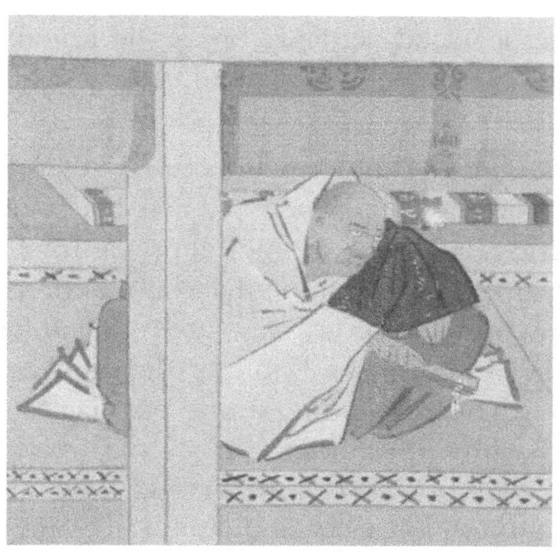

A depiction of Dōkyō.[83]

Many claimed that Kōken and Dōkyō had an even deeper relationship. They were believed to be lovers, though no concrete evidence exists to confirm it. What was certain was that Dōkyō's rise was faster than one could imagine. From a mere monk whose background was nothing more than a mystery, he was eventually appointed by the empress herself as Daijō-daijin (Grand Minister of State), which was the highest office in court. He was also given the title of Hōō (a Buddhist monarch), which gave him the power to issue edicts in the name of religion. At this point in time, Dōkyō had amassed such power that he was even allowed to appoint loyalists, including his brother, to court positions. This bypassed the traditional noble families who had long dominated the imperial court.

His pro-Buddhist reforms further agitated the court. Temples were granted land and tax exemptions. Meanwhile, the rest of the people, including the nobles, were faced with increasing restrictions on their holdings. Dōkyō also placed more monks in government positions. He was clearly pushing for a system where the state and Buddhist institutions worked hand in hand. Of course, this created a disadvantage for Shinto shrines and the aristocracy.

Many feared that it was only a matter of time before the empress stepped down and made Dōkyō her successor. It did not help that Dōkyō was already acting like one. Not only did he don garments similar to those worn by emperors, but he also dined in the imperial fashion and traveled in a palanquin styled after those of the royals. If Dōkyō were to be handed the throne, it would certainly break the imperial bloodline that had ruled Japan for centuries. Worst of all, his rise would possibly mark the beginning of a theocracy.

The public's fear almost came true in 769 CE when the court suddenly received a monk from the Shinto shrine, Usa Hachimangū. The monk claimed that the gods had given signs of approval for Dōkyō to become the next emperor. It is safe to assume that the empress was overjoyed by the message. The court, however, was far from content. Perhaps as a move to calm officials, Empress Shōtoku dispatched a trusted official named Wake no Kiyomaro to the shrine so that he could verify the prophecy. When Kiyomaro returned, he revealed that the prophecy was false and that the gods had spoken otherwise: only those with imperial blood could ascend to the Chrysanthemum Throne. The court was relieved, but Empress Shōtoku was not. She was said to have demoted Kiyomaro. Still, this was the beginning of the end for Dōkyō.

Usa Jingū, formerly known as the Usa Hachimangū.[84]

His final nail in the coffin came in 770 CE. His biggest supporter, Empress Shōtoku, died. Dōkyō eventually lost all his protection, and most of his supporters vanished overnight. He was then stripped of his titles and exiled to Shimotsuke Province, a remote area in modern-day Tochigi Prefecture. What happened to him afterward was not recorded, but some suggested he died two years later. His loyal supporters, who had been exiled as well, were pardoned later on when Emperor Kanmu rose as the next ruler. It was said that Kanmu recognized that Dōkyō's rise had been a symptom of a deeper issue. All those years had given the Buddhist clergy a chance to become too powerful. By the end of the Nara period, temples owned vast tracts of land, exerted influence over court decisions, and held enough manpower to pose a political threat. To Kanmu, the only way to reduce their grip was to start over far from Nara.

After Nara

By moving the capital to Heian-kyō, Kanmu hoped to create distance between the court and the growing presence of the Buddhist clergy. But even in the newly constructed capital, the influence of these Buddhist institutions was far from extinguished. Ironically, Kanmu himself played a hand in establishing Enryaku-ji Temple—this was the very same temple that would later rise to dominate the capital and get involved in the violent rivalries with Mii-dera and Kōfuku-ji.

The Golden Hall at Mii-dera, a national treasure of Japan.[85]

The move was done for several reasons. Spiritually, Kanmu authorized the construction of the temple to safeguard the city. Mount Hiei was considered a vulnerable direction in traditional geomancy (located northeast of Heian-kyō, the mountain was believed to be an entry and exit point for demons). To ward off evil, the emperor authorized the construction of the temple on the mountain itself. Politically, the temple was to serve as a counterbalance to the dominant institutions of Nara, though this only shifted the axis of power. Since the emperor also had close relations with the monk Saichō, Enryaku-ji became the center of the Tendai school of Buddhism. Yet, in time, it would also become a different kind of fortress altogether.

History repeated once more. Over time, Enryaku-ji amassed too much power. It accumulated vast tracts of land, attracted hundreds of novice monks—many from aristocratic families—and eventually developed its own internal hierarchy and paramilitary discipline. Of course, Enryaku-ji was not the only temple that flourished at that time. Kōfuku-ji, back in Nara, also continued to retain immense wealth, especially under the patronage of the powerful Fujiwara clan.

The Birth of the Warrior Monks

With the number of lands they possessed, these Buddhist temples could no longer rely on themselves to protect their sprawling estates. They hired armed retainers to protect not only their lands and grain stores but also traveling pilgrims from bandits. However, depending on forces outside of the temple had its own downside. These warriors usually had their own agendas and could switch loyalty in mere moments, provided they were paid more. By the 10th and 11th centuries, large temples like Enryaku-ji chose to produce their own troops of warriors. These men were not just normal warriors; they were also ordained.

The main hall of Enryaku-ji.[86]

These warrior monks were known in Japanese as *sōhei*. They were taught both sutras and weaponry. More often than not, these monks fought using the *naginata*, a polearm with a curved blade. This type of weapon gave them more reach and versatility in battle. Others wielded *yari* (spears), *bō* (wooden staff), bows and arrows, and swords—though swords were more often used by hired mercenaries. There were also those who fought with *shakujō*, a type of metal-tipped staff used in rituals that could double as a bludgeoning weapon.

Like typical monks, the sōhei shaved their heads. Some even tied white headbands tightly around their heads, especially during battle, to keep sweat from entering their eyes. They wore lightweight armor beneath their black robes, often simple iron cuirasses or leather vests. Although they could typically be seen in battle wearing their signature white cowls, beneath them were also helmets, though they lacked the ornate crests that generally adorned those of the samurai.

A statue of a sōhei.[87]

Monks from Mount Hiei's Enryaku-ji were especially disciplined in warfare. Apart from learning sutra and chants, these monks also underwent physical conditioning, practiced formation tactics, and trained with weapons as part of their temple lives. It is safe to say that their military strength was not merely for show. Almost similar to the imperial forces, these warrior monks formed organized units that were put under the command of senior priests or military abbots. They were capable of launching synchronized attacks not only on forces of rival temples but also on political targets who refused to comply with their demands. Even their monastery itself was fortified and structured almost like a military garrison.

Being one of the few major temples in Japan that held significant power (some of the others being Mii-dera, Kōfuku-ji, and Tōdai-ji), Enryaku-ji could exert direct pressure on the imperial court itself. Most of the time, its tactics to ensure that the court met its demands included open confrontation and intimidation. Its favorite strategy was known as *gōso* (sometimes spelled as *kōso*). This processional protest typically involved hundreds of monks wearing hoods known as *kabutō* marching out of their temples. They carried *mikoshi* (portable shrines installed on palanquins) into the capital. If the court refused to fulfill their demands or provide a response, the monks would leave the mikoshi in the middle of the palace. This would halt all activities and work in the court; ignoring the mikoshi was considered extremely disrespectful.

A mikoshi.[88]

If the procession did not work, the warrior monks would not hesitate to wreak violence. Apart from the imperial court, these temples often clashed with each other. Enryaku-ji frequently found itself at odds with the Mii-dera temple and the Fujiwara-backed Kōfuku-ji temple in Nara. The rivalry between these three temples soon became one of the bloodiest episodes in Japan's religious history. They turned sutras into war banners and temple bells into war drums. When they waged war against each other, even local governors hesitated to intervene. To their eyes, challenging a sōhei might offend not just a warrior but also the heavenly gods.

The Blood Feud of Sacred Powers

Among all the ranks and positions in a Buddhist temple—especially in the Tendai tradition—none held as much weight as that of the *Yama no zasu* (also known simply as *zasu*). By the time of the Heian era, Enryaku-ji had evolved into something bigger. It was no longer a mere spiritual sanctuary; it had become the nucleus of the Tendai sect with deep political ties and vast landholdings. To become a zasu or the abbot of the mountain meant more than just commanding Buddhist doctrine. The benefits included massive influence in court, complete control over temples and estates, and leadership over tens of thousands of monks.

Trouble, which later escalated into a bloodbath, soon brewed in the late 10th century. The imperial court had voiced its candidate to serve as Enryaku-ji's zasu. The man was Yōkei. However, Yōkei was not just another ordinary monk. He had previously served as abbot of Mii-dera, which was a rival Tendai temple located at the foot of Mount Hiei. Both Enryaku-ji and Mii-dera practiced the same religious traditions, yet they represented opposing factions. Enryaku-ji was the center of Sanmon, a Tendai branch descended from the teachings of the priest Ennin (also known as Jikaku Daishi). Meanwhile, Jimon, another branch of Tendai, taught by the priest Enchin, found its foothold at Mii-dera. For many years, their doctrinal differences became the root of their rivalry.

So, it is not surprising that the monks of Enryaku-ji strongly opposed the court's decision to appoint Yōkei as their leader. In their eyes, this was not only unacceptable, but it was also an insult to their constitution. As a sign of protest, two hundred sōhei descended into the capital in 981 CE, equipped with weapons in their hands and demands on their lips. Details are scarce, but it is safe to assume that the demonstration shook the court. Yōkei eventually took a step back. But still, the conflict did not end right away. For twelve years, the imperial court continued to pressure Enryaku-ji to accept Yōkei. Whether they were oblivious to the might of the warrior monks or were simply hoping to quell the sectarian rivalry through forced reconciliation, this move soon became the catalyst for a bloodbath. Enryaku-ji refused again and again. Surprisingly, it was not Enryaku-ji that launched an attack first.

Mii-dera, enraged by Enryaku-ji's stubbornness and the continued rejection of one of their own, chose violence. Their warrior monks ascended Mount Hiei in 993 and attacked Enryaku-ji. They laid waste to a temple where Ennin himself had once lived. Enryaku-ji retaliated by sending its highly disciplined sōhei to Mii-dera. Here, they torched more than forty temples, halls, and residences associated with Enchin.

That was not the end of their vicious rivalry. Over the course of the 10th, 11th, and 12th centuries, violence erupted again and again. Each time a zasu candidate was named, one side felt slighted or excluded. They fought over lands and taxes under the name of their different doctrines. This was a time when warrior monks displayed their roles; they transformed religious rivalries into full military campaigns.

Casualties were heavy on both sides, but Mii-dera suffered more. In the 11th century alone, the sōhei of Enryaku-ji managed to burn Mii-dera to the ground at least four times. To many, it seemed like it was impossible for the two temples to reconcile. However, history is rarely black and white. There existed moments when they shook hands and became unlikely allies. More often than not, they united to defeat a shared enemy.

This could be seen in 1081, when the powerful temple in Nara, Kōfuku-ji, burned Mii-dera to the ground and looted its temples. This was a calculated act of violence rooted in political tensions, possibly linked to Mii-dera's affiliations in a court dispute (Mii-dera had aligned with the Minamoto clan, while Kōfuku-ji had the support of the Taira clan). In a turn of events, Enryaku-ji—the temple also had a long-standing rivalry with Kōfuku-ji—offered assistance to Mii-dera. The two temples combined their forces and launched a retaliatory assault on Kōfuku-ji. This unique alliance was not a one-time occurrence. In 1117, Enryaku-ji and Mii-dera would again put aside their animosity to attack the great temple in Nara.

The rivalry between these Buddhist sects would flare up repeatedly over the centuries. It ultimately came to an end in the late 16th century with the rise of Oda Nobunaga, one of the three great unifiers of Japan. By the time Nobunaga had risen to power, the Buddhist temples were considered one of the main obstacles to unifying the archipelago. Their influence had grown uncontrollably strong, forcing the warlord to launch a campaign against them. In 1571, Nobunaga laid a siege on Enryaku-ji and laid waste to its monasteries. Records claimed he infamously massacred all the monks, scholars, priests, women, and children in the temple. Modern historians, however, doubt the scale of the massacre; the destruction was possibly less than some historical sources indicate. Nevertheless, his victory ended Buddhist militancy.

Conclusion

Through the stories we explored in the chapters of this book, it becomes clear that Japan's early history is neither simple nor uniform. Its history is defined by a diversity of beliefs, regional customs, political structures, and cultural practices. But still, these stories are far from enough to capture the full image of everything that shaped the country during its formative years. It is safe to assume there are still dozens of voices that we have not heard, events we have not yet covered, and regions we have not yet ventured into. However, that is the nature of history; there is always more to uncover and learn.

This book was never meant to be a complete account. The chapters were written to highlight the people and events that have been left out of mainstream narratives, not because they lacked significance but because they do not fit neatly into the story told by official records. By turning our attention to these almost-forgotten episodes, we can take a closer look at a more honest picture of what life was like in ancient Japan. These stories also help us better understand how Japan became the country it is today. Its cultural traditions, political structures, social values, and even sacred rituals did not appear fully formed out of thin air. Instead, they were shaped bit by bit through centuries of tension, adaptation, and negotiation. Sometimes, progress came through conflict. Other times, it happened quietly through the actions of individuals who never made it into the spotlight.

Of course, to unpack the entire history of early Japan requires hundreds of pages, but much of it still remains uncertain or incomplete.

Gaps in the written record, regional biases in historical documentation, and the limited survival of non-elite voices mean that large portions of the past are still out of reach. Archaeologists are still discovering more evidence that offers new clues to a certain period or region, and historians still debate the true meaning behind the lines written in ancient chronicles. Still, the act of revisiting these often overlooked stories has value; it reminds us that history is never fixed.

If this book has encouraged you to look a little closer, to question what you thought you knew, or to develop a renewed interest in Japan's past, then it has done its job. It is worth it to always keep in mind that the lesser-known stories may not always be the loudest, but they are often the ones that give depth to everything we thought we knew.

Free Bonus from Captivating History (Available for a Limited time)

Hi History Lovers!

Now you have a chance to join our exclusive history list so you can get your first history ebook for free as well as discounts and a potential to get more history books for free!

Simply visit the link below to join.

Or, Scan the QR code!

captivatinghistory.com/ebook

Also, make sure to follow us on Facebook, X, and YouTube by searching for Captivating History.

Bibliography

Part 1: Ancient India

Anand, Prakriti. "The King Whose Dream Was to Create Hell on Earth: The Story of

Ashoka's Hell from Ancient India." *Medium*, May 23, 2025. https://medium.com/@prakritipassion/the-king-whose-dream-was-to-create-hell-on-earth-the-story-of-ashokas-hell-from-ancient-india-659c15282391.

"Ancient Civilizations: India." *National Geographic.* Accessed November 16, 2025.

https://education.nationalgeographic.org/resource/ancient-civilizations-india/.

"Ashoka the Great - Rise of the Mauryan Empire Documentary." Posted April 18, 2019, by

Kings and Generals. *YouTube*, 17 min., 51 sec. www.youtube.com/watch?v=Ed6UZtVTI64.

Bin Naveed, Muhammad. "White Huns (Hephthalites)." *World History Encyclopedia*, June

22, 2015. www.worldhistory.org/White_Huns_(Hephthalites).

"Chanakya: The Political Genius Who Orchestrated the Rise of the Mauryas." Posted May 9,

2022, by Odd Compass. *YouTube*, 16 min., 34 sec. www.youtube.com/watch?v=gAeXw-txPLs.

Datta, Saurav Ranjan. "Ajatashatru." *World History Encyclopedia*, December 18, 2019.

www.worldhistory.org/Ajatashatru.

"Gupta Empire - Golden Age of Classical India - Ancient Civilizations." Posted October 22,

2024, by Kings and Generals. *YouTube*, 18 min., 58 sec. www.youtube.com/watch?v=Vu7myRpw4m4.

"The Hephthalites - Who Were These People and What Do We Known About Them so Far."

Posted February 28, 2024, by Boring Old History. *YouTube*, 22 min., 10 sec. www.youtube.com/watch?v=U2qHaAPQvvo.

Holmes, Robert. "Alexander the Great in India: Furthest and Final Conquests 327-325 BCE."

The Collector, December 4, 2021.

www.thecollector.com/alexander-the-great-india-conquest-achaemenid-empire.

"Indus Valley 3D: Walk the Streets of a 5000-year-old Civilization." Posted July 26, 2025,

by Odd Compass. *YouTube*, 33 min., 18 sec. www.youtube.com/watch?v=bBbE4iOm4cs.

"Introduction to the Story about the Elder Nun Kuṇḍalakesā." Ancient Buddhist Texts.

Accessed November 25, 2025.

https://ancient-buddhist-texts.net/English-Texts/Foremost-Elder-Nuns/09-Kundalakesa.htm.

Manhar, Sharma. "Dasarajna War (Battle of Ten Kings)." *Manhar Sharma* (blog), February

7, 2020. www.manharsharma.com/post/dasarajna-war-battle-of-ten-kings.

Mingren, Wu. "The Rise of Chandragupta Maurya, and the Golden Age of the Mauryan Empire." *Ancient Origins*, May 31, 2023.

www.ancient-origins.net/history-famous-people/chandragupta-maurya-002277.

"Porus: The Indian King Who Confronted Alexander the Great." *World History Edu*,

December 31, 2024. https://worldhistoryedu.com/porus-the-indian-king-who-confronted-alexander-the-great/.

"The Origins of War in Ancient India 5,000 BC—300 BC." Posted December 10, 2023, by

SandRhoman History. *YouTube*, 22 min., 12 sec. www.youtube.com/watch?v=KukBH8eyVOU.

Szczepanski, Kallie. "Biography of Chandragupta Maurya, Founder of the Mauryan Empire."

ThoughtCo, July 3, 2019. www.thoughtco.com/chandragupta-maurya-195490.

Vredeveld, Peter. "Ashoka - Preacher of Buddhism." *Original Buddhas.* Accessed November

20, 2025. www.originalbuddhas.com/blog/ashoka-the-great-emperor.

Wasson, Donald. L. "Battle of Hydaspes." *World History Encyclopedia,* February 26, 2014.

www.worldhistory.org/article/660/battle-of-hydaspes.

Part 2: Ancient China

"Ban Zhao." The University of Chicago, February 2, 2022.

womanisrational.uchicago.edu/2022/02/02/ban-zhao.

"Brave Men Never Return: On the Historical Trail of Assassin Jing Ke." The Hutong.

thehutong.com/brave-men-never-return-on-the-historical-trail-of-assassin-jing-ke. Accessed August 18, 2025.

"Bronze Sacred Tree Found in Sanxingdui Sacrificial Pit." *The History Blog,* September 9, 2021. www.thehistoryblog.com/archives/62185.

"Cai Lun - Improving Papermaking Technology." Chinese Learning, January 12, 2023. www.chineselearning.com/chinese-name/cai-lun-papermaking.

Cartwright, Mark. "Eunuchs in Ancient China." *World History,* July 27, 2017. www.worldhistory.org/article/1109/eunuchs-in-ancient-china.

Cartwright, Mark. "Women in Ancient China." *World History,* October 19, 2017.

www.worldhistory.org/article/1136/women-in-ancient-china.

Clementine. "Ban Chao: A Diplomatic Legend on the China Silk Road." China Xian

Tour, updated March 6, 2025.

www.chinaxiantour.com/xian-travel-blog/ban-chao.html.

Colville, Alex. "China's Renaissance Man." The China Project, March 1, 2021.

www.thechinaproject.com/2021/03/01/chinas-renaissance-man.

Colville, Alex. "Yu The Great, Tamer of China's Greatest Floods." The China Project, August 24, 2020.

www.thechinaproject.com/2020/08/24/yu-the-great-tamer-of-chinas-greatest-floods.

Ghose, Tia. "Mystery of Ancient Chinese Civilization's Disappearance Explained."

Live Science, December 24, 2014.

www.livescience.com/49247-chinese-civilization-disappearance-explained.html.

"How Was the Ancient Loulan City Discovered?" Silk Road Travel, June 22, 2020. www.silkroadtravel.com/silk-road-travel-guide/ancient-city-loulan.html.

"Inside the Elegant Concubine Rankings of the Six Palaces of the Tang Dynasty Imperial Harem." Amimisu, YouTube, July 17, 2025. www.youtube.com/watch?v=21V0qcBBKeQ&t=983s.

Jin, Alex. "Why Did Emperor Qin Shi Huang Not Determine the Empress?" Travel China Guide, August 4, 2025. www.travelchinaguide.com/attraction/shaanxi/xian/terra_cotta_army/qin-shihuang-empress.htm?srsltid=AfmBOoql3JkadV9tVAhpgTcPY-_HUFOT5X5k2lPxWiyIwLHOtffO5yEU.

Leung, Crystal. "Gay Emperors in Chinese History." China Publishing Group, June 27, 2019. www.theworldofchinese.com/2019/06/gay-emperors-in-chinese-history.

London, Helen. "Zhuo Wenjun, the Woman Who Got Her Man Back with the Beauty of Poems." *Nspirement*, September 6, 2022. www.nspirement.com/2022/09/06/zhuo-wenjun-poems.html.

Mark, Emily. "Xia Dynasty." *World History*, January 16, 2016. www.worldhistory.org/Xia_Dynasty.

Mark, Joshua. J. "Sima Qian." *World History*, July 6, 2020. www.worldhistory.org/Sima_Qian.

Norman, Jeremy. "The First Emperor of China Destroys Most Records of the Past Along with 460 or More, Scholars." Norman Jeremy. Accessed August 13, 2025. www.historyofinformation.com/detail.php?id=2491.

"Princess Pingyang Co-Founder of Tang Dynasty." Cool History Bros, YouTube, December 26, 2020. www.youtube.com/watch?v=Nt-nqgXoiM8.

Ryan. "Zhu Yingtai and Liang Shanbo – a Relentless Love in China's Folklore." China Partnership, February 12, 2015. www.chinapartnership.org/blog/2015/02/zhu-yingtai-and-liang-shanbo-a-relentless-love-in-chinas-folklore.

"Shocking Romance of Male Concubines in the Han Dynasty of Ancient China." Amimisu, YouTube, July 24, 2025. www.youtube.com/watch?v=WMCl-4SKjbs.

Stewart, James. "Li Yannian, House of Flying Daggers." Vermont Public, September
30, 2019. www.vermontpublic.org/programs/2019-09-30/timeline-li-yannian-house-of-flying-daggers.

"The Lost Kingdom of Loulan." Gwong Zau Kung Fu, May 10, 2021,
www.gwongzaukungfu.com/en/the-lost-kingdom-of-loulan.

"The Lost World of Sanxingdui." *World Archaeology*, November 23, 2023.
www.world-archaeology.com/features/the-lost-world-of-sanxingdui.

"The Musical Love Story of Sima Xiangru and Zhuo Wenjun." The Historian Hut,
March 31, 2020. www.thehistorianshut.com/2020/03/31/the-musical-love-story-of-sima-xiangru-and-zhuo-wenjun.

"The Mysterious History of Ancient China's Nine Tripod Cauldrons." History Skills, Accessed August 22, 2025.
www.historyskills.com/classroom/year-7/nine-tripod-cauldrons/?srsltid=AfmBOoriV64qLks-dRGV6wP69tpJPp8AAasAafFQN1E0QOSpugpqtWEZ.

Theobald, Ulrich. "Wu Zixu." Theobold Ulrich, November 13, 2010.
www.chinaknowledge.de/History/Zhou/personswuzixu.html.

Wee, Kek Koon. "Qu Yuan, Chinese Patriot Whose Death Is Said to Have Inspired
Dragon Boat Festival Customs." *South China Morning Post*, May 31, 2025.
www.scmp.com/lifestyle/chinese-culture/article/3312392/qu-yuan-chinese-patriot-whose-death-said-have-inspired-dragon-boat-festival-customs.

Wong, Noel. "How a Legendary Romance Ended China's Golden Age." *Free Malaysia Today*, February 15, 2022.
www.freemalaysiatoday.com/category/leisure/2022/02/15/how-a-legendary-romance-ended-chinas-golden-age.

Wu, Haiyun, and Ruolin Ye. "The Mysterious Ancient City That's Rewriting Chinese
History." *Sixth Tone*, July 7, 2021. www.sixthtone.com/news/1007903.

Xinhua. "Exploring the Lost Land of Loulan." *China Daily*, April 22, 2024.
www.chinadailyhk.com/hk/article/581516.

"Xuanwu Gate Incident - Tang Taizong's Bloody Rise to Power." Cool History Bros,
YouTube, January 5, 2021. www.youtube.com/watch?v=9gbSgtztHA8.

"Zhuo Wenjun: A Tale of Love and Betrayal." Kim Dramer, YouTube, January 1, 2021. www.youtube.com/watch?v=R_dV3gER2aI.

Part 3: Ancient Japan

Bernard, C. (2014, June 12). *Tomoe Gozen: Badass Women in Japanese history*. Tofugu. https://www.tofugu.com/japan/tomoe-gozen/

Cartwright, M. (2017, May 8). *Kukai*. World History. https://www.worldhistory.org/Kukai/

Chapter 1: Hot Springs as Tojiba (Places for Recuperation). (n.d.). Kaleidoscope of Books. Retrieved June 18, 2025, from https://www.ndl.go.jp/kaleido/e/entry/23/1.html

Eli. (2023, February 20). *E79 The Plague of Emperor Sujin*. A History of Japan. https://historyofjapan.co.uk/2023/02/20/the-plague-of-emperor-sujin/

Garcia, G. (n.d.). *Sohei: Buddhist Warrior Monks of Japan*. The History Corner. Retrieved June 23, 2025, from https://www.thehistorycorner.org/articles-by-the-team/sohei-buddhist-warrior-monks-of-japan

Hicks, J. (2016, February 5). *Goryo Shrine, Kyoto (Kami Goryo Jinja/上御霊神社*. Japanophile. https://nihonnozasshi.wordpress.com/2016/02/05/goryo-shrine-kyoto-kami-goryo-jinja上御霊神社/

J. Strand, K. (2024, April 5). *The Pillow Book of Sei Shonagon - Reprising an early review*. Karla J. Strand. https://newsletter.karlajstrand.com/the-pillow-book-of-sei-shonagon-a-reprisal-of-an-early-review/

Japanese Empress Jingū: All About The Legendary Onna-Bugeisha. (2024, March 8). Design Dash. https://designdash.com/wellness/mindset/japanese-empress-jingu-all-about-the-legendary-onna-bugeisha/

Johnson Lewis, J. (2025, June 10). *Empress Suiko of Japan*. ThoughtCo. https://www.thoughtco.com/empress-suiko-of-japan-biography-3528831

Linfamy. (2010, May 18). *Romance in early Japan (BEST dating ritual?)* [Video]. YouTube. https://www.youtube.com/watch?v=wEXcaMJbaYg&list=PLOWnSFzV-C9YfEch8cs8KNB6kFfkOTKd1&index=8

Linfamy. (2025, May 20). *Yobai: The Japanese practice of sneaking into women's bedrooms* [Video]. YouTube. https://www.youtube.com/watch?v=Fi8LdIbUM5A&t=34s

Mason, R., & Caiger, J. G. (2011). *History of Japan: Revised Edition*. Tuttle Publishing.

Meyer, M. (n.d.). *Hōsōgami*. Yokai.com. Retrieved June 15, 2025, from https://yokai.com/housougami/?srsltid=AfmBOoqpMo9oKIpkSmVSTiVIFaXVXPemTxxaUkkV9KplTmCmdL1FcRMG

Mori, Y. (2023, June 5). *Nagaokakyo: Why was this ancient capital city so short-lived?* The Japan News.
https://japannews.yomiuri.co.jp/original/perspectives/20230605-114311/

Neill Tincher, D. (n.d.). *Dokyo - The Rasputin of Japan Who Almost Became Emperor.* More Than Tokyo. Retrieved June 22, 2025, from
https://www.morethantokyo.com/dokyo-buddhist-priest-villain/

Neill Tincher, D. (n.d.). *Fujiwara Hirotsugu's rebellion and the forgotten role of the Hayato Warriors.* More Than Tokyo. Retrieved June 12, 2025, from
https://www.morethantokyo.com/fujiwara-hirotsugus-rebellion/

Neill Tincher, D. (n.d.). *Hayato - the forgotten ancient people of Southern Kyushu.* More Than Tokyo. Retrieved June 12, 2025, from
https://www.morethantokyo.com/hayato-southern-kyushu/

Sahir. (2023, March 23). *The Japanese smallpox epidemic of the 8th century: Cause and effect.* Ancient Origins. https://www.ancient-origins.net/history-important-events/japanese-smallpox-epidemic-0018112

Sensei, J. (2011, January 17). *The Sohei.* Together With Japan.
https://jp.learnoutlive.com/the-sohei/

Shaw, T. (2019, July 15). *10 Unusual and Fascinating Japanese Emperors.* ListVerse. https://listverse.com/2019/07/15/10-unusual-and-fascinating-japanese-emperors/

Szczepanski, K. (2025, April 30). *Beauty Standards in Heian Japan, 794–1185 CE.* ThoughtCo. https://www.thoughtco.com/beauty-in-heian-japan-195557

The Courtly World: Sei Shōnagon and Lady Murasaki: Sei Shōnagon. (n.d.). Bennington College. Retrieved June 20, 2025, from
https://libraryguides.bennington.edu/courtly/shonagon

Warrior monks of feudal Japan—These monks did not always practice peace. (2016, November 6). War History Online.
https://www.warhistoryonline.com/guest-bloggers/warrior-monks-feudal-japan-monks-not-always-practice-peace-x.html

Wright, G. (2022, November 30). *Hoderi.* Mythopedia.
https://mythopedia.com/topics/hoderi

Image Sources

1   Hafiz Mujahid Raza, CC BY-SA 4.0 <https://creativecommons.org/licenses/by-sa/4.0>, via Wikimedia Commons: https://commons.wikimedia.org/wiki/File:Ravi_River,_Lahore.jpg

2   https://commons.wikimedia.org/wiki/File:Defeat_of_Porus_by_the_Macedonians.jpg

3   https://commons.wikimedia.org/wiki/File:Le_Brun,_Alexander_and_Porus.jpg

4   Metropolitan Museum of Art, CC0, via Wikimedia Commons: https://commons.wikimedia.org/wiki/File:MET_1984_482_237872.jpg

5   Muhammad Bin Naveed, CC BY-SA 3.0 <https://creativecommons.org/licenses/by-sa/3.0>, via Wikimedia Commons: https://commons.wikimedia.org/wiki/File:Another_view_of_Granary_and_Great_Hall_on_Mound_F.JPG

6   Avantiputra7, CC BY-SA 3.0 <https://creativecommons.org/licenses/by-sa/3.0>, via Wikimedia Commons: https://commons.wikimedia.org/wiki/File:Indus_Valley_Civilization,_Mature_Phase_(2600-1900_BCE).png

7   Gary Todd, CC0, via Wikimedia Commons: https://commons.wikimedia.org/wiki/File:Harappan_(Indus_Valley)_Balance_%26_Weights.jpg

8   Gaffar772, CC BY-SA 4.0 <https://creativecommons.org/licenses/by-sa/4.0>, via Wikimedia Commons: https://commons.wikimedia.org/wiki/File:Moen_Jo_Daro_(The_Mond_of_the_Deads).jpg

9   Avantiputra7, CC BY-SA 3.0 <https://creativecommons.org/licenses/by-sa/3.0>, via Wikimedia Commons: https://commons.wikimedia.org/wiki/File:Nanda_Empire,_c.325_BCE.png

10 https://commons.wikimedia.org/wiki/File:Chanakya_artistic_depiction.jpg

11 https://commons.wikimedia.org/wiki/File:Ruins_of_Patliputra_at_Kumhrar.JPG

12 Photo Dharma from Sadao, Thailand, CC BY 2.0
   <https://creativecommons.org/licenses/by/2.0>, via Wikimedia Commons:
   https://commons.wikimedia.org/wiki/File:Ashoka%27s_visit_to_the_Ramagrama_stu
   pa_Sanchi_Stupa_1_Southern_gateway.jpg

13 https://commons.wikimedia.org/wiki/File:Dhauli_Ashoka_inscription_
   Puri_District_India.jpg

14 User:BPG, CC BY-SA 2.5 <https://creativecommons.org/licenses/by-sa/2.5>, via
   Wikimedia Commons: https://commons.wikimedia.org/wiki/File:Bimbisarajail.jpg

15 https://commons.wikimedia.org/wiki/File:Draupadi_and_Pandavas.jpg

16 Gita Press Gorakhpur, CC0, via Wikimedia Commons:
   https://commons.wikimedia.org/wiki/File:Sit_with_Rama.jpg

17 https://commons.wikimedia.org/wiki/File:Asoka%27s_Queen.jpg

18 Nomu420, CC BY-SA 3.0 <https://creativecommons.org/licenses/by-sa/3.0>, via
   Wikimedia Commons: https://commons.wikimedia.org/wiki/File:Amrapali_
   greets_Buddha_Roundel_36_buddha_ivory_tusk.jpg

19 Bernard Gagnon, CC BY-SA 3.0 <https://creativecommons.org/licenses/by-sa/3.0>,
   via Wikimedia Commons:
   https://commons.wikimedia.org/wiki/File:Shri_Ram_Ghat_01.jpg

20 Pravit, CC BY-SA 4.0 <https://creativecommons.org/licenses/by-sa/4.0>, via
   Wikimedia Commons: https://commons.wikimedia.org
   /wiki/File:Taklamakan_desert.jpg

21 Schreiber, CC BY-SA 3.0 <http://creativecommons.org/licenses/by-sa/3.0/>, via
   Wikimedia Commons: https://commons.wikimedia.org/wiki/File:
   Tarimbecken_3._Jahrhundert.png

22 No machine-readable author provided. World Imaging assumed (based on copyright
   claims)., CC BY-SA 3.0 <http://creativecommons.org/licenses/by-sa/3.0/>, via
   Wikimedia Commons: https://commons.wikimedia.org/wiki/File:
   LoulanCarvedWoodenBeam.JPG

23 Dan LundbergEric Feng, CC BY-SA 4.0 <https://creativecommons.org/licenses/by-
   sa/4.0>, via Wikimedia Commons: https://commons.wikimedia.org
   /wiki/File:Beauty_of_Loulan_(reconstruction_and_original).jpg

24 Tyg728, CC BY-SA 4.0 <https://creativecommons.org/licenses/by-sa/4.0>, via
   Wikimedia Commons: https://commons.wikimedia.org/wiki/File
   :%E2%85%A0%E5%8F%B7%E5%A4%A7%E5%9E%8B%E9%9D%92%E9%93%9
   C%E7%A5%9E%E6%A0%91.jpg

25 Tyg728, CC BY-SA 4.0 <https://creativecommons.org/licenses/by-sa/4.0>, via
   Wikimedia Commons: https://commons.wikimedia.org/wiki/File:%E9%9
   D%92%E9%93%9C%E7%BA%B5%E7%9B%AE%E9%9D%A2%E5%85%B7B.jpg

26 Gary Todd, CC0, via Wikimedia Commons:
   https://commons.wikimedia.org/wiki/File:2014_Jinsha_Gold_Mask_a.jpg

27 John Hill, CC BY-SA 3.0 <https://creativecommons.org/licenses/by-sa/3.0>, via Wikimedia Commons: https://commons.wikimedia.org/wiki/File: Statue_commemorating_Ban_Chao,_Kashgar.jpg

28 歷代聖賢半身像 冊 檀道濟, CC BY 4.0 <https://creativecommons.org/licenses/by/4.0>, via Wikimedia Commons: https://commons.wikimedia.org/wiki/File:%E6%AD%B7%E4%BB%A3%E8%81%96%E8%B3%A2%E5%8D%8A%E8%BA%AB%E5%83%8F_%E5%86%8A_%E6%AA%80%E9%81%93%E6%BF%9F_(Tan_Daoji).png

29 en:user: Kowloonese, CC BY-SA 3.0 <http://creativecommons.org/licenses/by-sa/3.0/>, via Wikimedia Commons: https://commons.wikimedia.org/wiki/File:EastHanSeismograph.JPG

30 https://commons.wikimedia.org/wiki/File:Letter_on_Papyrus.jpg

31 https://commons.wikimedia.org/wiki/File:Jingangjing.jpg

32 Gary Todd, CC0, via Wikimedia Commons: https://commons.wikimedia.org/wiki/File:Fu_Hao_Tomb,_c._1200_BC,_Reign_of_King_Wu_Ding,_Shang_Dynasty_3.jpg

33 https://commons.wikimedia.org/wiki/File:Ban_Zhao_-_Wushuang_Pu_(pref_1690,_1961).jpg

34 https://commons.wikimedia.org/wiki/File:%E7%95%AB%E9%BA%97%E7%8F%A0%E8%90%83%E7%A7%80_Gathering_Gems_of_Beauty_(%E6%BC%A2%E8%94%A1%E6%96%87%E5%A7%AC)_2.jpg

35 https://commons.wikimedia.org/wiki/File:Assassination_attempt_on_Qin_Shi_Huang.jpg

36 SY, CC BY-SA 4.0 <https://creativecommons.org/licenses/by-sa/4.0>, via Wikimedia Commons: https://commons.wikimedia.org/wiki/File: Nine_Provinces_of_China.png

37 https://commons.wikimedia.org/wiki/File:La_expedici%C3%B3n_de_Xu_Fu,_por_Utagawa_Kuniyoshi.jpg

38 Metropolitan Museum of Art, CC0, via Wikimedia Commons: https://commons.wikimedia.org/wiki/File:%E5%85%83_%E4%BD%9A%E5%90%8D_%E5%80%A3%E8%B6%99%E5%AD%9F%E9%A0%AB_%E4%B9%9D%E6%AD%8C%E5%9C%96_%E5%86%8A-Nine_Songs_MET_DP375119.jpg

39 vlasta2, bluefootedbooby on flickr.com, CC BY 2.0 <https://creativecommons.org/licenses/by/2.0>, via Wikimedia Commons: https://commons.wikimedia.org/wiki/File:Bamboo_book_-_binding_-_UCR.jpg

40 https://commons.wikimedia.org/wiki/File:Sima_Qian_(painted_portrait).jpg

41 dayu490301, CC BY 3.0 <https://creativecommons.org/licenses/by/3.0>, via Wikimedia Commons: https://commons.wikimedia.org/wiki/File: %E5%8F%B8%E9%A9%AC%E8%BF%81%E5%A2%93_-_panoramio.jpg

42 陈文 https://www.flickr.com/people/univers-finder/, CC BY 2.0 <https://creativecommons.org/licenses/by/2.0>, via Wikimedia Commons: https://commons.wikimedia.org/wiki/File:Wang_Zhaojun_Peking_Opera_13.jpg

43 https://commons.wikimedia.org/wiki/File:%E6%BC%A2%E6%AD%A6%E5%B8%9D.jpg

44 https://commons.wikimedia.org/wiki/File:%E7%95%AB%E9%BA%97%E7%8F%A0%E8%90%83%E7%A7%80_Gathering_Gems_of_Beauty_(%E6%BC%A2%E6%9D%8E%E5%A4%AB%E4%BA%BA)_2.jpg

45 Andrijko Z., CC BY-SA 4.0 <https://creativecommons.org/licenses/by-sa/4.0>, via Wikimedia Commons: https://commons.wikimedia.org/wiki/File:Monument_to_Liang_Shanbo_and_Zhu_Yingtai_near_the_Tombe_di_Giulietta_in_Verona,_Italy.jpg

46 https://commons.wikimedia.org/wiki/File:Meng_Jiang_Nu_Song_Dynasty_Lie_Nu_Zhuan.jpg

47 https://commons.wikimedia.org/wiki/File:Ch%27ien_Hs%C3%BCan_002.jpg

48 https://commons.wikimedia.org/wiki/File:Kano_Eitoku_007.jpg

49 https://commons.wikimedia.org/wiki/File:Hikohohodemi_otokowa.png

50 TUBS, CC BY-SA 3.0 <https://creativecommons.org/licenses/by-sa/3.0>, via Wikimedia Commons: https://commons.wikimedia.org/wiki/File:Kyushu_Region_in_Japan_(extended).svg

51 Fred Cherrygarden, CC BY 4.0 <https://creativecommons.org/licenses/by/4.0>, via Wikimedia Commons: https://commons.wikimedia.org/wiki/File:Hayato_Shield_Monument.jpg

52 https://commons.wikimedia.org/wiki/File:Japanese_buddhist_monk_hat_by_Arashiyama_cut.jpg

53 https://commons.wikimedia.org/wiki/File:Irukaansatsuzu.jpg

54 https://commons.wikimedia.org/wiki/File:Emperor_Sushun.jpg

55 https://commons.wikimedia.org/wiki/File:Nagaokakyo_Chodoin.jpg

56 https://commons.wikimedia.org/wiki/File:Yoshitsuya_The_Lightning_Bolt.jpg

57 https://commons.wikimedia.org/wiki/File:Shiramine-jingu_haiden.jpeg

58 Yu.nakai, CC BY-SA 3.0 <http://creativecommons.org/licenses/by-sa/3.0/>, via Wikimedia Commons: https://commons.wikimedia.org/wiki/File:Mt.Asama2_(From_saku_city).jpg

59 mamama (ままま), CC BY-SA 3.0 <http://creativecommons.org/licenses/by-sa/3.0/>, via Wikimedia Commons: https://commons.wikimedia.org/wiki/File:Nara_Sudo-tenno-sha.jpg

60 Naokijp, CC BY-SA 4.0 <https://creativecommons.org/licenses/by-sa/4.0>, via Wikimedia Commons: https://commons.wikimedia.org/wiki/File:Kamigoryo_Shrine_in_Kyoto_Two-storied_gate_01.jpg

61 https://commons.wikimedia.org/wiki/File:Yoshitoshi_Driving_away_
the_Demons.jpg

62 A photographer, CC BY-SA 4.0 <https://creativecommons.org/licenses/by-sa/4.0>,
via Wikimedia Commons:
https://commons.wikimedia.org/wiki/File:Mount_Miwa.jpg

63 Terumasa, CC BY-SA 4.0 <https://creativecommons.org/licenses/by-sa/4.0>, via
Wikimedia Commons: https://commons.wikimedia.org/wiki/File:Kougenji-
temple.jpg

64 https://commons.wikimedia.org/wiki/File:Series_C_10K_Yen_Bank_
of_Japan_note_-_front.jpg

65 663highland, CC BY-SA 3.0 <http://creativecommons.org/licenses/by-sa/3.0/>, via
Wikimedia Commons:
https://commons.wikimedia.org/wiki/File:Shitennoji03s3200.jpg

66 Art Institute of Chicago, CC0, via Wikimedia Commons:
https://commons.wikimedia.org/wiki/File:Painting_of_Chigo_Daishi_with_Goyuigo_
Inscription,_15th_century_-_Crop_and_contrast.jpg

67 Gyeongju City, KOGL Type 1 <http://www.kogl.or.kr/open/info/license_info/by.do>,
via Wikimedia Commons:
https://commons.wikimedia.org/wiki/File:A_scale_model_of_Hwangnyongsa_pagod
a.jpg

68 https://commons.wikimedia.org/wiki/File:Sakanoue_Tamuramaro_sw.jpg

69 Tomomarusan, CC BY-SA 3.0 <http://creativecommons.org/licenses/by-sa/3.0/>, via
Wikimedia Commons: https://commons.wikimedia.org/wiki/File:
Monument_to_Aterui_and_More2.jpg

70 https://commons.wikimedia.org/wiki/File:EmpressJinguInKorea.jpg

71 https://commons.wikimedia.org/wiki/File:Empress_Suiko_by_Tosa_
Mitsuyoshi_1726_Eifukuji_Osaka.png

72 Ishikawa Toyonobu, CC0, via Wikimedia Commons:
https://commons.wikimedia.org/wiki/File:Tomoe_Gozen_Killing_Uchida_Ieyoshi_at
_Battle_of_Awazu_no_Hara_(1184)_MET_DP135504.jpg

73 Ian Remsen, CC0, via Wikimedia Commons:
https://commons.wikimedia.org/wiki/File:Hiragana_and_katakana.svg

74 https://commons.wikimedia.org/wiki/File:Sei_Shonagon3.jpg

75 https://commons.wikimedia.org/wiki/File:Lady_Murasaki_writing.png

76 https://commons.wikimedia.org/wiki/File:Hyakuninisshu_001.jpg

77 Rijksmuseum, CC0, via Wikimedia Commons:
https://commons.wikimedia.org/wiki/File:Vrouw,_de_handen_warmend_bij_een_hi
bachi_32_moderne_types_(serietitel)_Imayo_sanjuniso_(serietitel_op_object),_RP-
P-2008-245.jpg

78 Suicasmo, CC BY-SA 4.0 <https://creativecommons.org/licenses/by-sa/4.0>, via Wikimedia Commons: https://commons.wikimedia.org/wiki/File:Yoshinogari_Ancient_Ruins_20170222.jpg

79 Metropolitan Museum of Art, CC0, via Wikimedia Commons: https://commons.wikimedia.org/wiki/File:%E6%A8%AA%E7%93%B6_%E9%A0%88%E6%81%B5%E5%99%A8-Recumbent_Bottle_(Yokobe)_MET_2015_300_259_Burke_website.jpg

80 ColBase: 国立博物館所蔵品統合検索システム (Integrated Collections Database of the National Museums, Japan), CC BY 4.0 <https://creativecommons.org/licenses/by/4.0>, via Wikimedia Commons: https://commons.wikimedia.org/wiki/File:Tebako_(Cosmetic_box)_Design_of_wheels-in-stream.jpg

81 Jean-Pierre Dalbéra, CC BY 2.0 <https://creativecommons.org/licenses/by/2.0>, via Wikimedia Commons: https://commons.wikimedia.org/wiki/File:Musicienne_de_Gagaku,_ensemble_%22Owari_Miyabie%22_(Maison_du_Japon,_Paris).jpg

82 https://commons.wikimedia.org/wiki/File:Empress_Sh%C5%8Dtoku.jpg

83 菊池容斎, CC BY 4.0 <https://creativecommons.org/licenses/by/4.0>, via Wikimedia Commons: https://commons.wikimedia.org/wiki/File:A-935_C0007076.jpg

84 Dana + LeRoy Bunward, CC BY 2.0 <https://creativecommons.org/licenses/by/2.0>, via Wikimedia Commons: https://commons.wikimedia.org/wiki/File:Usa_Shrine_(Nanch%C5%ABr%C5%8Dmon).jpg

85 663highland, CC BY-SA 3.0 <http://creativecommons.org/licenses/by-sa/3.0/>, via Wikimedia Commons: https://commons.wikimedia.org/wiki/File:Mii-dera_Otsu_Shiga_pref01s5s4592.jpg

86 663highland, CC BY-SA 3.0 <http://creativecommons.org/licenses/by-sa/3.0/>, via Wikimedia Commons: https://commons.wikimedia.org/wiki/File:Enryakuji_Konponchudo02s5s3200.jpg

87 shikabane taro, CC BY 3.0 <https://creativecommons.org/licenses/by/3.0>, via Wikimedia Commons: https://commons.wikimedia.org/wiki/File:%E6%AD%A6%E8%94%B5%E5%9D%8A%E5%BC%81%E6%85%B6%EF%BC%8F%E7%94%B0%E8%BE%BA%E5%B8%82_-_panoramio.jpg

88 663highland, CC BY-SA 3.0 <http://creativecommons.org/licenses/by-sa/3.0/>, via Wikimedia Commons: https://commons.wikimedia.org/wiki/File:Hiyoshi-taisha_juge-jinja-haiden02n4592.jpg